Stepping into Mystery

Four Approaches to a Spiritual Life

Monty Williams SJ

NOVALIS

© 2012 Novalis Publishing Inc.

Cover design: Blair Turner
Layout: Audrey Wells

Published by Novalis

Publishing Office
10 Lower Spadina Avenue, Suite 400
Toronto, Ontario, Canada
M5V 2Z2

Head Office
4475 Frontenac Street
Montréal, Québec, Canada
H2H 2S2

www.novalis.ca

Library and Archives Canada Cataloguing in Publication

Williams, Monty, 1944-
    Stepping into mystery : four approaches to a spiritual life / Monty Williams.

Includes bibliographical references.

ISBN 978-2-89646-328-2

    1. Discernment (Christian theology). 2. Spiritual life--Catholic Church. I. Title.

BV4509.5.W55   2012 248.4   C2011-908693-X

Printed in Canada.

The Scripture quotations contained herein (including the texts of the readings, the Psalms, the Psalm refrains and the Gospel verses) are from various translations taken from the Internet site http://www.biblegateway.com/.

The Ten Ox-herding Pictures illustrations are by Tomikichiro Tokuriki, in *Zen Flesh, Zen Bones: A Collection of Zen and Pre-Zen Writings* (North Clarendon, VT: Charles E. Tuttle Co. 1957, 1985). Used by permission of the publisher. The translations of the accompanying poems are by Monty Williams, SJ.

We acknowledge the financial support of the Government of Canada through the Canada Book Fund for business development activities.

5 4 3 2 1   16 15 14 13 12

Contents

Dedicated to

my father, Joseph Lewis Williams, 1909–1986
and
my mother, Lyma Dorothy Williams, 1912–2011
and
to all those with whom I have encountered love,
in gratitude
for the gift of your presence

Prologue

Discernment: A Guide for Life

We are on a spiritual journey. It is a long journey and, to speak truthfully, we do not know when, or if, it will end. We are created by God and for God. In God we move, live and have our being. Before birth, during this earthly life, and after death, this intimacy exists. Our life is to explore that relationship, and to see where it leads us as God's beloved. We know there are many paths with God, and many ways of being with God. As Jesus says, "In my Father's house there are many rooms" (John 14:2). Each human way is a path to God. For the Christian, the path is the Christian God who says in the person of Christ, "I am the Way, the Truth, and the Life" (John 14:6). Each of us, no matter what tradition we belong to, and even if we profess to belong to no tradition, desires to know the way to the fullness of life. We desire to know how to distinguish between truth and what passes for truth in the worlds we live in. We all desire to find and to live our path.

Each of us leans into the mystery of our lives, and each of us desires to know how to find our path through that darkness which calls us and lies ahead of us. Despite what we may think or even believe, none of us, by ourselves, can see into the future or create that future. As human beings we are limited and subject to forces outside of our control. We, and those forces, are aspects of creation and ultimately subject to the Creator. Within a relationship with that Creator, we can understand who we are and what we can do to live a life of meaning and fulfillment.

This is a book about discernment. It examines three questions: What do we do, now and in the future? How do we do it? Why do we do it? It works from the simple premise that our relationship with God determines us. It sees God as Ultimate Mystery manifesting as the Desire who desires for us the fullness of life. It sees us as human beings who are created to enjoy that fullness of life, but who often are existentially prevented from achieving it because of the forces of destruction present in creation. Often we have become complicit with those forces of destruction and so mistake what will bring us the life we desire. We find in our lives the tension between a greater good, which calls us beyond ourselves towards authenticity and that fullness of life, and a lesser good, which limits us by focusing on our narcissism. Because of that tension, we need to discern.

Discernment is more than decision making. Anyone can make a decision based on reasons ranging from the altruistic to the pragmatic and self-serving. Discernment, however, puts the context of decision making in terms of a lived relationship with the mystery we call God. Discernment occurs in the give and take of spiritual intimacy, and in the desire to deepen such an intimacy. If one desires to grow in spiritual intimacy, one discerns. Discernment is ultimately a lived relationship with God.

But how to discern? How to discover those forms of spiritual literacy where God and each of us communicate with one another like lovers, in unique, open, shameless and personal ways? What promotes that level of authenticity and what subverts it? One begins with a search for love that carries a person to seek the right lover. There are experiments. The seeker exhausts certain relationships. Other relationships reveal themselves as friendships. Then the seeker discovers someone who might be the right one. The two get to know each other, and slow, mutual self-revelations occur as they open themselves and become vulnerable to each other. When a mutual level of trust has been reached and two people find themselves comfortable with each other, they might decide to become a couple. They may grow to affirm that commitment in public ways acknowledging them as a unit, and out of that unity, establish a family or forms of generativity which bring life to others.

What happens among human lovers also happens in the relationship between us and God. God desires every aspect of us. Every aspect of us, from each individual cell to our whole corporate being, is created as a desire for life and, indeed, the fullness of life. We desire God and God desires us. We live both out of that longing and out of the delight of that longing fulfilled.

But this delight is often frustrated or rarely reached. We are prevented from reaching it by our own traps, which may be caused by personal trauma, family or social relations, or by the culture we live in. Yet all is not lost. Though we might find ourselves far away from God, God is always the root of our being.

Each spiritual journey is precisely becoming aware of how God is always present in our lives and of the efforts God and we commit to in trying to make that relationship more real.

To do that, we journey into Mystery—we step away from a world which has become familiar. We move into darkness. We become familiar with that new world the darkness opens us to. Familiarity promotes assimilation. Assimilation provokes exploration. Exploration carries us to new territory that we may appropriate and in time become familiar with. In each of those transitional stages, as we are drawn out of ourselves, we need discernment if we are not to get trapped by illusion. We need to be able to distinguish between what attracts us and what is good for us, between being true to ourselves and being true to what calls us beyond ourselves. To do this, we discern.

Introduction

This book examines certain aspects of the spiritual journey. It is divided into four parts.

Part I traces the spiritual journey as a movement through fear, clarity, power and despair.[1] Fear is understood as a force used to socialize us. Clarity occurs when we walk through our fear and begin to see things as they are. But this clarity still uses the constructs of the world we have left behind, on one level. Moving beyond clarity we discover we must be creative in our living. We discover the power we have to change the world we live in. The temptation here is if we succumb and use that power to recreate the world in our own image and likeness. Should we abandon such use of power and allow a new creation to emerge, often the forces of the world slowly overwhelm that new creation, absorb it and corrupt it. Our creativity becomes compromised or destroyed. Then we must face despair. We must start all over again, and, as T.S. Eliot tells us,

> each venture
> Is a new beginning, a raid on the inarticulate
> With shabby equipment always deteriorating[2]

But for us, it is not only *what* we do that matters. How and why we do it counts. We continue past despair to those new beginnings because we have fallen in love with God and have accepted God's love for us. The rest, as the book of Job shows, is not altogether our business.

Part I sees the movement through these four disorders as a path to liberation and to intimacy with God. Going beyond fear, we abandon security for a rootedness in God. Going beyond clarity, we move beyond meaning to live in mystery. Going beyond power, we explore creativity. Going beyond despair, we find ourselves as the biblical "poor of spirit," abandoning ourselves to the Divine Providence and delighting in the many manifestations of spiritual intimacy daily given.

Part II is based on The Ten Ox-Herding Pictures of Zen Buddhism. In Buddhism, these pictures trace the development of our coming to awareness of our true self and living out of that developing awareness. What I have done here is to translate those stages into a Christian context. This has been the basis of a series of retreats, workshops and presentations that I have given in recent years to the international Christian community. I see the spiritual journey as the development of awareness, and that awareness as the lived relationship between our drive towards God and God's desire for us to have fullness of life. Basically, the stages of that journey are as follows:

1. Becoming dissatisfied with the status quo and trying to move beyond what is then offered by it;

2. Experimenting to discover what eases the dissatisfaction of living;

3. Discerning between true and false consolations in our experiments;

4. Choosing the path of true consolation;

5. Training to follow the path of true consolation;

6. Becoming established in our relationship with God;

7. Forgetting God: that is, no longer concerning ourselves with such questions as "Does God exist?" but rather more with "What do I do now?";

8. Leaving even a sense of self behind and becoming "empty";

9. Seeing things as they are;

10. Entering the world with a sense of rootedness.

In effect, this section examines the dynamics of desire. There is a mutuality in desire, for God's desire for us is always interacting with our desire for what we hold to be God. The spiritual journey traces the development of that relationship. The dynamics of such desire are not restricted to a particular culture or religious tradition. They are characteristic of being human. We recall one gift of the Incarnation is Jesus' witness of how to live as a human being desiring the fullness of life. To follow Jesus and to become fully human requires discernment.

Part III looks at the rules for discernment and decision making that St. Ignatius of Loyola sets out in the Spiritual Exercises. Discernment is a necessary part of the spiritual journey, and every new stage of the spiritual journey calls for different modes of discernment, because each has a different way of understanding self, others and God. The literature on Ignatius's rules for discernment usually treat the rules as isolated observations within the general context, whether we are moving towards God or away from God. It has been my experience, both personally and in 40 years of giving spiritual direction, that the tension between moving towards God and away from God exists in every human being at every moment of existence, and so the rules need to be reworked to address every specific stage of the spiritual path. And because we are social beings, we need to look at discernment as a communal activity, since whatever we do has communal dimensions, just as whatever a community does has implications for the individuals who live in it. Added here is a section on the examination of consciousness as a way of remaining focused on the path.

Part IV sees the spiritual journey as a journey through time. Time is examined in terms of past, present and future. I explore these three dimensions of personal time using the categories of being redeemed, or graced, and of being unredeemed, or trapped. Each of us experiences dimensions of the past that have been, and still are, life-giving, but some dimensions of our past are not life-giving. The same can be said about our present and also about the way we anticipate our futures. This final section of the book, entitled "Redeeming the Time," looks at the ways in which we live time as a spiritual journey and as a path to liberation.

A Pilgrim People

We are a pilgrim people. This is one of the oldest understandings of what it means to be human. When we celebrate life, we remember, as did the early Jewish community in the Old Testament, that "A wandering Aramean was my ancestor" (Deuteronomy 26:5). "The wandering Aramean" is one of the earliest credal statements of the Jewish faith. It defines the identity of a people as "wandering" before being found by God, who then journeys with them. Here the word "wandering" also has the meaning of perishing, lost, vulnerable. It describes the human condition without God.

The result of being found by God is not a change in humanity, but a change in how to be human. Being found by God gives us a sense of identity, liberation and direction. It led the Jewish people to the promised land and to a celebration of life in that land, as the Deuteronomy text observes. God frees his chosen ones from captivity

> with a terrifying display of power, and with signs and wonders; and … brought us into this place and gave us this land, a land flowing with milk and honey. So now I bring the first of the fruit of the ground that you, O Lord, have given me. (Deuteronomy 26:8-10)

We, too, come from elsewhere. We, or our ancestors, were immigrants. We all left somewhere oppressive looking for a better life. Oscar Wilde, in his essay "The Soul of Man Under Socialism," writes, "A map of the world that does not include Utopia is not worth even glancing at, for it leaves out the one country at which Humanity is always landing. And when Humanity lands there, it looks out, and, seeing a better country, sets sail."[3] We are always restless for a greater good. Ultimately that greater good comes only from God. When we are found by God, we also celebrate, by the lives we lead, the gift of drawing closer to the fullness of life God offers to all. Gratitude is the response of the heart to being saved and to being able to share the path of spiritual intimacy with the One who saves us because that One, for some mysterious reason, desires us. Our pilgrimage is one that carries us to joy.

Part I

The Path of Contemplation

The rarest thing in this world is joy. Yet it is joy and joy only that can renew the world, heal it of its nameless ills, and make us what we are truly meant to be: living words of the Father. What stops joy is grief: the grief we experience when we see beauty ruined, innocence despoiled, hopes betrayed, and all that we hold dear cast aside for naught. These things happen not in the abstract but in our very own lives, in the lives of our communities and families, and in the world we inhabit. To come to joy we must walk through the paths of our grief that have so moulded us, the source of our perceptions is our pain.

We often see only through our hurt. To walk through the paths of our grief, we must first acknowledge each hurt in our lives. This is painful, because we have to admit we are severely damaged people. First we recognize this, and then we must accept it. Like a wounded child, we hold each hurt and live with it in the daily round of our lives until we can know it. Doing otherwise is simply a detached exercise of the mind evading the reality of our pain by pretending we understand and control it. We can admit how our pain shapes our lives. Only then can we name that hurt, as it is, without lies or drama or false humility. We can do so only if we do so lovingly—as a parent holds a bruised child. We allow each hurt to speak to us, tell us the stories of its suffering, and let us investigate its causes. We share its pain by letting it into our lives.

In the context of prayer and of being held in God's love we can unpack our hurts. Contemplation is consciously placing ourselves in God's love. Doing this opens us up and allows us to see beyond our anguish that we are more than our hurts. Then, and only then, can we set our pain free. Now it becomes a door through which the mercy of God enters into this world. All this must be learned.

The path to joy leads through grief. Yet the fruit of contemplation is joy. "Why do we need to walk this particular path?" one may ask. "Surely there are other paths to joy!" But other paths do not seem to be either the common experience of humanity or, indeed, the pattern proposed by the major religious traditions. Certainly it is not the way Christ lived in the world as that life is portrayed in Philippians 2:5-11. Christ enters into the condition of suffering humanity to raise us to the joy of his resurrection. As the Eucharistic preface for the Easter season tells us, the joy of the resurrection renews the whole world. The resurrection did not occur until after the life, crucifixion and death of Jesus. And even in the resurrection, his transformed body bears the physical marks of that suffering.

His path is our path. If we truly seek to follow him, to help him in the work of bringing the world back to the Father, we must follow his path. That path is made available to us through contemplation. We already have the material we need to work with and to open to transformation. It is ourselves.

First, we need to ask ourselves: What stops us from being joyful? To get an answer, we must examine ourselves and listen to our lives. Already we have taken the first three steps on the path to contemplation. In spending time with this dialogue, we have concretely declared our willingness to walk some way along the path. We cannot walk this path unwillingly. God does not force himself on anyone. He lets us be free. It is our fears and compulsions and anxieties stopping us from being free. The second step we have made in walking with God is being attentive to that history unique to each one of us. Within that history we find our personal path to contemplation. Thirdly, we walk this path with a deliberate purpose: to be with God, in whom is the fullness of life. We do not walk this path for the world's approval, or for the transitory security of fortifying the defenses of our ego, and certainly not to maintain, even unconsciously, the forces of destruction which can enter the world through us. We walk this path, ultimately, to be a special presence for God in whatever situation we find ourselves. In walking the path we become more and more attentive to God, and we discover more and still more how God attends to us and is present in the world.

Often we start something even before we know it, and so when we consciously decide to walk the path of contemplation, we do not have to make a new beginning, but merely continue to walk the path we are already on. What we must do is walk it more attentively, and more in tune with the forces of life surrounding us on so many levels. We are here to walk that path with faithfulness, with integrity, with creativity, with love. There is a pattern in our lives moving to contemplation; it is a pattern of attentiveness, faith, humility and creativity. If we follow that path, we learn to move with God, and we learn what that means for each of us concretely.

The first step is being attentive. We often think we are attentive and know what is going on in our lives and in the lives of those around us. This is often simply not true. Freud has an interesting thing to say about "repression." In *Remembering, Repeating, and Working-Through* (1914) he has an insight applicable to the spiritual life: "The patient does not remember anything of what he has forgotten and repressed, but acts it out. He reproduces it not as a memory but as an action; he repeats it, without, of course, knowing that he is repeating it."[4]

Repression makes us inattentive. Repression is different from suppression. Suppression occurs when we know something or feel something and use all our abilities to keep it from happening, or becoming public. Normally we are quite attentive to what we suppress, such as our sexual desires, our ambition or our anger. But whatever we repress we are not attentive to at all. The thing stopping us from getting in contact with what we repress is fear. So if we want to find out what limits our attention, we need to look at how we fear.

Looking at Our Fears

One normally thinks of fear as an enemy—and in a way it is—but our fears usually signal the way we must move.

Think of fear as a door beyond which is a group of children—aspects of ourselves—who have never grown up and instead have become wild, autistic. Their wildness, their withdrawal from what is human, results from not having been acknowledged, never having been known for what they are, never having been loved. A hurt is a desire that has never grown to love, and so it plays according to its own rules. It becomes wild. We defend ourselves from hurt through fear. On a spiritual level, on the path to contemplation, hurts are dimensions of our lives that have never known love, have never spent time with God. Those hurts are repressed, yet they affect our lives because they come out in the way we act. Think of the person in a religious community, or in a family, who is so organized that other people have become an intolerable burden. What has stopped her from being flexible? What lack of love has let her believe that concepts are more important than people? Her commitment to being responsible closes her off from Jesus' first commandment in Matthew's gospel to "Love the Lord your God with all your heart and with all your soul and with all your mind" (Matthew 22:37). And yet such people are usually convinced that they witness, in the face of crumbling community standards, a fidelity to the highest values of life. Consider the effect these people have on their communities, with their anger, their passive aggression and their unspoken sense of judgment. Or consider the member of a family who is always unhappy, always complaining, or always tired. Often the reasons for the behaviour are valid, but these truths are maintained without love, and truths without love are lies.

The positions of these personas we have just considered emerge from their strengths. We hide from our fears behind our strengths, and our strengths may be either positive or negative. Our strengths affirm us: the good teacher, the efficient administrator, the willing subject, the dedicated parent, the obedient child, the loyal employee, the politically committed religious. All set their institutional life as the highest value. They all seek to belong. But when we live

16

out of our strengths, rather than in a relationship with God, those very strengths do not let us enter into the areas of darkness in our lives that need to spend time with God. In contemplation, those areas of darkness meet God much as the wily Jacob meets God at Peniel, wrestles with him in the dark, is renamed and is transformed into Israel, the father of nations (Genesis 32:22-32).

The fight with God is named "contemplation." The word comes from the Latin *contemplari*, to observe carefully; the Latin comes from two words: *com*, an intensive, and *templum*, the open space marked out by augurs in the Near East to observe the stars and thus discern the fate of things. Roman augurs desiring to know what the gods wanted also opened a space, usually in birds' entrails, and looked carefully to see what the signs present in that opened space meant.

It is useful to reflect on this Latin word because the *templum*, the open space, became where the gods appeared: the temple. We must create that open space in which God appears, but that space is often covered up by our strengths, hidden by our fears and overlooked in our daily life. To get to that open space where we can experience God, we have to examine our fears, for we experience God through his saving work in his overcoming our fears. We experience God when he transforms us, when he heals our hurts so that our fears have no more destructive power over us.

How do we examine our fears? It is of little use merely to have an intellectual knowledge of our fears. That is rather like going to the doctor with a pain in your stomach and being told you have something with a long Latin-sounding name. Merely knowing the name does not stop the pain. Knowing your fears goes deeper than acquiring the names for them. To know your fears, you must live with them, rather than shut them out of the house you live in, though, of course, even if you shut them out, they will surround your house and inhabit it like ghosts. You cannot ignore your fears.

The temple is also a part of the body where we are very vulnerable. This area on the side of the forehead is very fragile, and we can be easily hurt there. Similarly, we can be hurt where we are most vulnerable; one way to discover our fears is to look at our vulnerabilities and at how we respond when we experience being vulnerable. Usually our fears manifest themselves at such times, and we seek to protect ourselves.

Once we see spontaneous responses to our vulnerability we must spend time with them. To "contemplate" is to spend time with. Indeed, the root, *temp*, to stretch or to extend, gives us the Latin *tempus, temporis*, a span of time, and *con* intensifies that sense of time so it moves from *chronos* to *kairos*, from ordinary time to revelatory time.

How can we spend time with our fears so time can become revelatory? Imagine being in a fearful situation. We go to the dentist. We sit in the chair, it tilts back, a bright light shines in our eyes and at something we cannot see. What we do see is a long needle moving at the periphery of our sight. We are helpless and are filled with previous memories of being injected. What do we do? We scrunch up our faces, close our eyes, grip the arms of the chair. We try our best to disassociate ourselves from that area of pain. We lose our sense of calm and become inattentive to how minimal the pain really is, because we become focused on rejecting or denying it. Ironically enough, according to psychologists, this effort to avoid pain actually increases our subjective experience of pain.[5]

Fears maintain themselves through panic. When we panic, we become blinded to everything else but our fear, which then controls us totally. In this way, panic limits our attentiveness by limiting our freedom, and thus it limits our possibilities of being fully human.

To spend time with our fear, we must see how fears walk through our lives and how they affect our relationships, our work, our self-image and our hopes. They affect the way we look at our past, our communities and families, our expectations of ourselves and others, the way we play, our sense of humour, even the way we keep our rooms. Our fears touch everything we do, and often it is our fears that act, and not we ourselves, because we are captive to them. Our fears cause us to maintain our sins. Here sin is not to be seen as opposing the "thou-shalt-nots," but rather as the lack of creativity, the inability to be loving, committed, responsible, intelligent or even aware. Those times when we have been such—and we can discover them when we look at our history—reveal to us our fear. Of course a question arises: Is not even the way we look at our history touched by our fear? That may well be so, but the way we look at our history is also touched by our drive to transcendence. There is a grey area in the story of our lives that makes us uncomfortable and becomes the site of our discovery of God. We enter that grey area when we start contemplation.

The root of "contemplation," *temp*, to stretch, also provides the basis for the word "temptation." When we set out to do God's will, to be a manifestation of his time in the world, we come into the grey areas of our lives, the places of our temptations. Contemplation leads to temptation. Jesus, after he is baptized in the Jordan, goes out to the wilderness—a place where he is without his strengths, a place where he encounters his fears—to discover God's will. There he is tempted as he tries to spend time with God. His temptations urge him to be less than who he is. Our temptations urge us to be less than who we are. Our fears make us less than who we are.

Like Christ, we are to be words of God; we are to be the signs of his presence in the world; we are to witness through joy to his transforming presence. The areas in our lives where we do not experience joy are areas mastered by fear. That fear can be transformed only if we spend time with it. We are always invited to become open spaces in which God becomes more present to the world. That openness can happen when we present our fear to the Father and remain with it in contemplation until he transforms it. God can enter our world only in what we call human time; it is one of the mysteries of the Incarnation that he chooses to do this. Actually it is the manifestation of his faith in us, his hope in us, his love for us, that he abandons himself to our time.

The first step in contemplation is to hold our fears up to the Father, rather than hide from him, as did Adam and Eve in the garden. In the time we give him, he is present to our fears. He transforms us, and the grace we ask for as we walk into the grey areas of our lives is to know and to be present to those fears. Of course, we can do that only if God is present with us, so in coming to be present to our fears we also come to be present to God in new and surprising ways.

Being Present to Our Fears

There are two ways of being present to our fears. We could look at them and wonder how we can be so stupid, and then make the plans of a perfectionist to ensure those mistakes never happen again—or, if they do happen, that they never become known. If anyone learned about them, we would excuse them as part of a bigger plan that only we know about. I think certain aspects of governments' foreign policy operate on these principles. This way of looking at our fears keeps us in our fears and we are not transformed. The other way of looking at our fears is to experience the amazement that no one has pushed us down the stairs or slipped some ground glass into our coffee, or that we have not destroyed ourselves. That amazement leads us to ask why. What is it that has kept us alive? The more we ponder it, the more we are filled with a sense of wonder—which gives us no answer. That wonder, that sense of amazement, is our first awareness of the presence of God in the space we have created by looking at our fears.

That sense of wonder is dynamic. It reaches out. It touches the things we took for granted or ignored. We then can look at things and get lost in them. Why? Because everything becomes unknowable according to the old rules that have ruled our lives and influenced how we looked at things. What had been insignificant now moves into significance: the light on a magazine cover, the pattern of voices singing out of key, the way our skin smells when we have just got up in the morning. What before was background noise to the tapes that ran your life now becomes voices, rhythms, music. All becomes something you notice. It is rather like children who watch the world with open eyes. Have you ever noticed the way young children stare? They have no shame or guile. And have you ever noticed the way you can stare back at young children? They do not turn away from a gaze. The eyes in icons do the same thing. They are filled with a sense of wonder. They gaze at you without judgment or suggestion, and that openness encourages you to be open, to gaze back. To gaze at something is different than looking at something. When we look at something, we are usually looking *for* something: an explanation, a distraction, the exercise of curiosity or power. Gazing at something provides none of these. To gaze—or, to use the more rustic word, to gawk, comes from the root *ga*, to rejoice. From it we get the Latin word *gaudete*, to rejoice.

To be attentive is to rejoice in the presence of something. When we are present in prayer, we are attentive and become aware of the dimensions, the forces, the powers, the presences constituting the space in which we find our identity. In the spiritual gazing contemplation allows, that space reveals itself to us. The patience we learn in contemplation is the time of that space. That time is not our time; it is not determined by *chronos*. Yet it is available to us and so is in time. The gazing we attend to in contemplation gives contemplation its freedom, and, in turn, we discover that we gain freedom at the same time. When our fears trap us, we become restless and obsessed; when we look at our fears, we need to do so from something other than our needs. We do not need at this time to say, "I have to find out my fears; I have to face them; I have to haul them out kicking and screaming into the open; I have to lay them out on the ground and line them up like dead rabbits at a shoot, so that everyone will know what a good and spiritual person I am."

If we are afraid of our fears, imagine how much more our fears are afraid of us. If we kill our fears, we become inhuman. What we need to do is transform our fears, and we can transform them only if we gaze at them in wonder. We can gaze at them in wonder only if we see them in the context of God's love for us. It is rather like floating in a deep lake. If we relax we are all right; we can simply enjoy the sun on our bodies, the cool water on our faces, the laziness of our limbs. But as soon as we start to worry about how deep the lake is, how far we are from shore, what bad swimmers we are, what if we get a cramp—as soon as we start to panic, we lose our sense of wonder, our sense of enjoyment of life. Suddenly, everything is the enemy.

Often as we relax into attentiveness, the gazing that is the beginning of contemplation, we are overtaken by a sense of panic. In this is the beginning of discernment. The good spirit leads us to relax; the bad spirit, to panic.

Our path to contemplation is found by following the good spirit. Yet we can use what happens to us when we panic. That thing is a fear. We can also ask ourselves: How did we get into that state of panic? How was the good we began with transformed into panic? From this we can get some insight into the way our fear controls us—not the general way, but the specific way. In this we are being attentive to ourselves and are beginning to understand our fear and how it works on us, the way it moves to take away our freedom. At this time we are not trying to discover the source of our fear or the private name we have for it; we are just trying to find out how it works, how it limits our attentiveness and stops us on our personal path to contemplation.

How does fear stop our contemplation? A small story may show you what I mean. Imagine yourself as a child again, out on an overnight camping trip. Supper is over; you have gorged yourself on hot dogs that you have burned over the campfire, you have had lots of pop and potato chips. Now that night has fallen and you have changed into your pajamas, you sit around the campfire and tell ghost stories until late at night, until you are almost asleep. You stumble into the tent, curl up into the sleeping bag, and soon are out like a light. Suddenly you wake up. All that pop you drank and the excitement of the day are having an effect. You have to go to the bathroom. But it is dark all around. You are in a strange place. There are strange creatures outside: bears, wolves, coyotes, snakes—ghosts, even.

You wonder if you can wait it out until morning; you try to find a comfortable position to get back to sleep. Nothing works. You toss and turn. You even consider wetting the bed. After all, it is not the first time you have done that. But you do not want to sleep in the damp that so soon gets cold. Besides, you know in the morning you will have to face the mockery of your friends. Finally you can take it no more. You stumble to a tree and wait there. Every sound is horrible; all around you sense the presence of terrible creatures ready to devour you. And nothing comes. Every second seems like an eternity. All you can do is wait.

But, as you wait, your eyes become accustomed to the dark. You see the camp just behind you; you are astonished by how bright and how close the stars seem; you recognize the tree you are next to; you suddenly discover the cool wind, certainly cooler than in the tent. You suddenly discover that you are smiling. This is not so bad, you think. It is exciting and quiet and, as you think that, you discover that you are doing what you came out to do and you are flooded with a sense of relief. You sigh and finish. You finish, but you hesitate to go back to the tent. You have a secret. The night is no big deal. You shiver, turn, go back to the tent, slip into your bag, stretch, and go back to sleep. When you wake up in the morning, you wonder where you are and then it suddenly all comes back to you: the night, your fears, your secret. You feel you are a different person in some way, no longer a baby. You tell no one about it. It is your secret.

We all face such nights, and there are depths of night. There is physical night. Then there is the night we enter into when we attempt anything new: nights that come upon us when we leave behind the securities of one way of living as we change jobs, communities, modes of living, even this life for another.

Our fears are doors to the night. In overcoming our fears, we discover living is more filled with wonder than we had previously imagined. Our fears stop us from seeing things as they are, and because they are so spontaneous, they stop us from being free. But our fears not only stop *us*, they also stop the people around us from being free. You know the effect one fearful person has within a community or a family. The old proverb sums this up: "One bad apple spoils the barrel." Fears are signs of arrested development. They stop us from growing to be who we are, and each of our fears stops our community, be it family, residence or project, from being fully alive and thus from being a kingdom of God.

Often we resent our fears, but more often we resent the fears of others and the impositions and restraints those fears have on us. As children, we are often forced to accept the fears of our parents; as members of society, common social fears shape our consciousness, and if we are religious and members of a community, we absorb fears that make our witness of spiritual intimacy ineffectual and our sense of joy shallow. This is, of course, one way to understand original sin and to suggest why—to get back to originating grace, which makes us children of God—we must move in contemplation along the path of grief.

Grief occurs because our original nature, as the Zen Buddhists would have it, is clouded by illusion; illusion shapes our perceptions. To change our perceptions, to see God and live, we must get rid of our illusions.

We do not lose all our illusions at once. This takes time. Fear creates illusions: the beasts and awful creatures of the night that lie and wait for us outside our tents of childhood. The process of seeing truly, of contemplating, is to see with the eyes of God. To see with the eyes of God is to see with the heart of God in whom all is held, including us, as we truly are. The way God sees us is as time. Time is more than the patience of God. Time is the eye with which God sees us and the eye with which we see God. Only in time can we spend time with God. Only in time and with time and through time can we be contemplative.

This means that contemplation is not at the end of a journey. Contemplation is the journey itself. The path is contemplation. We cannot arrive at contemplation. The saints in heaven, as they contemplate God forever, free fall, lost in wonder and joy. Here, in this existence, contemplation is the time we spend coming to terms with our fears that create illusions, those false ways of seeing. In contemplation we sink through layers and layers of self to a deeper sense of self in which the self becomes less and less selfish. We do this in an inner stillness that allows us to be attentive. Often, as we sink into contemplation, the disturbances we encounter, the fears. are nameless; we experienced them primarily as feelings. This is because the values we have manifest themselves spontaneously as feelings. To be sure, we may engage, if we want to, in exploring the education that has led us to become those values. Contemplation, however, is not psychoanalysis; it is more than that. The analysis we need most of all is to discern the right path. The basic antitheses on the level of feeling at this stage of contemplation are wonder and panic. The bad spirit creates panic; the good spirit encourages wonder. The inner senses of the spirit gaze on the fear, resting closer and closer. There is pain, but the pain comes as one holds the fear. The self shrinks away from the pain, but, in contemplation, comes back to it because it is the nature of grace to seek out what is lost and what is hurt in order to heal it and bring it to light.

In contemplation, we become attentive to pain. It is not that we like pain, as if we were masochists. The contemplative does not love pain, but realizes that the pain is healing, because it is felt only when the hurt covered with the scab of fear is touched by the love of the Father.

In contemplation, we finally embrace the fear even though it hurts. It hurts like hell, literally, for hell is a collection of hurts. We attend to the hurt like a servant, like a suffering servant. Hurt is the lack of love. In the attentiveness of contemplation, that lack of love meets love. If we think we can satisfy this lack of love of our own accord, we are mistaken. This lack of love can be satisfied only by the source of love, and that is why in contemplation we become only an open space, a temple, in which God can appear and the hurt can gain sanctuary.

When this hurt becomes human, the power its pain has over us disappears. Whether pain ever disappears totally, until the end of time, I do not know. It is not just ourselves as individuals who have to be healed. The need for healing is found in the people we are connected to, and the ones they are connected to, and the ones they are connected to, until at last we stretch back and forth from the beginning of time to the end of time. Time is where all creation groans in an act of birth. In contemplation we stretch. The etymologies of "contemplation" we discussed earlier are rooted in *temp*. Its original meaning is to stretch, and from *temp* we get not only "temple," "attempt," and "temptation," but also "tapestry." In contemplation, as we stretch, go beyond the barriers of our ego maintained by fear, and sink into time, we discover ourselves not as individuals—which is an abstraction and illusion—but as a tapestry in which all of creation is woven. In weaving, the temple is the device for keeping the warp taut on the loom. Contemplation stretches us and keeps us taut in our vocation. That vocation manifests itself in a spiritual journey where we move past the traps of our fears and discover, next, the worlds those fears construct.

The Danger of Clarity

We live in constructed worlds. As we grow, we are educated into values that cover everything from when and how we go to the bathroom to our attitudes about ourselves, others and God. Even the language we think in and the words we use, those signs we share to communicate, are constructs. We suppose that, because our feelings are spontaneous, they are natural. Yet even our feelings, our acts of perception, are learned. Feelings are simply values refined to spontaneity. Those values are learned, and even spontaneity is learned. We are constructs, the world we live in is constructed, and that construct—our world, our cosmos, everything—is called creation.

We derive our sense of identity, our sense of direction, our sense of vocation, and even our sense of how to satisfy our desire for happiness, from these constructs. The radical importance of those forms, which give our life its meaning, cannot be overemphasized. We need only think of the sense of dislocation we feel when we go to a different place or to a new job or when someone close to us dies. There is a gap, an emptiness, that is alienating and frightening. At least, we have been conditioned to think of that emptiness (if indeed we think of it as emptiness) as scary.

The relationship between fear and the constructs by which we attune ourselves to our experiences needs to be examined. We need to get in contact with what it means to live in a constructed world. This will take some work, and it is work, for as John's gospel tells us, our work is to believe in Jesus (John 6:29), the one in whom creation is established. Fear keeps us in an unhealthy relationship with creation. It creates an idolatry in which aspects of constructed reality take the place of the creator. When that happens, fear makes us seek security. To find security we grasp at this constructed world of ours instead of maintaining our relationship with its creator. In that lie we may find a certain peace of understanding, but not the peace which passes all understanding (Philippians 4:7). The peace of the world is not the peace of contemplation. In the gospel of Luke, Christ says,

> "Do you think I have come to give peace on earth? No, I tell you, but rather division; for henceforth in one house there will be divided, father against son and son against father, mother against daughter and daughter against her mother, mother-in-law against daughter-in-law and daughter-in-law against her mother-in-law." (Luke 12:51-53)

Similarly, in John's gospel, Jesus tells his disciples, "Peace I bequeath to you, my own peace I give you; a peace the world cannot give, this is my gift to you" (John 14:27).

The next few steps on the path to contemplation involve coming to correct terms with the construct of creation. If we have spent time with our fears, rather than hiding from them or allowing them to hide from us, we have moved out of the familiar routines of our lives, and already we are in a different place. We are in a different world. If we look at the lives of those who have walked the path of contemplation, we discover that, at the beginning, they always experience a withdrawal from the normal, the habitual or the commonplace. Teresa of Avila says in her autobiography, "The Lord became desirous of preparing me for that state of life which was best for me. He sent me a serious illness."[6] The same thing occurs with Francis of Assisi and Ignatius of Loyola. In fact, in his Spiritual Exercises, St. Ignatius insists on this withdrawal if the soul desires "to approach and be united with its Creator and Lord" (Sp. Ex. #20).[7]

The effect of this dislocation is to realize the limitations of the myth that gives our life meaning. To take away the supports of meaning throws the questing soul onto itself and, more specifically, onto a critical examination of the myth through which the soul structures experience into meaning. Despite the anxiety such dislocation might cause, we grow to realize that we can and do survive without this myth. The night does not devour us.

If the first door to contemplation is fear, the second door is clarity. Clarity I take to mean the ways we understand things. I have two friends who are Freudians, and I am always amazed by how they seek to understand the world according to Freud. Or one might think of those people in religious communities who transpose their anger onto the arena of social justice, seeing the world only in terms of politics and economies, of oppressor and oppressed. Some people construct their world out of anger, others out of pleasure, some out of knowledge, and still others out of pain.

The way to understand the trap of clarity is to look at the way ideology entraps. Ideology gives clarity. An ideology presents clear and definitive norms of behaviour, establishes appropriate responses to counter positions, offers security in the midst of complexity, and situates the human in a system that effectively controls life. The trap of clarity substitutes a world view for reality. The person striving for holiness who submits to a world view instead of living a faithful relationship with God translates dogmas into logical propositions instead of reading them as signifying in a particular historical moment the loving compassion of a community of believers. When we live according to a world view instead of in a living relationship with the Father, we have, to be sure, the ease of living life according to social norms, but those norms also cause pain and oppression. They make us less then we are. We become like those scribes and Pharisees whom Christ condemns because "for the sake of ... tradition [they] make void the word of God" (Matthew 15:6).

We need to ask ourselves what the myths are informing our lives. Myths are not evil in themselves. It is when they seek to displace the mystery of reality that they trap us. So we need to ask a further question: How do we hold the myths we use and which shape us? Religious generally take vows of poverty, chastity and obedience. Does our obedience make us irresponsible? Does chastity make us sexless, unloving and unlovable? Does poverty make us misers? If they do, then we do not hold our vows as contemplatives; we hold them as prisons. We are trapped in clarity. The same is true for a lay person who, as a model citizen, can also abrogate responsibility and so become complicit in destructive social and cultural norms. We see this in racial discrimination, ethnic cleansing, sexual subjugation and class privilege, which conscripts us to the violence of exclusivity.

Why do we hold onto what traps us? Because we have not yet learned to trust the Void, which is the way God comes to us as we walk through the second door of contemplation. The path of contemplation does not ask us to be stupid, naïve or ignorant. What we discover as we walk that path are the limits to our intelligence, the inability of the ways in which we understand the world to deal with everything we experience. Often, our inattentiveness, manifested in the things we overlook, happens because we do not know what to do with what we might see or discover. We falsely believe if we cannot make sense of the world, how can we deal with it? Yet we are not called to make sense of the world. The only one who can make sense of the world is God, and we are not God.

The myths we use to function in the world are broken myths. They cannot account for everything. Our legal system is biased towards the rich, our educational system towards the average, our medical system towards efficiency, our religious systems towards the establishment. But there are many who do not benefit from these systems: the ignored, the abandoned, the alienated, the outcast, the marginalized, the gifted.

The present world we live in does not have much use for God as a living reality. It finds a dead God who can be used to justify dead systems more manageable. That is why the path of contemplation is so difficult—because to walk that path we have to come to the edge of those myths which give our lives meaning and look down into the nothingness surrounding them. Only in contemplation, when we spend time in this nothingness, do we discover that this nothingness is really the mystery we call God.

But to name that nothingness, that mystery, as God really does not help us at this particular point of our journey. It substitutes one sound for another, for it is rather like telling a person learning the alphabet about semantics, or a person who knows addition and subtraction about probability-chaos theories, or a child who is hurt about love. It is just a word, a sound, another theory. The last thing the soul questing for God wants is another theory. What it wants is the experience of God, and that experience of God can only be found by living with God, living—spiritually—out of nothingness rather than out of myths, institutions, world views and conventional social norms.

To live in that radical insecurity is painful, because we not only lose a way, we lose even the name of the way. We lose all sense of direction. We are lost in the dark. It is like waking up from a dream to find ourselves on a street corner in a foreign country stark naked and without money or any understanding of the language. This is a time of enormous discouragement and depression, but what happens in that long time of pain is that our vision and our heart becomes purified in that long time of pain. At this time, the temptation to return to inadequate myths—like a dog to its vomit—is very strong. If we return again and again, we discover these do not satisfy. We are restless in them, rather like wearing tight clothes even though they might be fashionable. Finally, we just have to take them off, go out into the darkness and complain bitterly to God for not being there. Of course, God *is* there. The complaining comes from our limited perspective, which prevents us from seeing that presence. It is not as if God could appear otherwise, because for God to appear in ways we can understand at this stage, God would appear as sin. God, in that infinite mercy, has done just that through the gift of the Incarnation. The second letter to the Corinthians says, "For our sake he made [Jesus] to be sin who knew no sin, so that in him we might become the righteousness of God" (5:21). Jesus was misunderstood and killed for this.

We can only wait in that darkness beyond a particular broken myth until our perspective changes, until our attitudes change, until we come to the lived awareness of how conditional our existence is. We discover that we can take nothing for granted—neither our lives nor the things we hold most dear: our friends, our health, our present path through life, even our sanity. Even our understanding of how the love of God should manifest itself changes. If we hold love to be the affirmation of our selfishness—there to be warm and affirming, peaceful, nonjudgmental, happy and simple—we discover that we experience the presence of God as cruel and painful; it teases us with a desire it never satisfies. In our quest to satisfy that desire, we are stripped to basic desires—past even our dependency upon our sexuality—to define ourselves. We discover ourselves as desire for God. As we are stripped, we journey past the rawness of our sexuality, past shame, even—as Christ was on the cross—and however we entertain temptations, fall into them or not, we discover even they do not satisfy our hunger.

We have a hunger for what we do not know. That hunger not only takes away the myths by which we organize reality. It also takes away even the desire for knowledge, for knowledge is now seen to be ineffectual against our need. At this stage, even the wisdom of the wise does not help.

As can be expected, this is also a time of personal crisis, for with the terrible insistence of the hunger and its lack of compassion, we can at this stage see the falseness, the inadequacies, the errors and the compromises of the communities or the paths of life to which we are committed. We wonder if this is our path, but at this stage we have no other path to go down. We must tell people at this stage that no reason to stay on a particular path is no reason to go to another. The desire for flight is enormous. Anything, even the sense of movement, seems to give us the satisfaction of at least attempting to satisfy that hunger, and invites, only to frustrate, that intolerable urge.

Nothing helps. We just have to stay there in prayer. In this stage on the path of contemplation, nothing seems to be happening. Even prayer seems to be blank. We cannot spend time in prayer the way we spend an hour knitting or reading or watching TV or gardening. We become conscious of time in prayer. Contemplation now becomes an intensification of time; time seems to stretch on and on, filled with temptations and distractions, but with no ease or satisfaction.

This particular stage of contemplation spills over into our daily life and actually is a sign of the weaving together of our life that has been previously fragmented and compartmentalized by fear. At this stage our call is to fidelity, to be faithful to that hunger, and its purifying process. It is the opposite of clarity, wherein the self sees and understands reality in terms of myths, institutions and conventions, and there we can get an answer for almost anything. The opposite of that clarity is faith, in which we say yes to the unknown. When we step out of a particular fear and are not trapped by it, we tend to see things more clearly. Often we use that clarity to attack those who are trapped in that fear—the way reformed cigarette smokers are the most aggressive anti-smokers. We move on, then, from one trap to the next. We learn to move out of that trap through contemplation.

Contemplation moves us through being attentive to things to being lost in wonderment at what is present to us, and from that to a deeper wondering: about ourselves and about our path. That wonder shows us to be mystery and in mystery, where answers do not occur on any other level but the mysterious. Our entry now into the mysterious—in the act of contemplation—is through fidelity to our hunger. In that darkness we learn to use our spiritual senses.

In the preface to his novel *The Fratricides*, Nikos Kazantzakis has placed this poem:

God speaks:
He who seeks me, finds me.
He who finds me, knows me.
He who knows me, loves me.
He who loves me, him I love.
He whom I love, I kill.[8]

Passing Through Death

The journey towards God in contemplation leads towards death, and so we face death constantly on the path of contemplation. This refers not only to physical death, but also to the deaths of the various levels of the self. If, in contemplation, we discover we live various deaths, through contemplation we also move to resurrections beyond those deaths. When we move to give up fear, we face a form of death; we become outsiders. We no longer participate in the common sense and the myths of the world we live in, which keep us socialized through fear. When we give up clarity, we also die the death of finding the meaning for things.

We become a sacred fool. Yes, no, maybe: all become equally valid answers to almost any question. Someone asks you: What does so and so mean? You answer: Well, it depends. And it does depend on the perspective you want to take, or not take. When you say, "Well, it depends," often you are treated as if you are silly.

As we move through life, we are called to face many deaths: the deaths of family and friends, the deaths of projects, relationships, ideals, the deaths even of certain self-representations of self and of Church.

At whatever level of self is engaged in the act of contemplation, we experience those stages of coming to terms with death that Elisabeth Kübler-Ross has written about: denial, bargaining, anger, depression, acceptance. Of course, there are stages beyond acceptance. Beyond passive acceptance, there is active acceptance, and beyond acceptance there is indifference, and beyond indifference, creativity—or what Christians would call resurrection.

As we move from level to level of contemplation, we go through stages of death to creativity. Each death opens greater and greater areas of freedom and exposes us to subtler and subtler temptations. If, in this description of the path of contemplation, I am concentrating on the temptations and on the pain involved, it is because these things cause greater confusion than the peace and joy and the sense of life which accompany freedom. When directing someone on retreat, I often ask that old question, "Well, how is it going?"

The person answers, "Great! I am feeling peaceful and happy."

I ask, "Do you want to talk about it?"

The person usually says, "No, not really." The person looks at me with that air of kindness that implies, "What is there to talk about? This is what I have come on retreat for, isn't it … to have experiences of bliss, peace, contentment?" Then there is a little silence and the retreatant gets up and says, "Well, see you tomorrow … or whenever." After the person leaves, I wonder about that bliss. Where is it coming from? Where is it carrying that person?

In his rules for discernment, St. Ignatius says that those in consolation should prepare for ensuing desolation (Sp. Ex. #323, 324).

33

It is a different case for those who come in desolation. They usually want to know how to get out of it. They do not want this experience. They understand it as a clear sign that God is not with them, because they understand God in terms of sweetness and light.

The path of contemplation does not exist to give anyone experiences. If experiences come, they come. We all have experiences. Everything is an experience. The path to contemplation is about making the time we find ourselves in more and more resonant to God's time. It is about how to see God in everything, how to see everything in God, how to see everything as God sees everything.

The path to contemplation is not just to see God more clearly, or to feel God's presence more passionately; it is also to see the world as God sees the world. When we struggle to move from a perspective of ideology to one of faith, this involves not only changing, correcting or expanding our notions of God; it also involves changing, correcting or expanding our attitudes and our notions of the world.

To see the world with the human eyes of faith is to accept, first of all, the limitations of the world. It requires that we let go of false expectations of the world, even when the world solicits those expectations. If, for instance, we were to read the arts and entertainment section in one of the major newspapers every Sunday, we would soon discover dozens of movies and plays touted as "The Year's Best!" or "The Best of the Decade!" or even "One of the Most Significant of the Century!" If we were to go to only a handful of these, and only those that have won major awards, we would soon realize how disappointing most of them are. Oddly enough, the good ones seldom get that kind of attention or awards. Or consider the things we buy or do to be happy. Often they cause us more grief than pleasure, except the dubious pleasure of knowing we are conforming to someone else's myths about what will make us happy. Oscar Wilde once noted that "Most people are other people. Their thoughts are someone else's opinions, their lives a mimicry, their passions a quotation."[9] The path of contemplation allows us to become ourselves—no one else, and certainly not God.

The world, creation, we ourselves are not God. To put on others or ourselves expectations that are godlike is to court disaster, or at least depression, because such expectations are impossible to fulfill. What we learn on the level of faith, through the pain of purifying our vision, is a new evaluation of ourselves, our communities, our works and our God. How we put to use what we have learned thus far exposes us to the temptations of power.

Power

To be faithful is to have only one God. To be faithful is to allow ourselves to be possessed by God and only by God. To be faithful is not to possess God as if he were a divine puppet we could manipulate to show our power or as if he were a teddy bear we could hug every time we want to be comforted. To be possessed by God is to die many deaths; it is to engage in a passion that nothing in the world can destroy—neither pleasure nor humiliation, good health nor bad, approval nor disapproval.

When we think of Christ on the cross, and of his hunger and desire to remain faithful to the Father in the face of the unknowingness of death, the mockery, the humiliation and the sense of abandonment, we see what he has done is commit himself radically to the Void. He has given up power. Even the concept "God" is inadequate to comfort him in the face of the Void. He cries, echoing the psalmist, "My God, my God, why have you forsaken me?" (Matthew 27:46), and gives up his spirit. He lives towards, and past, a death his vocation calls him to. Our vocation also calls us to this death to truly become ourselves.

Giving up our spirit to the Void, or Father, is the dissolution of self, the dissolution of those forces or energies that make up our ego by being directed inwards. In living death, what constitutes our self is radically directed outwards. Every movement in our lives that effects this change of direction is a death. In so dying we give up the power to control our lives or the lives of others.

Our deaths do not come until we are ready for them along the path of contemplation. As we become what God wants us to become, co-creators of the universe, the deaths we face, learn to accept and live out of are the deaths we deal with in purgatory. Purgatory is nothing other than those moments on the path of contemplation when we are immersed in a love that burns our selfishness away. We are at all times immersed in that love. But there are those who are interpenetrated by those fires of love and do not realize it. They cling to their selfishness and to their sense of their identity, and are in hell. Love can be felt as heaven, purgatory or hell. When we accept the love that calls us beyond ourselves, and accept our vocation as that journey into love, the path of contemplation makes us realize and accept the gift of pain, especially spiritual pain. In this life, such pain means we are on the way. For one who believes, that pain ends only when everything and everyone are united to the Father by being aspects of Christ. In the meantime, we suffer from our own blindness, the blindness of others and the hate that stems from that blindness, until all are converted, redeemed and made one with the Father.

If we were to ask ourselves why we should go through this pain, these deaths, a purely selfish answer would be that no one will get to heaven, the fullness of life, until everyone gets to heaven. Heaven, the fullness of life, will always be incomplete if our worst enemy is not there, transformed, filled with the glory and love of God. And if our worst enemy is not in heaven, we are not there either, because a part of us is not in heaven. Because we are perverse creatures—in fact, Jeremiah says that there is nothing so perverse as the human heart—we might think, "Well, I can give up a little piece of heaven to see some of the people I hate in hell. It serves them right, and I do not mind paying that little price. After all, I am with enough friends and, in a pinch, I can get by with just one friend."

That pearl of little price! When we have just one fragment of hate, in truth we do not have even one friend. Hate is selfish; it wants no friends, and it will work and work on us until we are absolutely alone. The path to contemplation is the way to make friends with ourselves, with others and with God.

But, like Mary at the Annunciation, we can ask: How is this possible? Fears, on one hand, are easy to recognize, to pray over, to deal with. But how does one deal with clarity—to use it against itself—as a friend? We can ask ourselves: What do I not understand? We can make a list of all the things that we do not understand as well as the things that make us angry or fearful or that we dismiss as unimportant: stock car races, why so-and-so behaves in such and such a way, why we are not more happy or unhappy about certain things in ourselves, in others, in God, in the Church, in the world. Doing this brings these things to attention. We bring them to light to wonder about them, but we are doing something more important. We are confessing our limitations and our inability to have all the answers. We are acknowledging our ignorance, our weakness, our brokenness, our inability to discern in detail the evolving plan of creation in which we are intimately involved. We are escaping from the trap of clarity and from the temptations power offers.

To confess is not just to acknowledge; it is to bear witness to. We admit to ourselves that we are not God. Now, this can be a very liberating moment, and an exciting one, because we are giving up the pretense of having it all together. What destroys us is not our brokenness, but the illusions and pretenses we use to hide that brokenness from ourselves and others. Rather than leaving our wounds open to the healing love of the Father, those illusions cover our wounds, which then fester and eat into the very bones of our lives. To live our brokenness openly is to manifest in our lives the scandal of the cross—and the scandal of the Father's love. To live out of our brokenness maintains our fidelity.

Fidelity, then, is not merely an intellectual assent to dogma. It is not a mere recitation of the creeds for the believer, and, for religious, the constitutions of their religious orders. It is a way of bearing ourselves; it is the attitude we take to the myths of the world. The work of the faithful ones is the refusal to live out of those myths and the determination to point out their deceptions. To do this is not to create another myth, but to live towards the calling we are: manifestations of the mystery of God's presence in the world. At this stage along the path, contemplation is the presence of mystery to mystery.

If we wait faithfully in the darkness, following the path our hunger takes us, what gets transformed in us is the notion of time.

We discover a vital life after the deaths we endure. We discover that we can live without answers, and so we can live differently in time. Time becomes not the stretch given us to do things in, but—every moment of it—an entry into the mystery of God's presence. Time becomes the encounter with wonder. This allows us to put things in perspective: the humble mending of a shirt is as important as organizing a community or running a school or a hospital. Everything allows us a chance to encounter God.

At this stage, contemplation is not letting our minds go blank or tuning in to our alpha waves; it is going beyond the borders of our mind. It is not being enticed by the mind to try to enter more fully into the mystery of God through some systematic exposition that creates just another intellectual construct. The mystery of God is the source of the mind, and the heart, and all of their products. By sinking into that mystery, which the mystics describe as "void," "nothingness," "darkness," we can, for the first time, enjoy the mind, because if we persevere in fidelity, mind becomes tamed again and ordered again. Its products, then, are not to justify itself but to build up the kingdom of God.

Living Death Decisively

If we can enter into our death and stay with the agony—however it may manifest itself to us as pain, boredom, exhaustion or something else—in time we discover life in that death. Life has been there all along, for Christ has been there before us, waiting for us as the Father waited for him. If we can live through our deaths in patience and humility, we discover a new face of Christ and a new face of the Father.

Yet it is one thing to be aware of the ultimate context within which the insights into life are to be had and quite another to have to make concrete and appropriate decisions based on our awareness of that context. We all know that our values are to be manifestations of our intimacy with God, and so help create the reign of God on earth, but how to live that reign in our daily life is quite a different matter.

On this stage of the path, the temptations we must contend with are to dismiss any decision as insignificant when faced with the void, or to regard any decision as so crucial that we are faced with scruples. Both are blocks on the path to transcendence, because both deny the Incarnation, which affirms for us that God does speak in the world so that it is possible to do his will in time. The last four words are important. Because God has chosen time to manifest himself in time, time is important, and because his word is incarnated in time, it is his time. And though God's word may be misunderstood, abused or manipulated by his creatures, yet God's speech is time.

Discernment asks how to use time properly; we can use time properly only if we understand time properly. Time presents the invitation to transcendence. It opens us to the word of God calling, inviting, disposing and leading us. To ignore time is to ignore God's invitation, and so is to ignore God. Therefore, we cannot do nothing; we cannot be apathetic or other-worldly and live a spiritual life. On the other hand, we cannot live a spiritual life and work out of our fears or ideologies or selfishness. The question is, of course, what do we have to do now?

We need to ask this question because the path to contemplation leads to action. In fact, contemplation comes to its fruit in action. Contemplation is neither quietism nor being worldly. The temptation that comes at this stage of the path emerges from trying to decide what is the right thing to do. The temptation of power is to impose upon the Void our own ambitions, rather than becoming empty and allowing God to pass through us into the world. So what are we to do?

It would be easy to answer, "Everything." Everything and anything done in freedom is the right thing to do, and that is true. But often we are not free. We are—or should be—aware of just how much a sinner we are. The awareness of the degree to which our compulsions, known and unknown, enter into our actions makes the contemplative, who wants to do the work of God, hesitate. What is the right thing to do?

At this stage, there is a clear need for what St. Ignatius calls the discernment of spirits, because in dying, we are tugged by many different forces. The underlying pull is often between pride and humility, between maintaining our illusory ego at the present or more pleasant levels of existence, or entering the void, and becoming an integral part of the creativity of God in time. What causes tension is the growing awareness of the void opening within us. It is only when we accept the void within us and within the lived spaces of our lives that we can move to a further level of intimacy with God. What is of concern here are the difficulties encountered in living the void in a concrete manner. The forces of the ego, of self-preservation, engage in a life-and-death struggle not to accept the reality of the self as void, because the ego sees this literally as death.

Prayer opens us up to death. We learn to face death in prayer and to face that sense of being totally dependent upon life beyond our control. At this stage, in effect, we live that prayer in our lives. It is here we discover the meaning of the beatitudes for us: what it means to be poor in spirit, to be meek, to mourn, to hunger, to thirst for justice, to be, in spite of the burdens we bear, merciful, clean of heart, peacemakers, and truly to suffer persecution for the sake of heaven. To live the beatitudes is to acknowledge death. Yet this is not to seek death, which would be an instance of pride, since martyrs are made not by human will but through God's dispensation. We do not have to seek death. What contemplation does is uncover the death, and the resurrection, we already are.

If we want to discern, we need to do it out of death, out of our awareness of the void at the centre of us. If we can live consciously with the emptiness that centres us—for it never goes away—we discover through it we are connected to the Father. What we experience existentially as our emptiness, understood as our radical poverty of spirit, is connected intimately with the Void we name Father. Christ emptied out on the cross opens to the void and discovers in his humanity the redemptive love of the Father. The matters we have to discern and to decide upon must be tested by the encounter between our emptiness and the Void. What emerges from that encounter comes from God, since in that encounter all evil is overcome and only what is rooted in God's life survives.

Often when we consider these things we become scared or skeptical. We think we have neither the courage nor the special skills to walk the path of contemplation. In truth, each of us is called to walk that path, and in walking it we discover we have whatever we need to walk it. This is how contemplation changes our self-image, opens our imaginations to greater dimensions of wonder and liberates our lives to greater freedom and love.

Contemplation allows us to live our lives spiritually. Whatever happens to us, we live our lives. Often, in practice, we tend to live our lives in cultural roles, as professionals, as teachers, administrators, and so on. We tend to invest this professional status with the emotional expectations appropriate to the spiritual life. Yet, on that professional level, things do not make spiritual sense and we become frustrated. It is as though, in spite of our calling, we were seeking the most secular forms of satisfaction first and trying to apply those forms of satisfaction even to our understanding of our spiritual life. Think of the guilt we sometimes feel when we remember the commandment to love our neighbor, a member of our family or community, and we know emotionally just how much we cordially hate that person. To live our life merely at the emotional or professional level is to become trapped in a diminished self-image. We are saved not by how we feel or by what roles we assume in the marketplace, but only by the Father's love for us. It is rather frightening to come to understand how helpless we are to save ourselves. Contemplation, in opening us up to the void, gives us the humility to live spiritually. Within that humility we discover the passion, the courage and the humour to make decisions and live our lives in accordance with God's will.

Humility overcomes scruples and apathy. For the person with scruples, God's will is completely caught up in a dead tradition. It is as though God's plan for creation were a predetermined blueprint that one must discover and apply with rigid fidelity. If one holds this, then one holds that the Father predetermined his Son's death, and what we worship then is a selfish God enmeshed in an abstract justice. This is the God of institutions. If we worship such a God, that act denies both God's freedom and our own, keeps us spiritually undeveloped, stops us from making adult decisions, and thus prevents us from being responsible. To be scrupulous is to deny our responsibility, and to be responsible is to cooperate with God's invitation to be free. Our institutions, our constitutions, our vows, our relationships with those in authority, secular or ecclesial, are valid only if they bring us and themselves to freedom. We should not confuse idolatry with obedience.

The decisions we make on the path we are walking are of value only if they bring us and the people and the occupations we work with to freedom. It is an illusion to think only of personal freedom, for freedom involves everyone, not just ourselves; and so when we make decisions that claim to be responsible, we need to make them with a concrete context in mind and, indeed, if possible, with every factor and person making up that context. The decisions must bring all in that context to freedom.

Freedom is a very frightening thing, for it calls us to be supportive to what builds up God's community and to withdraw our support from what does not. No one within himself or herself has that kind of energy, and often we sacrifice the freedom to which we are called for security. Our energy to make and endure discerned decisions comes from the passion we discover within ourselves when we move to an intimacy with the Father. When we open ourselves to the hunger to be with the Father, we are carried and sustained by that hunger. When that hunger we have meets the hunger the Father has for us, we enter into a context of love that is the presence of the Holy Spirit. We share, then, the spirit of holiness.

When we love somebody, we know what that person is thinking and feeling because we think and feel just as that person does. The same heart, the same approach to life is shared. When people are in love, there is an incredible simplicity between them, an incredible openness to each other, an incredible playfulness and ease. When we are in love with someone, whatever that person does is all right, and whatever we do is all right for that other person. When St. Augustine tells us, "Love and do what you will," he is speaking about this level of responsiveness that is available to us all as we open ourselves up to the void.

That is why—when we discover that the void in us is the door through which God enters our life—when, instead of hiding from that void or hiding that void from us, we learn to accept it, live with it, cherish it, seek it out in all areas of life, we start becoming more and more intimate with God. Then it does not matter what we do or what God does. Then the decisions and the doing are not important. What is important is being with God. It is rather like going on a holiday with a friend. It really does not matter what you do; you can do everything or nothing. What is important is the time you spend together. Contemplation, here, is shared time. Our time is God's time, and no other time is as interesting, as nourishing or as alive as that time.

To be contemplative, to be alive in the void, extends the range of our emotions and the depth of our emotions, because every aspect of our life is touched by God. Nothing is withheld and nothing repressed. You may say, "But surely in the contemplative life our sexuality is repressed." It is not. Our prayer becomes so emotional as to satisfy in a most delicate and strong way the generative instinct each of us has. We discover that our sexuality is a part of everything else that we are. It is not cut off and put in the freezer. In that sexuality, which moves towards integration, we discover the sense of joy, of belonging, of sharing all we are. Similarly, despite what people might say about poverty, we discover that we have enough—in fact, more than enough—for our needs. In the state of contemplative love, we discover that obedience never becomes elaborate power plays or passive-aggressive games. We discover that it is no big deal to do this or that. We discover that God can be found here or there or anywhere. This radical dependency upon God, and our experience of God's constant care for us, is not restricted to those in religious life. It is available to everyone. It is the gift, from God, of being human.

This enthusiasm for the void is not naïveté or idealism, nor is it unrealistic about what sharing God's time with him, or God's sharing our time with us, can do. Contemplation transforms, and that transformation becomes the beginning of ever deeper, more all-encompassing transformations. The path to contemplation never ends; we never get bored. There is, in contemplation, no dead end, no final death. We discover that what looks like death from the outside, when approached and reached out to, is really a door to fuller life. When St. Francis embraces the leprous old woman in rags—how he describes Lady Poverty—she becomes beautiful.

The temptation we must see through in discernment is to stop before death. If we stop before we go through the doors of death, we end up not glorifying the power of God through the resurrection, but fostering inadequate notions of ourselves hemmed in by fear, and so we do not give the Father the freedom to be in the world. Difficult times are not difficult if God is with us, and God is with us in every stage and in every aspect of our lives. Our difficulty is that our fears stop us from recognizing his presence, and so we often mistake something else for him.

In contemplation we do not choose death; we choose the Father. There is a subtle spiritual pride that invites us to choose death at times, to say yes to the things we know can destroy us and most likely will. We want the world and God to see what good spiritual people we are. Sometimes our reasons are much more blatant. We might figure we need a change, or feel we should be further up the corporate ladder than we are, and so we say yes to a job or we become ambitious. Of course, superiors and administrators are usually quite glad and even relieved that we accept to do this or that thing. So we walk into death and soon become mauled, disillusioned, burned out and cynical. The glamour, the acknowledgement we sought to satisfy ourselves cannot support us, and we cannot support ourselves. We get destroyed or addicted.

What went wrong? What went wrong is that our eyes were fixed on the job rather than on the Father, and so we set off on a path that, little by little, carried us to our deaths and our deaths only. I am not suggesting that we should not take difficult jobs, but that we should take those jobs only when they involve oneness with the Father. This, of course, should be true not only for difficult jobs but for any job, even flossing our teeth.

People often ask: How are we one with the Father? When asked what they think about it, they usually describe being one with the Father in terms of high mysticism, raptures, ecstasies, visions, transports, voices, miracles and healings. What they want is rather like Harlequin romances, as if God were a drug that induced a high. Often those people have to be asked: What is it like

awareness of love-as-time when we become attentive to the strands of our lives interwoven with the strands of others' lives. When we contemplate what rises from the depths, what comes to us from the void is the presence of other lives in our present life. As in true community, they support, give direction and comfort. They share time with us—like the breaking of bread together, the sharing of a meal with each other. That is why the Eucharist is so important. In it, all the acts of contemplation are made actively present.

In the Eucharist, God is made present, life is celebrated, a bonding with others occurs, sins are forgiven, the gifts of the Spirit are shared, and there is created in our time an open space for the world to enter and become humanized. In contemplation, the same things occur. This is the last stage of contemplation—before we move again through deeper levels of fear, to deeper openings to wonder; and then the whole process begins again and again, spiralling out until everything and everyone is involved, and all past, present and future are aflame with God's love. No one will be fully himself or herself until this happens. The path of contemplation opens us out to all of creation and reality, and opens all of creation and reality to God. That opening out and the interweaving of our lives create community, which allows us to be more alive and to risk more.

It is a tremendous gift to be on the right path and a bigger gift to be aware that we are on the right path, but it is awesome to encounter one or two others on the same path, and then more and still more. It does not matter what sex or age they are, what job they do, or where they are from. There is a living bond, which makes creativity and the celebration of life possible.

By making us members of a community, the path to contemplation ties us into a tradition. A tradition is not something static, nor is it handed down like mother's silver, with the stern admonition that "This is the way things are done." That is not tradition; that is ritual custom. Tradition is alive and ongoing and capable of welcoming disparate elements in its development. Often, people trapped by fear try to keep tradition alive by freezing it to make it secure. Yet if we truly walk the path of contemplation, we open ourselves to a tradition that carries on the saving work of Christ who was raised to life. It is a tradition the prophets carried on before him and that the saints, mystics, martyrs and holy men and women continue on after him until the fullness of the Second Coming.

All of these share one thing in common. They are creative. The path to contemplation leads to creativity, the highest form of action. To be creative—and this is different from exercising power—extends over all activities: cooking and sewing, being a nurse or teacher or administrator, giving or receiving spiritual direction. It is only secondarily to be innovative, for the root of creativity is not originality—which is a Romantic reinterpretation of that activity. To understand creativity, we need to look at the original creator, God as Father and as Mother. To be creative is to give life and to allow life to be lived most fully: the highest form of creativity is community.

When contemplation moves us to such creativity, we ask ourselves how to establish and maintain community. When we forgive ourselves and when we forgive others, we give ourselves and others the time, the space, the encouragement to be healed and to live openly without guilt. When we do that, we bring people back to life; we raise them from the dead to new life. Often when we say we are sorry we just mean: Can we be civil to each other again without too much tension? But to reduce forgiveness to a social convention does not give life, because the space then opened is just a social space. To forgive, we must open a spiritual space, and to do that we have to hold our own pain and the other person's pain, the institution's or the culture's pain, together with the pain that causes the other person, institution, community or culture to hurt us. We cannot do it alone, and so we need the support of the community we find as we walk the path of contemplation. What we create, we create out of brokenness, alienation, disease. We create, as T.S. Eliot puts it, "with shabby equipment always breaking down."[10] What a good artist or musician does is create openings, spaces through which we can see life, live it, enjoy it and share it. When we move in contemplation, we move to the same activity in the world.

To be creative is to move beyond the clichés of what constitutes a spiritual life. For instance, it is always interesting to observe the ways in which different religious communities live in a postmodern culture with the same problems of overwork, lack of vocations, financial difficulties and aging members. Some of these communities are life-giving; others are deadly. What causes the difference? In those that are alive, we find a self-sacrificing love that is echoed in 2 Corinthians 6:4-10. The communities with life are not afraid to talk about their spiritual lives and the pains of their lives. They share the pains and the joys of their lives. They celebrate what they have and they celebrate who they are. It is the same thing with families, or any other social group.

One of the biggest blocks on the path of contemplation is the lack of celebration, a fear of celebrating joy, enjoying parties, going out to dinner, entertaining, spending relaxed and relaxing time with those others whose paths we cross. There is a peculiar cliché about the spiritual life that says it must reject anything fun or enjoyable. The rationale varies: it is unedifying, it shows a lack of seriousness, it violates the vow of poverty; spiritual people so identify with the suffering of humanity and of the Christ on the cross that they do not behave this way; there are more worthy things to be done with one's time. There is a very strong and perverse myth that insists that the proper witness to God's love excludes fun. When did you last hear someone laugh in a church service? Why is it considered inappropriate? That creeping fear spreads itself across relationships and denies them for the sake of "a witness to chastity" even though we are emotional and sexual and social human beings. That same fear suggests "in the name of obedience" that we do not take responsibility for our lives and for maintaining life in our communities and so we hand over power to the institutions we belong to in order to determine how this is to be done. This fear under the guise of poverty encourages parsimony. This false myth makes us walking dead, and we read this life just as "a vale of tears."

What is lost is humour, a delight in our absurdity and in the absurdity of the world. Everything becomes heavy and serious. The freedom we attain in contemplation allows us to delight in our lives in the way God as Father and Mother delights in our lives, the way a parent delights when a child is enjoying itself. This delight in life allows our existence in time to be play, and contemplation becomes play—for play is the most liberating form of creativity.

In spiritual direction, it is always interesting to ask this question: "Do you ever play with God?" It is also interesting to ask, "Whom do you play with? Do you ever play? When is the last time you played?" Thomas Aquinas tells us that there are two kinds of activity that have no end or purpose outside themselves. One of these is contemplation, and the other is play.[11] Contemplation is play. When we enter a state of contemplation, we allow God to play with us, and in playing with God, we come to forms of spiritual intimacy not found anywhere else. Serious people do not play, and we do not play with serious people; we also do not play with silly people. We can only truly play with people who have a sense of humour. How can we ever enjoy God, delight in the mystery God seduces us with, risk ourselves in him, or even understand him as the one we can play with, if we are always serious?

Such seriousness damages us, others and everything we do. It builds up such resentment that it distorts us so we cannot function normally. There is a story about a spiritual director who, on an eight-day retreat, met someone who was so angry about having to do a retreat that she claimed she hated the director, hated the reasons that brought here there, hated God, and even hated herself for being there. Now, this director, who was slightly crazy himself, took one look at her, got up from his chair, went over to his wallet, pulled out some money, and gave it to her, saying, "For at least once in your life, try to have a pleasant day." She took the money, went downtown, bought ice cream cones, went shopping, had a nice little lunch, went off to a show, came back, and apparently had a good retreat after that. In fact, this story comes from her. What did she discover with her day? Quite simply that God likes fun, too. The God she started to discover that day is one who does not hurt and who does not delight in anyone's suffering, but is rather the one who heals our hurts and whose salvific work is best witnessed to by our laughter.

Laughter cannot be forced; joy breaks down barriers; play occurs when people recreate, without competition, envy, jealousy or anger. When we trust God, we can trust ourselves in God. And when we can trust ourselves with God, we can relax, we can recreate, and then we can recreate into something joyful what has been broken and damaged, what has been dead.

Contemplation makes us witnesses to the true face of God, because as we delight in him, we learn to delight in our lives. Because of contemplation, our life is no longer a grind, a task or a distraction from boredom; it becomes an adventure, a holiday—even though at times it may be difficult or riddled with anxiety.

In that joy, and because we can trust, we explore further and further what it means to be alive. We go down deeper and we expand. As we do this we uncover new hurts to be healed, new forms of repression to be dismantled, new invitations to power to be refused, and newer and newer ways of being creative and thereby making this world, our culture, our institutions and our communities more alive. As they say in the sequel to *Star Trek*, the journey continues. It is a journey into joy, for in it and through it the dead rise and share its life. The joy of the resurrection renews the whole world. We are invited to enter into that joy and, through living that joy, transform all of creation into a home for all.

Conclusion

Walking the path of contemplation makes us see reality with spiritual eyes. Contemplation does not give us two worlds: the practical world in which we wash our underwear and dislike broccoli, and a spiritual world to which we withdraw to escape. Contemplation makes washing our underwear a spiritual act. It opens levels of awareness on the level of the commonplace. We have only one world, and it is in this world that God spends time with us. Insofar as we share the passion Christ has for the Father and the passion the Father has for the world, and insofar as we share their Spirit, the places we live in will be touched by the healing and transforming presence of God.

Through contemplation, we become the living words of God in our world, and we are sent by that vocation to become the continuing presence of Christ, not only in our work, in our apostolate and in the places we live, but in everything we do. If we have to tell people about God, let us tell them about what he has done for us, about what we have personally experienced: the transformation of our fears, the freedom from the prisons of false myths, the passion of our hunger and where it has led us. That is, if we have to speak to people about God. Otherwise, let the people we encounter know about God through the lives we lead: by our willingness to bear the pain of forgiving, by our joy in the humblest of tasks, by our laughter even in the darkest moments.

What we have been given is not given only for us. It is given to be shared. Only in that sharing do we experience what it means to be Church, and if we are truly Church, then we can transform the institutions we now have and thereby create those open spaces— those temples and sanctuaries—in which God, who promises to be ever with us, can dwell and in which others who are now lost and alienated and searching can dwell and fulfill themselves creatively.

The path to contemplation never ends. Christ himself is in agony until the world is brought back to the Father. The saints and the martyrs in their contemplative states share our joys and struggles on earth just as we share, through contemplation, their joys and passion in heaven. Those with whom God shares his time, as we go farther and farther on that path to contemplation, will find ourselves called to hold different fears up to his love, allow more and more of the constrictive scaffolding we have relied on to drop away, enter into deeper and deeper deaths, become more and more simple, and discover ways beyond present telling of being creative in the situations in which we will find ourselves.

The path of contemplation does not only lead to life. The path of contemplation *is* life. It carries us past our fears and our desire for clarity. It allows us to transcend the temptations to power, and frees us from the traps of despair. Walking that path, which is offered to all, we learn to celebrate life. We can do that by becoming attentive to the life we live here and now.

Part II

Being Rooted, Being Attentive: Covenant Moments

Introduction

The Principle and Foundation of the Spiritual Life is Attention. We are attentive not only to ourselves and to the circumstances we find ourselves in, but also, consciously or not, we attend those who concern themselves with us. Not the least among these is the God who desires us. In fact, our attention is a form of mutuality. In every stage of the spiritual journey, being attentive to what we are present to, and are presented with, allows us to have a relationship to the God who is always present to us. Moses in the desert encounters a God who describes himself as "I Am Who Am." That God is not only always present, but is the presence in whom we live and move and have our being. That God is not only the ground of our presence but is also the One we encounter in the different ways and in the different relationships as we go through the different stages of our spiritual journey. The Spiritual Exercises of St. Ignatius, which gives a path to spiritual intimacy, translates this attentiveness in its Principle and Foundation:

> Humans are created to praise, reverence, and serve God our Lord, and by this means to save their souls. And the

53

other things on the face of the earth are created for humans to help them in prosecuting the end for which they are created. From this it follows that humans are to use them as much as they are an aid to this end, and ought to rid themselves of them so far as they are a hindrance to that end. For this it is necessary that we make ourselves indifferent to all created things in all that is allowed to the choice of our free will and is not prohibited to it; so that, on our part, we want not health rather than sickness, riches rather than poverty, honor rather than dishonor, long rather than short life, and so in all the rest; desiring and choosing only what is most conducive for us to the end for which we are created. (Sp. Ex. #21)

If we can look beyond the provocative nature of its moral rhetoric, which challenges our easy assumptions about life, we see that this Principle and Foundation basically asks us what we are attentive to and how we are attentive to it. What we are attentive to reveals who we understand ourselves to be, shows us what we value, and thus reveals where we put our life.

Created in the image and likeness of God (Genesis 1:26, 27), we are desire as God is Desire. God desires creation to be fulfilled, and creation can be fulfilled only by being in full relationship with God. That relationship is offered to us in the Christian tradition by our incorporation in the resurrected humanity of Christ, who has been commissioned to restore all to the fullness of life. Paul's Letter to the Ephesians tells us this. It notes, "to each one of us grace has been given as Christ apportioned it" (4:7) … "to prepare God's people for works of service, so that the body of Christ may be built up until we all reach unity in the faith and in the knowledge of the Son of God and become mature, attaining to the whole measure of the fullness of Christ" (4:12-13).

Our whole being, from our corporate spirit to every cell of our physical body, desires God. Often we think of desire as a feeling, but feeling is only one small manifestation of our identity as desire. Like light that extends beyond the visible spectrum, so, too, does desire extend beyond the sense spectrum of feeling. We are more than our feelings. Our feelings, operating within the horizons of our being as desire, are limited indicators of who we are. Yet those feelings reveal to us something of what we value, for feelings are our values refined to spontaneity and experienced bodily. I encounter other people and I immediately feel something for them. Their presence touches something in me and I respond. That response is shaped by my lived experience, my culture, my gender, my family upbringing and even by my genetic makeup. Sometimes those responses are life-affirming; at other times they are not. This raises the question of the way we feel and of its relationship to our being created as desire for God. Why do some of our feelings of desire turn us away from God?

We are Desire and Desire intends God. We are created by God as the Desire for God, and we are oriented to God through our desires. On one hand, we can operate out of the narrowing of desire by limiting our awareness of ourselves as desire to seek satisfactions that run contrary to satisfying us fully. Those satisfactions appease only a limited aspect of ourselves. This is not bad. It becomes bad when we devote our whole life to such limits and ignore other dimensions of ourselves. They distract us from ourselves. Then, like Esau, being hungry, we exchange our birthright for a mess of pottage (Genesis 25). On the other hand, we can also operate out of the expansiveness of who we are, and then we can also experience that sense of rootedness in God through our feelings. Feeling can reveal to us if we live our lives as desire or as distraction. Indeed, in the spiritual journey our feelings can act as a moral compass.

When we are good and are moving towards God, we often experience feelings of consolation, because there is a resonance between us and God that exhibits itself in peace, joy, delight, simplicity. When we do bad things but are still basically good people, there is dissonance between us and God, and we experience feelings of guilt, shame and remorse. The opposite occurs when we are committed to lesser goods that take us away from our heart's desire. Then we are affirmed by those lesser goods and have a sense of satisfaction when we give into them. However, we experience desolation when, so turned away from God, we happen to become aware of the all-encompassing presence of God.

To escape that desolation, we often indulge ourselves more and more in those soul-destroying activities and end up becoming addicted. In short, how we respond to our lives as desire shapes our feelings and determines the range of our feelings. Too long an exposure to lesser goods deadens our feelings, and we may be left with hearts of stone. Encounters with the divine transform those hard hearts to ones of flesh, able to empathize with the joys and the sufferings of humanity.

Our feelings show us what we actually pay attention to, and when we learn to become attentive to our feelings we have a way of discerning how to become more deeply engaged in our spiritual journey. Reading our feelings is not an exercise in narcissism or morbid introspection. Our feelings are the text that God, the world and others use to communicate with us. Feelings give us the texture of our lives, the habitual world out of which we spontaneously operate. We can be habitually depressed, angry, confused or apathetic; we can also be in a state of constant wonder, serenity, gratitude, rootedness. Most of the time we find ourselves in a mixture of both. When we start paying attention to how we feel, and why we feel the way we do, we can start becoming intentional about our lives. That drive to live fully sets us out on a spiritual journey. At each stage of that journey, we find ourselves torn by two forces. One draws us to an ever deeper rootedness in God; the other tempts us to find our security within our selves. At each stage of the journey, our feelings illuminate where and how we stand on our path. They become our spiritual compass.

As we become more in tune with the Desire who desires us, the focus of our attention changes and our feelings change. They become more all-encompassing and more nuanced. There are times when they even fall below the range of affectivity, and we might find ourselves waiting to feel. This does not happen because we are no longer in contact with God; rather, the contact is occurring at levels of our desire beyond feeling. Then all we can do is wait for our self-awareness to grow to arrive at those levels of intimacy. At other times, the awareness of being embraced by God feels like pain. As in Purgatory, this embrace both brings to light our disorders and works to eradicate those disorders that are so woven into our psyche that their transformation feels like a "refining fire." God says he puts those who desire him more fully

> into the fire,
> and refine them as one refines silver,
> and test them as gold is tested.
> They will call upon my name,
> and I will answer them.
> I will say, "They are my people";
> and they will say, "The Lord is my God." (Zechariah 13:9)

When we start to become attentive to God in our lives, we feel that peculiar mixture of affirmation, when what is good in our lives is noted and celebrated, as well as desolation, when what is contrary to our spiritual well-being is also noted and felt as suffering.

This attention shows us where we are in our relationship with God. We attend God. We are waiting on God, and being trained by God as servants to one in authority. The focus on what holds our interest is a manifestation of that relationship of service. Or, to put it another way, in those consolations and desolations we experience how we are disposed to love, and how we spontaneously react to our call to be loving and lovable. When we love, we live out of our most comprehensive desire that connects us to God, and our other desires become integrated within this horizon of desire that calls us and attracts us to God.

Basically, we intend God. We are incomplete within ourselves. This is experienced as desire, which intends to be satisfied. We seek that satisfaction of completeness by having a life-giving relationship with the Creator. As St. Augustine of Hippo points out at the very beginning of his *Confessions*, "Our hearts are restless until they rest in Thee." In this he echoes St. Paul: "Even we ourselves groan within ourselves, waiting for the adoption, namely, the redemption of our body" (Romans 8:23). This dissatisfaction is both the awareness of our creaturehood and the call of the Divine. Such dissatisfaction manifests itself in what we concretely pay attention to in our life. It calls us on a journey.

Attention is a Journey

When we start to become aware of our dissatisfaction, this stage of attention leads us to embark on a spiritual journey in which we wait *for* God and we wait *on* God. Techniques cannot bring God to us. God's attending to us is a gift. I would say, humbly, that God is always present to us. We are blocked from our awareness of that presence because of illusions and distractions. We cannot bring ourselves to that noticing. It lies beyond our will, though not beyond our intention. We can dispose ourselves to notice, and wait to see what happens. We need teachers and guides to help us unpack what we experience during that active waiting. As one Buddhist said, enlightenment is an accident, but techniques make us accident prone. There is a process of coming to notice. That process is often dialectical. We are tugged in two directions. One desires God; the other seeks to subvert that desire. Each level of attentiveness is gained by a hard-won struggle, often established after many reversals, and usually not appropriated until after we have left it. As each level of attention is addressed and consolidated in our consciousness, we open out to another, which contains deeper and broader aspects of our being in relationship to God. This journey never ends, because as creatures we cannot comprehend the infinity of the Creator. As God's beloved, we never reach the limits of God's love.

Attention as Relationship

There are many ways of depicting this journey into relationship. The journey goes two ways. As we attend to God, God also attends to us. God presents God's self to us in different ways as we journey into that life. In the Scriptures, this journey is presented as the Promise, the Incarnation, Baptism, Transfiguration, Passion, Resurrection, Ascension, Pentecost, The Second Coming, and Recapitulation. These are ten radically different ways of God's self-presence to us in the humanity of Christ as we journey into our relationship with God. Here we see God attending to us in his Divine Mercy. On the human side, we could look at stages of faith and spiritual development as proposed by Erik Erikson or James Fowler, for example, to see how humans journey.

The Development of Attention

In this section of the book, I have chosen the Ox-herding pictures of Buddhism to explore some stages of attentiveness in the spiritual journey. They can be traced back to a Ch'an master in the Sung dynasty of China (1126–1279 AD), but they have their roots in the early Buddhist texts. Buddhism explores the nature of human consciousness as relationship without attaching itself to specific religious dogma. When each stage of attentiveness has become appropriated, it opens out to a newer form of awareness. The letting go of the habits of older forms of attention and the acceptance of those newer forms can often be disturbing and can take a long time to be fully appropriated. Exploring each of these stages, I use St. Ignatius of Loyola's Meditation on The Two Standards, which occurs in his Spiritual Exercises. This mediation breaks open the tension that dwells in every human being: the tension between a call to God and the denial of that call. Each stage of attention exposes that dynamic in ways that are different from the previous stages.

Attention as a Form of Rootedness

Oddly enough, these ever newer forms of attentiveness, while they root us ever deeper into more comprehensive forms of relationship, often uproot us from the familiar and the habitual, and cast us more and more deeply into the world of mystery and into the stance of wonder. A brief example from Kierkegaard might be helpful here. It comes from one of his reflections on faith, called "Fear and Trembling." He notes that there are three different modes of being: the aesthetic, the ethical and the faith-ful. There is a significant shift in awareness from the aesthetic person to the ethical person. The first seeks a life of pleasure and sensuality; the second lives a life of conformity to social norms. This is commonly referred to as growing up after sowing one's wild oats. But then there is the third level of awareness, belonging to the knight of faith, where someone, like Abraham, is asked to go beyond all the values of his culture and sacrifice what he holds most dear. For Abraham it was his son Isaac. Abraham's relationship with God carries him to a level of attentiveness that seems, at best, absurd to the world he lives in. But only with the offering of his son does he show his commitment to his relationship with God and become the knight of faith. Because of that rite of passage, Abraham now has a relationship with the future of Israel that was not his before. The radical uprooting of all Abraham has known and believes in leads him to his new sense of self.

We find this same pattern of rootedness/uprootedness in the spiritual journey of Moses. After it is discovered that he has killed an Egyptian, he abandons his life of privilege and flees into the desert. There he encounters God in the burning bush. That God describes himself as Abiding Presence. "I AM WHO AM." The stripping away of previous forms of attention by a desert life opens Moses' vision to become aware of what is always there. That particular encounter moves him to a different level of self-awareness, and opens him up even further to his own spiritual journey. He returns to the place from which he had exiled himself and liberates those who are trapped there. He leads them through a desert experience that he also has endured. But even there he is again being transformed into what it means to be a prophet. He keeps relinquishing his life in his spiritual journey. He never enters the promised land.

Jesus, as the new Moses, gives up his life to enter resurrection. Jesus' followers do the same. Paul is converted, and then martyred. Francis of Assisi, Teresa of Avila and Ignatius of Loyola endured illness that took them from their previous lives to a new way of being in the world. In their growing attentiveness, they became, each in their own way, more and more attentive to God and more and more disposed to the desire that named them, called them and brought them further into the fullness of life to which each human is invited.

For anyone who is consciously on the spiritual path, attentiveness is the principle and foundation that provides the rootedness for our discernments, our work, our relationships, our identity and our stance in the world.

To become attentive is to be intentional about where we find ourselves, and to be aware of the dynamics of desire that situate us in the world in which we are incarnated. This does not lead to a stasis, but towards a continual coming home to ourselves. It involves us in a journey. We are always leaning into the darkness calling us beyond ourselves, or, rather, beyond those places where we are trapped in ways of perceiving and living that no longer offer us life. To become rooted is to become uprooted. As Martin Buber said, "To be holy is to journey." This journey towards ever-deepening intimacy with God often carries us to places where the familiar God is absent. The loss we feel is both a mourning for what is past and an invitation to enter into those seemingly empty spaces. There we wait for our sensibilities to become accustomed to that unfamiliar state in which a new relationship with the divine already waits for us.

This journey to a new awareness moves through stages. Each stage is dynamically constructed. The consolation of living out of a particular sense of self and the consolidation of aspects of that sense of self lead us into a rootedness that allows further dimensions of the self to emerge and be explored. Then we leave behind the complacency of the familiar and enter into a period of desolation where the disorder of deeper aspects of the self are brought to light. These must be acknowledged and dealt with. These deeper forms of disorder did not accept assimilation into the previous sense of self. Encountering them is felt as desolation. We cannot withdraw from that desolation into an earlier stage. We might try, and often do try, this tactical withdrawal, but to grow we must return to the desolation. We enter it to allow the Desire, which calls us, to form a new synthesis and let us live at a new stage of intimacy. Again and again, held and drawn by the Desire who desires for us, and for all, the fullness of life, we are drawn further, and ever further, into the divine love.

As Ruth says to her mother-in-law Naomi in the Old Testament, we can say to God, "Don't ask me to leave you and turn back. I will go wherever you go and live wherever you live. Your people will be my people, and your God will be my God. I will die where you die and will be buried there" (Ruth 1:16-17).

Naomi's Israelite faith was strong enough that Ruth, her Moabite daughter-in-law, came to faith in the God of Israel. Ruth's own faith was strong enough to cause her to leave her homeland and religious idolatry, and endure hardship to care for her mother-in-law. And what was Naomi's own faith? Although she was beaten down by the loneliness and helplessness of widowhood, she never abandoned her awareness that God was in control.

The two travelled together and returned to Bethlehem, Naomi's homeland. Naomi was recognized by the town's women. They wondered if it was really her.

She replied, "Do not call me Naomi [meaning sweetness]. Instead call me Mara [bitterness] for the Almighty has made life very bitter for me. I went away full but the Lord has brought me home empty. Why should you call me Naomi when the Lord has caused me to suffer and the Almighty has sent such tragedy?" (Ruth 1:19-21).

Yet out of that tragedy Ruth met Boaz and they wed. Naomi was cared for. Out of that union between her kinsman and her daughter-in-law came David, and from the house of David, Jesus the Messiah was born.

The pattern in the spiritual journey is from consolation to desolation to consolation. It is a pattern we see with Joseph in the closing chapters of the book of Genesis. He is the favoured son, but is sold into slavery, then rises to a position of security in his new world of Egypt. There he is cast into prison because of false testimony, but rises to greater heights because Pharaoh's wine steward, who was in prison at the same time, remembers him. Joseph becomes a minister in Egypt because of his ability to read dreams and his administrative skills. He rescues the Israelites at a time of famine and is reunited to his family. The book of Genesis ends with the Israelites moving to Egypt because of Joseph. The next book in the Old Testament, Exodus, begins with the Israelites becoming so numerous and powerful that they inspire fear and envy, and they are enslaved by the new Pharaoh. Out of their own good fortune comes misfortune, and out of that misfortune comes Moses, who rescues them from Egyptian bondage. Through this Passover, God creates a liberation that becomes a symbol for the Christian paschal mystery.

It is the nature of grace to seek out the unredeemed and to bring it to life; it is the nature of love to call us to deeper and deeper intimacy by carrying us to those places that cry out for salvation. As Jeremiah says,

> You have seduced me, Yahweh, and I have let myself be seduced; you have overpowered me: you were the stronger. I am a laughing-stock all day long, they all make fun of me …. I would say to myself, "I will not think about him, I will not speak in his name any more," but then there seemed to be a fire burning in my heart, imprisoned in my bones. The effort to restrain it wearied me, I could not do it. (Jeremiah 20:7, 9)

As we are driven by desire and called by Desire, we enter the pilgrim path where we know ourselves in a certain way only to lose that knowledge in ever newer ways of being and living. Our understanding of ourselves, others, the world, God and creation changes, and our ways of relating to these and loving them changes. What we are attentive to, and how we are attentive, differs from one stage to the next. As each stage is different, each stage has a different mode of discernment and can be reached only after living the previous stage as fully as possible. It is in the fullness of each time and stage that the process we call Incarnation happens in our personal lives. When we open ourselves to the presence of God in our lives, we are carried to levels of attentiveness that embody an ever-deepening relationship with God. Attention is simply the place where our desire encounters the divine Desire.

Intentionality

Attention is how intention becomes incarnate. What we attend to reveals our world and our values. But it also reveals to us God's desire for us. God desires us. The way God manifests that desire for us is by bringing to our attention how he is present to us. God draws our attention to him by making us aware of what we are attentive to. Our perceptions are not a collection of sensations. As William Blake says, we see not *with* our eyes but *through* our eyes. We see with our vision. That vision is a product of our imagination.

We all live in imagined worlds, and those worlds change as we walk our spiritual paths.[12]

Often, the way we see the world and the way God offers creation to us differ. What seems to be suffering is really the covering of love. In a confusing Hasidic story, the devout Rabbi Elimelekh prays to find out why there is evil in the world. In a dream, his dead master appears to him. Rabbi Elimelekh cries out, "Why are you silent in such a dreadful need?" He is answered, "In Heaven we see that all that seems evil to you is a work of mercy."[13]

How can this be? We do not see as God sees. We are caught in a particular time and at a particular place. Our seeing is limited. Our desire for God is conditioned by the contexts that have created us. These are personal, familial, social, cultural, historical, ecological, cosmic. These nestle in each other; and holding them all in love is God. What is explicit is what we see. What is implicit but even more real is that everything is held in God's creative transforming love. This is not to deny that evil exists, or that God does not see evil. The difference between us and God is that for God there is no evil that cannot be transformed. The power of the resurrection reveals this. There, death is transformed from the end of life on earth to the beginning of a new life on earth. One of the gifts of Jesus' resurrection for us is that we no longer have to understand ourselves and live our lives as beings thrown towards death, as Heidegger claims in *Being and Time*.[14] We are beings invited to the fullness of life, which places death in a broader context. It is the context of God's love bearing in on a creation damaged by sin. God bears in on our lives to affirm what is good and to transform what is damaged. He intends us to have life and to celebrate it. How do we react to that gift? Do we even see the gift given? What do we actually see?

What we see reveals our intentionality. How we respond to what we see reveals God's communication to us. We respond by evaluating what we see. That evaluation is incarnate in our feelings. Nothing is neutral. It reveals God to us and us to God. As Meister Eckhart once observed, the eye by which I see God is the eye by which God sees me.[15] We may unconsciously pick and choose what to notice and be attentive to, but what is given extends beyond those limitations. God communicates with us through everything. Thus St. Ignatius can talk about finding God in all things.

This does not mean that Ignatius is a pantheist, believing that all things are God, or even a panentheist, believing that God is materially present in all things. It simply means that our relationship with God, and thus a path to life, can be discovered by the way we value things. What we value and how we value those things reveals to us where we find life, and not only life, but also the delight in living. God gives the delight in living in all the ways of our living. We may find such delight only in a few things and people and situations. The spiritual journey invites us to further that abundance of delight. Often this means walking through the pain and the darkness of this world. God enters that pain and darkness. When we meet God in those places, a transformation occurs. New life is given.

> a man must make his way
> through the world.
> he must learn how to use
> what is given:
> the cold spring water; the scorpion
> under the stone; the shadows
> on the wall that walk towards him
> and through him – taking with them
> their kin – leaving him
> empty filled with light

The Ten Ox-Herding Pictures of Buddhism

What follows next presents one reading of the spiritual journey. There are many others. The New Testament offers The Beatitudes (see *The Gift of Spiritual Intimacy*, Novalis, 2009). We also have St. Augustine's *Confessions*, Ignatius of Loyola's Spiritual Autobiography, Teresa of Avila's *Interior Castle*, and John Bunyan's *The Pilgrim's Progress*, to name a few. In literature, and on a secular level, we have the *Bildungsroman*—the novel that follows a person's growth to maturity. In the popular writings of the day, there is Tolkien's Lord of the Rings series, the Harry Potter series, and the writings of Ursula LeGuin. Despite their secular nature, they describe the consolations, desolations, temptations and trials to be overcome for characters to come to a sense of their identity and mission in life. Psychology, which might be regarded as the secularization of spirituality, offers us similar paradigms in the writings of Jung and his followers, such as Eric Neumann and Joseph Campbell, or in the works of James Fowler and his stages of faith development, or Erik Erikson and his depiction of psycho-social maturation.

The Ten Ox-Herding Pictures are Buddhist depictions of the stages of the human spiritual journey to enlightenment. Buddhism reflects on the nature and development of human consciousness from a human perspective. It is an experimental science. It does not impose an ideology on experience, but rather allows reality unconstrained by ideology to manifest itself to the questing spirit. This is not so very different from Teresa of Avila's comment that mysticism is an experimental science. We have to discover what works for ourselves in our journey to spiritual intimacy.

Ignatius of Loyola's famous Spiritual Exercises and rules for Discernment also emerge from an intensely lived and reflected upon personal experience. He experiments and pays attention to the results of those experiments. They have given us a path to spiritual intimacy. Unlike the Exercises, which are existential in their method and have been examined in *The Gift of Spiritual Intimacy* (Novalis, 2009), the Ox-herding pictures do not offer a method of growth but depict stages of growth in an equally authentic search. They make no claim to expose the dynamics of that movement.

The present reading of the Ox-herding pictures[16] attempts to show the dynamics of desire, which carries us through those stages towards a spiritual maturity, and to explore those different stages of attention within a Christian context, noting how the nature of discernment changes with each stage.

1. The search for the bull

Driven by conflicting desires, and frantic,
I search for a path with life;
Nothing satisfies. I am alone, tired and dispirited.
In the dark all around me, the business of an alien world.

Attention as longing

We are God's desire, and we desire God. Nothing or no one else ever fully satisfies that desire. Our whole life is determined by that mutual desiring between lover and Beloved. Created as love and for love, we find that anything less does not satisfy. Our longing is first felt as frustration at the way things are presently experienced. It can be read as psychological—"I want to be a better person." It can be read as social—"I want the world to be a better place." It can be read as ecological—"I want there to be harmony among all levels of creation." All of these are expressions of the spiritual. The spiritual takes these up and goes even further. It states, "I want there to be right relations between creature, creation and Creator.

I desire an intimacy with the Divine that satisfies all my desires." The construction of the "I"—how I see, understand and experience myself—is as someone driven by desire. No one escapes desire, though that desire may seek to satisfy itself in many different forms. Comfort, security, meaning, freedom, self-esteem, power, beauty—all are objects of our desire. These are not bad. They are just not full expressions of the presence of God to us, and so we should not treat them, individually or collectively, as gods for us. We should not expect them to make us complete. Only a relationship with God completes us. The culture we live in and our own personal inclinations can propose to us various satisfactions for our longings, which are the felt experiences of our desire. Their narratives suggest to us ways of understanding ourselves that stimulate our longings and subvert our identity as desire for God. Thus we are led to believe that if we have wealth, prestige, fame or a socially approved self-image, we will have gained our heart's desire.

What stops us from living fully our desire? We can confuse longings and desire. Longings, manifested as wants, are often confused with needs, and then the hierarchy of needs is often determined by cultural norms. Society may say that when I feel hungry, I should eat what society promotes. But eating such foods can be unhealthy and destructive to my well-being. Similarly, my value system might place the need for security or social affirmation over the need to be rooted in God's love, and so I limit the expression of my life as a desire for God to a state of making sure I look after my own immediate interests first. Such was the state of the rich young man whom Jesus saw and loved in Luke's gospel (Luke 18:18-23). The rich young man turned away from that love.

We are a brood of conflicting urges. All call to be satisfied. As social beings, we are educated into which urges are to be satisfied, and how they are to be satisfied; which ones are to be suppressed because they contravene social norms, and which are repressed because they are taboo. We start our spiritual journey when we find that how we are constructed as social beings does not fully satisfy the longing in us, the craving to be acknowledged and fulfilled. When we give into that longing, we step into a darkness away from what we already know. We experiment. The only criteria we have for finding life is how that longing responds to what we do. In this state, we are caught between the fear of the unknown and that urgent desire that calls us into the unknown. We try some things and discover they do not work. They might give us some satisfaction and pleasure, but we find that they are not enough. Mistakes happen because we do not know what we are doing, and the only way to find out how to ease that intolerable itch that possesses us is to find what relieves it. We often confuse the loudest call with that deepest call. Looking back on our earlier life, it seems like a wonder we did not destroy ourselves. We did not know then that the God who desires us was also protecting us. We realize now that the greater mistake would have been *not* to experiment, for then we would never have discovered our true relationship with God.

Those mistakes we uncover as we experiment are very useful, for they give us the basis of discernment. After being wounded at war in 1521, Ignatius of Loyola used his experience on his sickbed, where he was recovering from knee operations, to discover which urges led to God and which led to transient pleasures. Both the reading of courtly love romances and the lives of the saints gave him pleasure. But the pleasure that came from reading the lives of the saints and the Bible lasted longer and affected him more deeply than the secular literature he had access to. Similarly, his experiments on how to live a spiritual life—his extreme fasts and penances—in 1522 at Manresa almost destroyed him. They caused him to see that evil could appear under the guise of good. This led to the rules for discernment found in his Spiritual Exercises. But underlying his mistakes and his insights and the correction of his mistakes was his desire for a fulfilled life.

Similarly, Moses first had his own desert experience of exile and loss when he fled Egypt after killing a citizen. This served as a basis for leading the Israelites through their own desert experience after they crossed the Red Sea. The Buddha's experiments with yogic asceticism, which almost destroyed him, led to his advocating a path of moderation, the Middle Way.

But there is another set of experiments—not ascetic—that implicates us in the values of the world. Material success, prestige, power, fame, sexual conquests and addictions are all thrilling and absorbing, but engagement with them demands more than they return, because they can never fulfill our identity as desire.

What we learn from these experiments are ways of going beyond the socially approved limits of the world as we currently experience it. We discover that those borders are porous, and that within our culture, though often overlooked or misinterpreted, they are people who attract us at a deeper level. These are the saints and holy people within our own tradition or from others. They attract our attention, for their values seem different from the dominant values around us. They call us beyond ourselves. We might long to emulate them, but their lives seem too far removed from ours for this to be possible. As we become more attentive to our own longing, we also become aware of the fears that would stop us from following the path of our deepest desires. We see how we are conditioned by fear and how it drains us of our creative energies. But our deepest desire is to be in right relationship with God—and, like Francis Thompson's "Hound of Heaven," it will not let us be satisfied with anything less. So we set out past our fears.

The first Ox-herding picture depicts a young person setting out to seek his fulfillment. We notice that, while his feet are pointed forward, his head is turned around in the opposite direction. He is torn by conflicting forces and, like the prisoner leaving prison, he carries the prison with him in his habits and ways of seeing and relating to the world. He carries with him a map of the world that lacks a real place to fulfill his desire. He needs to lose that map. He needs to become lost to be found.

In becoming lost there are discernments we need. These are twofold. First we must be able to admit our conflicted state. Then we must be able to experiment with the different forces that move us without becoming trapped by them. This is possible only if we are attentive to what our awareness is telling us as we explore what it means to be human and alive. If we do pay attention, we will not get trapped, because the Desire who desires us saves us from getting caught. We are not on this journey by ourselves. At every stage we are held in the dynamic love of God: that love is there to hold, rescue, redeem and encourage, and thus guide us on the path of life. We are saved here, often, in spite of ourselves.

Secondly, because we are socially conditioned, we have urges that do not support a culture constructed by its dominant ideologies. These urges may be countercultural; admitting them sometimes carries us into the areas of shame, guilt and taboo. Thus, one of the difficulties in becoming an individual is contravening the social norms that constrain us to conformity. At times, counter-conformity manifests itself in destructive behaviour—terrorism and theft, to name just two. But at other times, what the individual desires is not necessarily immoral or illegal; rather, it is unacceptable to the common sense of the times. Sometimes being counter-cultural involves opposing the immorality that has become the dominant norm. Such would be the case of resisting an oppressive regime, or working against culturally sanctioned sexism or racism.

Resisting is possible only if we first become attentive to those dimensions of the socially unsanctioned desires in us. We must be able to distinguish between conformity and risk, and with both conformity and risk, we must be able to discern which aspects are life-giving and which are destructive. The first discernment to be made here is between accepting our dissatisfaction and denying it. Then we are caught in the tension of repression that strives to maintain a status quo by denying the energies that demand to be acknowledged. We become conscious of our vulnerability and of the forces that pull us in many different directions. Either the comfort and the social acceptance of the known would keep us frozen—and supposedly safe—in a predetermined world, or the tribulations and social alienation that would emerge in admitting our dissatisfaction might drive us to we know not what. This is not to say that security and comfort are bad things, or that insecurity and unease are good things. We need to know how the desire God has for us touches our own desire for the fullness of life. We need to know what desires to follow.

The second discernment, then, is within the realm of risk. How do we know what non-conventional activity leads us to life and what traps us in destructive behaviour? Here is where the hidden guidance of God comes in because in, this area we are truly confused. When we look back at this time of our lives, we see how the divine providence operates in looking after us by providing us with happy coincidences and with what seemed like lucky breaks, or even obstacles to a path we thought might offer us a viable way forward. In retrospect, we discover God's hand directly at work.

But in other areas of risk we had to discern. Having become aware of those conflicting dimensions in ourselves, we need to find some way of discerning which ones we should explore, and which we should leave to a later time. It is the desire of God that all our energies be attuned to the energies of the divine. This is the work of a lifetime. It cannot be done all at once. So the issue is which ones should be engaged first. This is not something we can decide, because our disorders can convince us that what we need is to focus on one thing, while, in effect, the immediate concern of the divine is something quite different. For instance, perfectionists might want to reorder the world, society and even themselves according to their convictions, while it is the tendency to idealism, which creates perfectionism, that perfectionists need to deal with before any reordering occurs.

How do we discern which areas of dissatisfaction need to be addressed first? By experimenting within the limited areas of freedom that we have. We do not do this in the vacuum of love. The God who desires us also arranges what enters our path; these things provide us with the material for discernment. While we think we are wildly following our instincts and urges, looking for satisfaction and meaning, in retrospect we realize that the people, places and situations we encounter at this stage of our spiritual journey have allowed us to develop our own sense of what gives us life and what does not. It is as if God gives us certain experiences, rather than answers, that move us along our spiritual path. While we could have been destroyed by our naïveté we were not destroyed. Only later do we realize that we were protected and cared for even as we blindly sought whatever would give us life. The wonder we experience in that recollection is different from the wonder we experienced when we were starting our spiritual journey in that state of heightened self-consciousness, susceptible to any sensation.

The sense of wonder that reveals desire to us is what we experience when we are carried out of ourselves in our encounter with God. This discovery of wonder carries us to the second stage of our spiritual journey. The delight in the beloved reveals the path of desire. It is the path that calls me through my frustrations, longings and dissatisfactions that I find myself committed to travel with. My desire for a better life disposes me to walk that path. At the beginning of our spiritual journey, we all experience desire as longing, as question. We ask ourselves: Who am I? What am I to do? What is to become of me? We experience our lives as a question. That question leads us on a quest where we are led by desire. We are not given answers, but experiences. Dissatisfaction becomes the principle of discernment. Nothing satisfies. The tensions build up in us in a way that cannot be denied. We are driven to become attentive to the desire that is not satisfied, no matter what we do. Often we become exhausted in the search for an answer, and that exhaustion manifests itself in giving up the willed search. We let matters take their course. Here is the first giving up of our self-will. In experiencing our dissatisfaction, we allow the desire of God to become more apparent in our daily world.

Questions for reflection

1. What were the dissatisfactions that led you to begin your spiritual quest? What was the allure of the world you lived in that made you unwilling to admit your dissatisfaction?

2. What were the fears you faced? How did you face them?

3. What happened when you started to face your fears and the power they had over you?

4. How did you discern what was life-giving and what was not in the darkness you experienced after leaving the ordered world of established values?

5. How did you experience the hidden presence of God then?

2. Discovering the footprints

Looking heavenwards as I walk the path of desire
I discover traces of the life I seek.
They are everywhere hidden in full view
Waiting to be found. Each one a gift!

Attention as testing

When we start becoming attentive to the dissatisfaction we experience in our daily lives, we enter unknown territory. We discover in ourselves a peculiar sense of dislocation and distance from the events of our daily lives. We become moody because we feel that sense of being dislocated. At times we are pleasant and affable; at other times we just want to be left alone. We are becoming strangers to ourselves. Yet, even though we have made an important shift in our awareness, we still bring with us the habits of a lifetime and the conditioned perspectives and responses of the cultures we live in. It is rather like being in a city by day and now being in the same city at night. Our attentiveness to what is around us and inside us becomes sharpened. We become aware of things we had not noticed before. Some of these may be paths to the divine. Some may not. We explore those paths because they touch something in us. They might be an answer to the need that drives us. We might read of saints or holy people in different traditions who seem to be living the life we seek. We look for people who might share the same interests. We search for a knowledgeable person we can trust to help us find what we are looking for. In allowing our dissatisfaction to surface, we discover that our dissatisfaction has many elements to it, and so we begin to be attentive to the different strands of desire, all of which cry out to be satisfied. We look at the ways they call us, and we look at the ways in which they are satisfied.

What we are doing here is sifting our desires. We follow them all and learn from our experiences. Some desires bring pleasure, but not life. They may leave us feeling soiled or ashamed or simply not interested. Others are pleasant, but we feel ambivalent about them. Still others intrigue us and catch us at deeper levels of awareness than we were normally accustomed to. Unusual things move us in strange ways. We become vulnerable to a sense of difference. In this way, we may explore different traditions of spirituality or of life to see if any of them offers a path we want to follow. We know that what we seek may not necessarily be defined by society as religious or even holy. We are seeking a love that will touch us intimately and deeply and totally. It may be with another person, or in a community, or even in solitude. What we are looking for is a path that will make sense of the different aspects of our lives. Our interior and our exterior life; our private and our public life; our spiritual and our secular life. We are looking for a way that will allow what is in us to find a voice. We now know that before we find our voice, we first have to find a language and then to learn that language. But none of this is articulated as yet. All we have is the feeling of dissatisfaction at our present condition, and, like a baby desiring to be nursed, we blindly turn to what will suckle us.

In this testing we discover traces of what we are looking for. In everything we do, we find ourselves asking this question: Does this carry me closer to that goal, whatever it is? We are being led by desire and answered by Desire. At this time, the coming together of these two desires as satisfaction is temporary, because we do not yet have a system or a way of living that allow those experiences to be appropriated and integrated. These experiences of being met by God as desire further deconstruct the habitual world we are moving out of. The experiences could be momentous, like the death of a loved one or a significant illness. But they could also be quite simple in effect, and quite positive.

For me, the chance reading of Thomas Merton's *The Sign of Jonas* (because I felt guilty about playing bridge during a sixth form prefect's retreat) was such a moment. It was almost my last year of high school. I chose the book from the school library simply because it had a woven hemp cover. In reading that book I experienced a flood of peace I had never experienced before. That night I realized this peace was what I deeply wanted. I resolved to find that peace again. I considered becoming a Trappist, even though at the time it seemed quite impossible. I was not a Catholic and was not particularly interested in the Catholic world. I could not—and still cannot—sing and I knew singing in choir was an important part of the Trappist vocation. I was not at that time keen on a vegetarian diet, and more significantly, I loved chattering, and so the world of monastic silence terrified me. Years later, rereading the same text left me unmoved. But when I read it the first time, it gave me a trace of the Divine in the world, and that trace pointed me to a life that could be fulfilling, though how that was to occur, I did not know.

If we reflect on our history, we discover things that have happened to us that show God is also seeking us through our experiences in the world. But while we are still at this second level of attention, these seem to us to be coincidences or fortuitous incidents. Those chance encounters open paths for us that lead us to glimpses of what satisfies our deepest longings. Yet these are not clear indicators. There is the element of risk and suspicion in accepting what is presented to us. But what is presented has a level of insistence that cannot be overlooked or ignored.

Those traces of God's desire for us are all around, but the ones that get our attention are the ones significantly dissimilar from our daily or habitual experience. Their unusualness catches our attention. This raises for us the question of "otherness." How do we deal with the "other" outside of our regular experience and yet within the range of our perception? Do we treat it as an invitation or as an enemy? Otherness can fill us with wonder or can threaten. When we are walking towards God—even though we may not experience it as such—we read those experiences that get our attention as coming either from God or from the enemy of our human nature, the one who stops us from becoming fully human. The first letter of St. John advises we test every spirit to see which one comes from God and which does not (1 John 4:1); Paul in his first letter to the Thessalonians says the same thing. "Test everything and hold onto the good" (1 Thessalonians 5:21).

But how is this testing to occur? Because we are in the middle of an experience, we do not have the skills to be able to evaluate it. This is where a good spiritual director is useful. Such a person, like Ignatius of Loyola, has the lived knowledge of doing such a thing. He knows what it is to be gifted with experiences that come from the good spirit and what it is to have experiences that come from forces pretending to be good. He suggests it is helpful to see where those experiences lead us. If they lead us to a deepening of our sense of adventure, and if they give us a sense of our call in ways that are life-giving and fill us with gratitude and peace, then they come from the good spirit. If, as we allow the experience to reveal itself to us, we find ourselves dispirited and closing in on ourselves, then that experience, even though it initially seems good, likely does not come from God. Having negative experiences that appear good is very valuable. After being caught several times by such experiences, we become more sensitized to what evil disguised as good feels like. Then we can refuse to entertain those experiences before they take a deeper hold of our spirit. Also, these kinds of experiences teach us how to distance ourselves from our feelings. We do not deny them but discover that we do not have to identify ourselves with them. We are more than what we feel, both good and bad. We are the desire for God, not what we feel. Feelings change; our identity as desire does not. It is precisely our identity as desire and as desired by God that allows us to discern at this stage. What comes from God is rooted in our identity and lasts; what does not come from God does not have those roots, and so, after a while, is revealed as deceptive.

The little poem that accompanies this Ox-herding picture depicts our desire for God as "looking heavenward." Looking heavenward gives us the perspective for discernment. We aim towards the fullness of life in our life's journey. That fullness of life always and everywhere offered to us becomes the criteria for choosing what we do and how we do it. We can examine ourselves and ask this question: Does the experience that seems good, or bad, lead us to God or not?

Admittedly, at this stage we may entertain a wrong or truncated image of God. This image may come from our personal and social history, or we may have confused our super-ego with God. But what our upbringing and our "education" cannot control is the Mystery who enters into our history and refuses to be confined by it. We experience our relationship with that Mystery in terms of desire and of being desired. Nothing and none but God can fulfill and maintain that relationship. What comes from God stays.

What does not come from God falls back upon itself and so is exposed for what it is. In all of this, God is not passive. God desires us—not needs us—and the desire God has for us enters into our living situations and makes itself felt. At this stage, God is not silent but communicates constantly. However, we are so constrained by our disordered life, and by the patterns of that disordered life and by the power of worldly forces, we get only occasional glimpses of God at this deeper level of our calling.

We do not have an ordered self that allows those experiences to be integrated and become habitual or commonplace. They strike our attention precisely because of their unusual and often dramatic nature. They stand in stark contrast to our habitual way of experiencing life. They offer us traces of the Divine.

Questions for reflection

1. What were the significant experiences in your personal history that focused your quest in a particular direction? Looking back at them, why do you think they were significant? How did they come across to you then? How do they come across to you now?

2. How did they clarify the path of desire? Negatively? Positively?

3. As you sit with these experiences, do they draw out others from your store of memories that do the same thing?

4. As you continue to sit with these, do you discover family incidents—some in which you were not involved, or some that happened even before you were born—that have shaped your life and given some shape to the path you now walk?

5. Do you find moments in your cultural history that have done the same things?

6. When you reflect on yourself—as an individual, a member of a family and a community, and a culture, and as a member of the human race—how do you understand yourself as belonging to a flow of desire that extends through time and space?

7. How do those past experiences in which you discovered traces of God and the illusions of good shape the way you discern now?

3. Perceiving the bull

Following the traces, I come to a sense of life
Bigger than I could ever imagine. Though far from me,
it colours all I now see and understand.
It calls me beyond myself.

Attention as glimpsing

On some of the paths we explore, we experience moments of consolation, awareness, connectedness, meaning, direction, peace. These moments show us what we are looking for is possible. The question is how to hold onto those momentary feelings of intimacy. The ways of our present life do not enable us to live or maintain a deep sense of connection. The peace I experienced reading Thomas Merton's memoirs as a Trappist monk seemed beyond my reach. I was not a Catholic then; I was a chatterbox for whom silence was an impossibility. I could not sing, and a life of vegetarianism was totally foreign to me. Such glimpses reveal an intimate but elusive reality and engender frustration, because we have tastes of what we desire but do not have the skills or the discipline or the disposition to maintain that state of awareness. However, those moments are so powerful as to confirm our suspicions there is something there for us. In fact, we use those experiences, and the memories of them, as a touchstone to judge what is important to us. They give us a way of moving towards what we desire. We try to find something that resonates on an intuitive level with the feeling we had during that experience. We hold onto it and pursue the path it opens. Those experiences become the touchstone and the basis for our discernment about what to do next. We strive to do what connects us back to those experiences, and we use those experiences to evaluate the worth of what we do with and in our daily lives. When we do this, our attention—the way we look at and experience life, ourselves, others, even our relationship with the Mystery we call God—is being transformed. We have had the experience of being found. But there are layers to being found.

If, in the second stage of attentiveness, we were shown a wrapped present, in this third stage, we are like children at Christmas receiving that present. Inside, waiting to be ours, is our heart's desire. But it is one thing to receive a present and another to open it.

Receiving something and being able to say it is yours are two different things. The prisoner incarcerated for a long time daily desires freedom, but because he desires it does not mean he has it. The process of justice through the legal system still has to be brought into operation before he can be freed. He must wait to be let out of prison. And even though the system might get him out of prison, he is still not free. He carries the world of the prison within him. Still, looking through the bars of his cell window, facing outwards, he glimpses the world of possibility available to him. He hopes to achieve what he has seen.

At this third level of attention on the spiritual path, we are led by hope. We know intellectually an intimacy with God is offered, and can be found. We desire to receive it, but that intimacy is not realized in our habitual life. The experiences we are given come and go beyond our control. We know intellectually God is holding us, but except for those intense and dramatic moments, we do not experience being held. What we normally experience, rather, is a sense of separation from God and a sense of alienation from life. We do not see our life as patterned by God; we just see the scribbles of daily living. The concept of the awareness of God as the ground of our being—or to put it another way, the sensed awareness of a consoling God holding us—has not become a realized insight. We believe it to be so because, as we say to ourselves, it just has to be. Nothing else makes as much sense. But we do not spontaneously live with the awareness. What we realize is the overwhelming nature of the momentary experiences we have of being touched by God.

Beyond the sense of consolation we experienced in the previous stage, here we encounter a sense of the giver of those consolations. We can speak of it only in similes. It is as if we are a drop of water and suddenly find ourselves to be a part of an ocean. Or it is as if we suddenly experience ourselves as not being separate from anything else. It is not as if there is a boundary, like a glass wall, between us and everything else. There is nothing. We can be shocked by what we experience. With its sense of immediacy and enormity, it so deconstructs the narratives and myths we live out of that we might feel as if we are having a profound psychological illness. For some, this is a gradual process wherein the many consolations of the previous stage of attentiveness consolidate into a preparation for this particular moment of revelation. For others it is sudden and dramatic. Still others may experience it as a combination of the two, where we have what might be called religious experiences against a background of consolations and desolations.

This raises a very troubling question: Is this a psychological malaise—much like a psychotic break—or is it a sudden felt insight into the enormity of God's love that overwhelms us? The closed myths we have lived out have been made porous by all the experiences we have had so far. Aspects of ourselves become vulnerable to God's love. God's passionate desire for us breaks through that fragility. Through these cracks floods in a light so strong we are blinded. What we have lived before, and how we have lived before, is inadequate to comprehend what we presently experience in those moments. These seem so radically "other," we wonder if we are going crazy. How do we distinguish between a psychological illness and a spiritual experience when the spirit so incarnates itself in our psychological makeup as to be indistinguishable from it? The destabilization of our personality manifests itself in its effects. We feel it.

The difference between a psychological collapse and a religious experience, both of which can contain extraordinary effects of a similar nature, is in the context. What comes from God does not destroy our identity. The God who desires us to have the fullness of life does not take us beyond what we are capable of bearing, though evil can and does. And even though we may fall into desolation as our known worlds are deconstructed, we are sustained in that desolation until we can reach a state of consolation.

At this stage of our spiritual journey, we arrive at some clarity. We have a deep and profound sense of what we want. We want God. Nothing else satisfies. Rather like the person who has just encountered another and feels the firm assurance the person he has just met, or has even just seen, is the one to spend the rest of his life with, there is a similar recognition here. The path that opens resonates with the particular disposition of the person. The concordance feels just right. It marks the beginning of a long, hard struggle to accept, open and live the gift presented.

The tensions at this stage rise between what we deeply desire as our reality and how far we are from realizing that dream. The obstacles seem insurmountable, and, in fact, the dream seems quite unrealistic in practical terms. We are caught between desire and frustration. We can do nothing but wait. The temptation is to abandon the desire, if it were possible, and to try to assuage the frustration we feel by throwing ourselves into forms of self-destructive behaviour. These behaviours can range from excessive manifestations of normalcy, such as conformity to politically correct social values denying the drive to individuation, to their opposite: stereotypical wild behaviour and driven self-indulgence. At times, we even hope the desire we feel would disappear. In retrospect, the destructive behaviour can be seen as an attempt to kill the desire in us. It is an attempt to deny our identity as desire by reducing it to the satisfaction of a single need: the flight from self-awareness. In all of this, unnoticed at this time, is the compassionate mercy of God defending us from our self-destructive tendencies. In fact, what is being transformed here is the image we have of God and the expectations we have of this God. God is not Santa Claus, or the mythical womb we want to return to. We are being educated in a hard way to be liberated from those images and expectations. All the while, we pray desperately for whatever is calling us, and whatever in us is responding to that call, to go away or to take us completely. Even prayer here is a flight from self-consciousness and from the attention that defines our life at this stage.

But the attention and the tension remain. They are felt in the midst of a freneticism that seeks to displace or overwhelm this tension. We resign ourselves to a long, maybe endless wait. We slowly come to accept this sense of call through desire will not go away, and slowly accept the fact that what we experience in admitting and accepting this desire moves us to adopt a new and different way of living.

In this sense of waiting, we learn to discern how to be patient. Against the urge for closure and the urge for some movement lies a counter dynamic. A dreadful stillness settles in, bringing with it a new presence of God and a new sense of attentiveness. Like Elijah, we discover the presence of God in the stillness.

> The Lord said, "Go out and stand on the mountain in the presence of the Lord, for the Lord is about to pass by." Then a great and powerful wind tore the mountains apart and shattered the rocks before the Lord, but the Lord was not in the wind. After the wind there was an earthquake, but the Lord was not in the earthquake. After the earthquake came a fire, but the Lord was not in the fire. And after the fire came a gentle whisper. When Elijah heard it, he pulled his cloak over his face and went out and stood at the mouth of the cave. (1 Kings 19:11-13)

In that new-found stillness, God appears. If we return to the metaphor of leaving prison, the struggle we endure to come to that stillness is a gift, like giving a prisoner new ways of seeing and living to overcome the self-destructiveness he or she has taken for granted as natural. We have been offered a gift. We have just received it and acknowledged it. We now have to accept it. Now we must learn how to grow into the freedom to which we have been introduced as stillness or calm. In the Ignatian paradigm of the growth to spiritual intimacy, we have just left the First Week of the Exercises. We have discovered ourselves as lovers who have been trapped by sin, but invited to be liberated by love.

The next stage is discerning how to live that love we are called to, knowing full well that in our very being there is a centripetal force to narcissism. This force seeks always to turn us away from the forms of authenticity that constantly take us beyond ourselves as we know it.

Questions for reflection

1. When did you first discover a personal God, more intimate and real to you than the one you were taught?

2. What were the struggles you endured in coming to accept that gift?

3. How did you experience the movement from ideology to intimacy?

4. Was there a significant moment when you gave in? What was that moment like?

5. What discernments did you have to make at this stage, and what was the process of discernment like?

4. Catching the bull

The path carries me through many hard times, to strange places and people. Among them I am weak and alone,
and the God who has hooked my heart distant and forbidding.
I am struggle on only through a passion for life.

Attention as finding

We are vulnerable to our new image of God and to our newly emerging sense of self. As we integrate the calm we experience in coming to know God personally, we enter a new stage of attentiveness. At this stage we find ourselves in a crisis, because the path that opens to us challenges us. We have to change our life, the things we do, the people we associate with, and how we view ourselves and others. We are called to a commitment involving great risk. It feels as if we are starting life over again and do not have the skills to live it in an authentic way. It is one thing to discover we are loved, but it is quite another thing to know how to love. This is very much like being engaged. We have found the one we want to live with, but a great deal of work has to be done if the relationship

86

is to be established. There are times when our infatuation makes life wonderful. There are other times when we must learn to adapt and to become accustomed to the new life to which we are called. There are times when we resent what we are called to. Life seems to be passing us by.

The same is true of the spiritual life. We know we must be schooled in love if we are to live the life that has called us in the midst of our disorders. We must learn how to make a huge existential leap to living a life of faith that seems like folly to ourselves and to the world.

Kierkegaard talks about this state in *Fear and Trembling* when he discusses Abraham's decision to sacrifice Isaac on Mount Moriah. God asks Abraham, who was already an old man when he became a father, to give up his son. If he does this, Abraham destroys his relationship with his wife, with his family and clan, and even with himself and his future, since that son represents God's promise that Abraham will be the father of a nation. He will become nobody if he willfully destroys all the relationships that give him his identity. In killing his son, he even gives up the religious traditions that assure him of his relationship with God. He is asked to hand over all he believes in to an unknown who does not tell him what will happen after he offers up that sacrifice. The Other who bears in on him in such a radical way could be malign or the projection of his own disordered, aging mind.

Abraham's angst is our own at this stage. We risk our very lives, our future and the respect of others. We hand ourselves over to the unknown.

This is rather like selling all we have in order to buy the pearl of great price. But our willingness to do this—costing, as T.S. Eliot said, "no less than everything"[17]—disposes ourselves to be found by the Mystery who is also seeking us. It might seem easy to talk about this, but the actual process is quite difficult. In the radical vulnerability of standing stripped of everything, we present ourselves as disposed to being given a new identity in God. Perhaps this is one way of looking at the dark night of the senses John of the Cross talks about, wherein the senses are the incarnate embodiment of what we value. Those values manifest themselves through our feelings. As we are stripped of our previous values and our perceptions of the world through those values, we lean into a darkness. In that stance of attention, we become aware of all the demons within us and around us. They are attracted to this level of vulnerability and become more openly manifest in our daily life. Because we are moving against the values of the world and even the values we have been conscripted to, our change of direction brings what we have understood as natural and normal into the foreground. We have confused the habitual with the normal, and the normal with the real. We are now moving away from that confusion. The new sense of the real emerges as a darkness. We cope as best we can, stumbling in this new darkness, and we suffer the mockery of being different without any self-justification for our odd behaviour. We expose ourselves in this manner to those forces outside of ourselves, both good and bad, attracted by our lack of defenses.

Attentiveness at this stage occurs at a broader level than our mere conscious willing. We dispose ourselves to an emerging sense of identity, even when aspects of ourselves are still caught up in security and comfort, and we find this larger movement of ourselves to be a trial. But we endure and wait in that darkness. Our learning to follow the Christ feels like an obstacle course. That deepest desire we are for God, which transforms us so we can find God, is the movement from one narrative to another. Our story encounters the story of God and, out of this encounter, a new narrative to live by slowly emerges.

In the Spiritual Exercises of St. Ignatius, this shift occurs in the second stage of the journey to intimacy with the Divine. The Exercises facilitate the journey by having us contemplate the life of Christ. In these Exercises, we imaginatively allow God to integrate our life and its concerns into the gospel story. There our energies encounter the energies of God in an imaginative construct, and we experience affirmation of certain ways of our being and the need for transformation in others. Those "religious experiences" of intense nature stand in contrast to the daily lives we lead. They give us significant moments of consolation and desolation. But that transformation need not occur only in doing the Spiritual Exercises.

For some people, the Exercises might facilitate the journey to intimacy, but for others, just being at this level of attentiveness produces these spiritual experiences.

Only in retrospect, sometimes years later, do we understand, in both the consolations and desolations of this time, we are held by God. The consolations occur when what is spiritually healthy opens us further to God's self-giving; the desolations occur when we experience the blocks in our awareness to accepting that self-giving. Then we experience ourselves as being torn apart.

The discernment we must make at this level of attentiveness is how to remain faithful to the calling without submitting to or feeding the false or limiting narratives, which arise with power to subvert us. Those forms of persuasion suggest our inability to walk the path of such desire, or they offer false and self-serving motives for such a choice of a way of life. The reality of that way of life and the spiritual intimacy it offers seem unattainable from our present position. We can do nothing at this moment but submit to being confirmed and by disposing ourselves to accept what is given by being attentive to the consolations and desolations and seeing what those tell us about ourselves and what to do next.

The second form of asceticism needed now is to find what fosters a spirit of perseverance without being trapped in counter-cultural stands. Those offer merely the substitution of one set of distractions for another. We need to find what is appropriate. If our feelings reveal to us a lack of self-esteem and we unpack these to see that the stories we live by shape and support that poor self-image, we might be tempted to acquire material things in reaction to that poor self-image. Against the cowardly and people-pleasing personality we may have developed, we might do foolhardy and imprudent things that could offend others. Instead, we learn at this time to cultivate practices that allow us to wait in patience and in calm for the clarity bred of detachment to emerge. These will show us the next step.

A twofold asceticism is required here. First, we must maintain the discipline of perseverance in the face of opposition from within the self, from others, or from the dynamics of the world we find ourselves in. This is essentially negative. This means learning to recognize and investigate the feelings that dominate our awareness at this time. We need to say what those feelings are and how they affect us. We need also to become aware of how those feelings were created. This allows us to have some sort of understanding of the way we experience ourselves based on what we know about our early histories and the cultures we live in. We do this to stop being trapped by those feelings and to stop thinking that we are those feelings. The feelings, which indicate to us how we have become conditioned to value certain things, are not us. They are just one section of the spectrum of desire that makes up our constructed sense of self. We are more than those feelings. As we discover at this time, with the rapid and dramatic flux of our feelings, we do not need to identify with any one set of feelings, or even with all of them put together. When we do not give authority to those feelings, even though they affect us dramatically, we can choose how to avoid responding instinctually to the stimulus that provoked those feelings. Simply put, we do not give into those feelings that manifest values we are moving away from. This discipline engenders in us a sense of what our dominant culture would call depression. But on the spiritual path, we are moving towards liberation.

Questions for reflection

1. Do you remember significant religious experiences you might have had? When you look back at them, can you see how they have shaped the way you now are?

2. Do you recall the arid times that came before and after those experiences? How did you experience those arid times?

3. What were the struggles you had at this stage of coming to terms with your new emerging sense of self? How did these manifest in terms of your self-understanding and in relationship with others?

4. What did you find helpful at this time?

5. How did the providence of God manifest itself to you in your daily life?

5. Taming the bull

Leaning into the love calling us through this darkness,
We slowly discover habits of living which open us
To spiritual intimacy. Such discipline is hard,
But, transformed, we learn to trust what is given.

Attention as commitment

The work we do at the previous stage slowly consolidates. This takes a long time. The hard work of asceticism pays off, and we find ourselves with a growing ease in the new path we walk. When we have a grasp of our vocation, when we know what we want because of the life, the sense of direction and the identity it gives us, and when we have an emerging sense of self rooted in God's love for us and in our own love for God, we enter the stage described in this fifth Ox-herding picture. The turbulence associated with becoming radically oriented to God's love and to living our life in response to that love subsides. It takes years to attune the diverse energies of our desires to the gifts given to us in those earlier dramatic religious experiences of encountering God. We slowly become ordered and integrated by the desire God has for us. That desire orients our energies, not to forms of narcissism, but to the community we call Trinity. In the resurrected humanity of Christ, we are invited as humans to partake in the life of that community. This does not mean we become God, and it does not mean we have become perfect. There is always within us the tendency to disorder and self-will. As the first letter of John tells us, "If we refuse to admit that we are sinners, then we live in a world of illusion and truth becomes a stranger to us" (1 John 1:8).

Conversion is not once and for all. The separated aspects of ourselves, our unintegrated energies that manifest themselves in renegade forms of desire, are sought out piece by piece and woven into a new and emerging self. Over the years, we find ourselves becoming attuned to that mysterious Other who has desired and called us. We find ourselves in a constant state of tension between the impulses of our separated desires and our desire of God. But we also find ourselves becoming more and more aware we are held by God, and that God's desire for us interacts with our own desires. Consolation occurs when our desire for God resonates with God's desire for us. Desolation occurs when our desire for what is other than God encounters God's desire for us. The process of attunement is a lifelong work, because every action in our lives is caught in the tension between consolation and desolation.

In his Spiritual Exercises, St. Ignatius considers something he calls "The Two Standards." In each stage of our spiritual growth, we are caught in the tension between the Standard of Satan and the Standard of Christ. This tension between our narcissisms and our desires for self-transcendence never disappears. But as we live attentive to the spiritual path and to the passion that roots us, we discover ways of personally identifying the dialectic that occurs at every moment of our lives, and is different at each stage of our spiritual journey.

Narcissism, which seeks to establish the ego at the centre of our world, uses its gifts, and the privileges those gifts gain in the social world, so that its perspective on life is maintained. Thus a rich person could use wealth for social status, and that would substantiate her belief in a particular sense of identity that is ego-centred. An angry person could use the violence of anger to intimidate others, and so get what he wants. But a victim could also be so filled with self-pity as to maintain a social image that confirms a false sense of identity. Like the self-justifying power of that rich person, self-pity is equally seductive and destructive. We all have the tendency to narcissism; at this stage of our attentiveness, we need to see how that tendency manifests itself even in the little things we do. We also need to discover forms of asceticism that prevent us from slipping into selfishness.

On the other hand, our drive for self-transcendence manifests itself in the lived desire to align ourselves to God. We note Paul's injunction to the community at Philippi.

> Do nothing out of selfish ambition or vain conceit, but in humility consider others better than yourselves. Each of you should look not only to your own interests, but also to the interests of others. Your attitude should be the same as that of Christ Jesus:
>
> Who, being in very nature God,
> did not consider equality with God something to be grasped,
> but made himself nothing,
> taking the very nature of a servant,
> being made in human likeness.
> And being found in appearance as a man,
> he humbled himself
> and became obedient to death—
> even death on a cross! (Philippians 2:3-11)

Opposed to narcissism is humility. Humility comes from the profound awareness that we as creatures do not have our identity within ourselves but only in a vitally lived relationship with God. Jesus' human identity comes from the relationship the Father gives him in calling him "Beloved Son." Jesus responds to that calling by addressing God as "Abba," "Daddy." Our humility comes from the realization of our radical dependence on God. It is this dependence—this "poverty of spirit," and not our gifts or our social status—that defines and roots us. This is not to reject our talents or social forms of acknowledgement, and certainly it does not mean that we ought not to celebrate them. Rather, the use of these qualities has value only within the primary relationship with God. Our identity is not to be confused with our gifts, or our lack of these, or with our social position, whatever that may be.

It is the nature of the world to assert we are our gifts, and to define our identity by establishing our social status and what this means according to those gifts. Often we spend our lives trying to satisfy our desire for the fullness of life by cultivating our gifts as the path to happiness, and by thus trying to gain social approval in order to belong. Such an approach ignores the first commandment stated by Jesus: "Love the Lord your God with all your heart, and with all your soul, and with all your mind" (Matthew 22:37).

To love in this way requires our energies and desires become aligned to God. This requires the asceticism of opposing whatever dynamics of narcissism prevail in our lives. The enemy of our human nature seeks to take away from us the fullness of life and the path that would lead to the fullness of life. In his rules for the discernment of spirits, Ignatius says that "the enemy of our human nature investigates from every side all our virtues, theological, cardinal, moral. Where he finds the defenses of eternal salvation weakest and most deficient, there he attacks and takes us by storm" (Sp. Ex. #327:14). The theological virtues are faith, hope and charity; the cardinal virtues are prudence, justice, fortitude, temperance; the moral or eschatological virtues are gratitude, humility, vigilance, serenity, joy.

I mention this because often—and this has been my experience—we do not ask ourselves what we must do to counteract those temptations against these virtues. Virtues maintain relationships. Instead, we seek perfection by trying to eliminate what we consider "bad" feelings. Perfection becomes distorted to feeling good. We want to feel good, not realizing that the myth of feeling good all the time is an illusion. We are always in tension, and, as the Buddha's First Noble Truth says, everyone suffers. We cannot avoid suffering. So instead of avoiding the tension in our lives and the suffering that is part of the human condition, it is much healthier spiritually to do the positive work of cultivating those virtues. They are not simply given as grace; they need to be sought after, accepted and allowed to flourish. It is hard work to develop these virtues, and hard work to eliminate the forces in our lives and around us that erode these virtues. This is difficult work because we often identify ourselves psychologically with our feelings. When we treat spirituality as psychology, we ignore the broader dimensions of our being creatures in a contemporary world. We exist only in relationship. Our evolving identity is created through our relationships with God and with the many dimensions of God's creation. Cultivating the virtues puts us in right relations with God and all others. But how to do this?

The Examination of Consciousness (discussed in Part III) is helpful here. In this discipline, we allow our gratitude to show us how our day has been. Elie Wiesel, the 20th-century Holocaust survivor and writer, observes, "If the only prayer you say throughout your life is 'Thank You,' then that will be enough."[18] In this he echoes Meister Eckhart, who made the same observation almost 600 years earlier. For them, and for us, too, gratitude is the human manifestation of all virtues. It is our response to the Beloved's desire for us. Gratitude shows us where we are in tune with God; the lack of gratitude shows where we are not in tune with God. Gratitude refines our attunement. It is better to allow gratitude to do this rather than using our intellect or our "conscience," because the latter two often carry us to places of idealization, self-flagellation and duty. It is the beggar who knows gratitude. The one who realizes his "poverty of spirit" (Matthew 5:3) in the depths of his being realizes the good given to him daily, as well as his radical dependence on that good and the giver of that good. This knowledge grounds his way through the world and becomes the basis for discernment of spirits.

Remaining in gratitude not only shows us our day clearly, it also reveals to us appropriate means of asceticism to become more deeply rooted in attention. To approach this attunement otherwise focuses on perfectionism and forms of self-will to improve our condition. Then we unwittingly succumb to Michael Serres's observation that disorder favours certain forms of order.[19]

At this stage of attentiveness, when we become aware of the habitual patterns engrained in ourselves that prevent us from a domestic familiarity with the divine, we can clear away some of the dust that clouds our vision. But some of what clouds our vision also shapes the way we see, and we cannot of ourselves do anything about this. What needs to be done has to be given. All we can do is dispose ourselves to receive that gift and to live out of it.

This approach requires the discipline of being where the gift is. That gift is the connection we have discovered between God and us. The work at this stage of attention is to recognize the gift when it appears; to accept that gift for what it is and not for what we want it to be; and finally to be able to use the gift. Learning to use the gift occupies our attention at this stage of our spiritual journey. A connection has been made and recognized. How this unique and passionate relationship develops into the familiarity of lovers takes time and discipline. One experiments to find out what works. As Teresa of Avila once said, mysticism is an experimental science. We can allow it to reshape our sense of presence to ourselves and to others and to the world. The years of discipline are not undertaken to find love. It is done out of love and in love, to learn how to become more loving.

Questions for reflection

1. When you look at the virtues, which ones are the least developed in you?

2. What do you need to do to build up those virtues?

3. How do those asceticisms bring you to a deeper and more joyful rootedness in God?

4. How does the Examination of Consciousness help here?

5. What are the areas in your life where you feel gratitude? What are the areas where you do not?

6. What happens when you ask gratitude what is the next step to undertake in those areas?

7. How does the tension between narcissism and authenticity manifest itself in your life?

6. Riding the Bull Home

The love I have found transforms me slowly into a witness
Of life. My every act is a blessing, and reveals the eternal blessings
Always present. They invite all to join the way
which leads through the darkness to their heart's desire.

Attention as habit

As we lean always into the darkness that calls us beyond ourselves, we fall into the habits of love, fostered by the daily practices
of prayer, spiritual reading and the asceticisms that slowly eradicate some of our tendencies to self-destruction, fostering care for
ourselves and others instead. We no longer suffer the dramatic ups
and downs of beginners walking a spiritual path. We discover and
become more aware of the tendencies and patterns in our lives
that lead to selfishness. We also discover the ways in which we are
invited to overcome those stumbling blocks so they do not throw
us off our spiritual path. We discover the spiritual path is defined
by relationships, and so the work we do is to discover and maintain
right relationships with those around us.

This sixth Ox-herding picture offers an image and a poem representing this stage. One continues on the journey to the fullness of life as the light of the world we had previously known slowly fades. But we are not disturbed, because we feel within ourselves a growing rootedness to the source of life and a sense of the community of those who truly belong to God, which we are becoming part of.

At this stage, life does not become easier; rather, we are becoming seasoned as practitioners of a particular spiritual path. This does not make other spiritual paths and traditions irrelevant. In fact, as we become more attentive to our own spiritual path and explore it existentially, we see just how other spiritual traditions and practices can supplement it.

Attentiveness as habit leads to an openness seeking to develop our relationship with God without restricting that relationship to the biases of our cultural conditioning. If the previous state of attention deepens us, this present state broadens us.

Our perception normally is focused within a limited range of attention. As we cultivate our spiritual life, that range of attention broadens. We start discovering the presence of God's life in more than our prayer, liturgies and spiritual reading. Our being attuned at the depths makes us aware of aspects of the world around us that also manifest God's life. The boundaries between the sacred and the secular become more blurred. We find God in more and more things, because we seek to discover the way God is present in all things.

The Roman poet Terence wrote that nothing human was foreign to him. When we live our attention as habit, we find the same thing. We discover the broader dimensions of being human. The path of becoming fully human, beyond our fears or socialized self-interest, makes us interested in the world outside us as aspects of ourselves. Attention as habit focuses outward like a child discovering what feeds it and gives it life. Its curiosity is the manifestation of its becoming grounded in the love that not only holds and celebrates it, but calls it forward ever deeper into the life that surrounds it. Becoming comfortable with our emerging spiritual identity, we explore the world around us to find connections, allies and confirmations about the path we walk.

We start to become aware of our connections to all of humanity and creation. This happens not just in an intellectual way, but
also at those deeper levels of being opened up and integrated at
the earlier levels of attention. Our relationship to nature becomes
shamanistic; we explore different religious traditions and spiritual
techniques. Zen sitting, yoga exercises, Sufi poetry, Orthodox icons,
the world of the desert Fathers and Mothers, tales of the Hasidim:
all feed us and illuminate our path. The world of the mystic in our
own traditions achieves a depth and a flexibility of understanding
from communion with other traditions. It is as if the voices and
presences from different spiritual paths and cultures are in dialogue with us as part of the human family. We are in the process
of coming home to ourselves, beyond alienation or shame or self-
justification. We find ourselves being able to sit more comfortably
with the saint and the prostitute, the creative and the corrupt, and
we experience a sense of wonder and simplicity. We discover our
kinship with the created.

We become aware of how elements or incidents in our past that
we might have regarded then as negative, or as making no sense,
or as detrimental to our well-being, were actually gifts that now
stand us in good stead. What was previously held as unredeemed
or unredeemable is now discovered to be of value and of use. Now
we see connections between those incidents and the present path of
our life. We understand why it is important that they happened, or
even how our new present awareness brings good out of these. In
my own life, growing up in a multi-ethnic culture that was home to
many different traditions—Christianity, Hinduism, Islam, Chinese
ancestor respect, African tribal religions, and Amerindian spirit
worship—prepared me to see the value in that diversity. Being a
child of mixed race is no longer something to be ashamed of, but is
actually a source of exploration and celebration of the many voices
that make up my life. One comes to realize from this that unity
does not need conformity to be community. Identity comes from
accepting the other as invitation rather than viewing the other as
enemy. But coming to this position takes time, and to hold it without a spiritual underpinning makes for relativism; with a spiritual
grounding, one sees life as relational. From here we seek to see how

the diverse elements of our life—our past and our present living conditions—can develop our present state of attention.

Now we do not ask why something good or bad has happened, but rather how we might use all that has happened to us, all that we are, for the good. For instance, the difficult moments in our life allow us to empathize with others who are going through similar difficult moments. How we coped, or did not cope, revealed to us strategies for living, the knowledge of which is helpful for others. Our connection with others' brokenness exists precisely through our own brokenness. While we are not necessarily healed, neither are we trapped by the false narratives our brokenness can solicit within ourselves or others. Attention as habit breaks open some of the closed myths that have controlled our lives. We discover the quiet abiding presence of God even in those times we thought God was not there. We see our past, our present and our future from a new perspective. Part IV of this book explores this aspect of our life journey to redemption.

Once we become aware of this presence, without falling into introspection about ourselves, or intrusively investigating others' lives, we discover a sense of wonder at our present life. While we do not primarily question what this or that means, we do find ourselves positioned to allow all elements of our lives to reveal themselves to us. We ponder not only what arises in our hearts but also what displays itself around us in our daily lives. At the centre of our lives, a quietness and a stillness create the space for such revelations. These come to us charged with symbolic import and energy, as if we are riding and manifesting the currents of energy that shape the worlds we live in.

Our response to this expanded sense of awareness manifests itself in the spirit of gratitude, which shapes the way we do our daily examen and spiritual practices. We sit in the spirit of the gratitude that arises in us, and we let that spirit show us how our day went. We rejoice in what is revealed as a celebration of gratitude and in what still calls us to gratitude.

What is shown to us is that we are still on the journey to ever deeper levels of spiritual intimacy, and that journey consists in the

Beloved becoming more present to us as we go to him. The journey is marked by transformation, often painful and bewildering, as we give up more and more of what we know of the world. We are being taught not to be caught by conceptual worlds, but rather to see that the conceptual frames of reference that structure our reality open out onto mystery; as we relax into that mystery, we discover we are mysteries to ourselves also.

For each of us, that sense of mystery is unique. We might be tempted to think that this is not so, but as every snowflake, every leaf, every fruit fly has unique characteristics, so does each and every one of us. Our relationship to mystery is also unique. Coming home to ourselves, we experience the growing realization that each of us is unique, as is everyone's path home.

The temptation at this stage is twofold. First, we can be so overwhelmed by the desire to belong that we think we have reached home before we are there. Then we act in certain ways before the grace for such is given, accepting a self-realization that is not ours, or we take on a narrative, approved and confirmed by the tradition we find ourselves in, as our own. To do so is to live a lie. In this state, we adopt a certain complacency and rootedness we assume is our own, or will be soon enough, as though this does not matter. We behave as if we have arrived. But we have not. This presumption short-circuits the unfolding of what we need to be attentive to at this stage. The second temptation occurs when we act out of that misconception of having arrived. We try to offer others a way to their way, when we have just lost our own way.

What are we to do then? The Desire that desires us is blocked by our arrogance, and the effects can be felt in our discernments. We desire to be approved by the world for this accomplishment, as it validates our sense of self. We show off our giftedness. We become spiritual brats. But no matter how the world informs and deigns to acknowledge us when we behave this way, our relationship with the Desire who desires us brings us into a desolation. Our energies are not in accord with the energies of God. This felt discord needs to be recognized and admitted. Things are not the way we want others and ourselves to see them. The feelings of desolation must be unpacked. The stories contained in them need to be deconstructed so we can discover and dismantle the dynamics that lead us to behave in the ways of the world. This may be difficult and takes time, and the work is done often in an unconscious manner. Yet the release from the traps that halt the journey home brings a greater sense of peace and an awareness of the mystery we are to ourselves and to others. Being liberated from the traps means being liberated from conceptual worlds that predetermine how we are to behave or approach life.

That freedom allows us to become like little children—without being naïve or childish—delighting in life and exploring the possibilities for living that open on the path. We see "otherness" and "difference" as an invitation to explore what it means to be a neighbour and to learn ways of accepting those neighbours, as flawed as we are, as companions on the journey.

This journey has as its guide a humility that allows us to be aware all is a gift from the God who desires only what is best for us. We learn to relax in humility and to delight in the life given us on our path. We see the life we experience as a symbol of that greater life of which we are a part, and notice the interplay between us and that larger life occurs on the level of mutuality, covenant and interconnectedness, much the way a baby is in the womb of its mother.

As we learn to accept this sense of mystery, and not to be threatened by the sense of unknowing it affords us, we see life is not a maze with dead ends but a journey into intimacy that never stops. It can be compared more to a labyrinth where we are always moving towards the centre even though at times it seems we are going away from it.

In fact, every apparent end we arrive at opens to another beginning. At this stage of attention, the joy we celebrate at being on the journey home is always coloured by mourning for the worlds we leave behind. We, being human, want the comfort of security, of familiar ways of understanding ourselves and others and the world. But the darkness we lean into and that calls us to rootedness does not allow such false comfort. We become more and more accustomed to a state of coming to an end and starting anew. We discover the truth of Heraclitus's observation: All that is known goes nowhere. We never step into the same river twice. Realizing this, and holding the known more and more lightly, we settle into a deeper pattern of endings and beginnings. We are always coming home. There is a move here from structuralism to post-structuralism. We move from a way of knowing to a way of unknowing, from structures and seemingly secure conceptual worlds we have become familiar with to post-structures and the rawness of mystery. Living in that mystery, we slowly create new structures to accommodate this new life. These in turn become codified, and then must be transcended. We struggle against the temptation to systematize the experience of attentiveness by removing it from the experience of an evolving relationship into the truncated objectifications of dogma. Rather than holding dogmatic assertions about our identity and God, we tell stories of the Lover and the Beloved and of their struggle for intimacy. The Ox-herding pictures I use here present one such narrative.

The journey home is one of constant transformation. The path we travel on opens us to the possibility of a greater intimacy with God. Consolation urges us to those places that need transformation. We go there and find ourselves in desolation. Desolation reveals a pattern to be transformed. We remain in that desolation until the pattern that traps us is deconstructed. We discover liberation and then the consolidation of those aspects of our lives so liberated. We experience consolation. That spirit of consolation that affirms and celebrates our new life carries us once again to what cries out for life. We move on and are transformed. It is the nature of love to go to the unloved and unlovable. Thus our anger, for instance, shows us what is not compassion, but reveals elements of narcissism and self-clinging that cry out to be liberated into community. Our certitude reveals what is yet to be permeated by mystery. Our greed reveals what has yet to be transformed into generosity. This is done not by acts of will but by a humility that invites us to the available ways of liberation that bring a delight in living. It is the path not taken by the rich young man in Mark's gospel (10:17-27). Jesus invites him to give away all he has and live out of a relationship with Jesus. He is a good person and on the way. He lives an upright ethical life. He is invited to live a fuller spiritual life, but he turns away, unable to take the next step.

That movement to a fuller spiritual life is the one Peter endures after his encounter with the risen Jesus on the Sea of Tiberias. In that gospel story, Jesus asks Peter three times if he loves him. The first two times, Jesus uses the word *agape* for that love. Peter responds that he loves Jesus, but uses another word: *philia*. *Agape* translates into a self-transcending love. *Philia* is used for friendship. The third time Jesus questions Peter, Jesus uses the word *philia*. And Peter, breaking down and crying, knowing his past betrayals and his inability to live *agape*, replies, yes, he is Jesus' friend. Not lover. The rest of Peter's life is that movement from friendship to a deeper love. It is the movement from *philia* to *agape* (John 21). It is from a friendship that is a relationship marked by self-knowledge to a love marked by self-transcendence. This is the movement from sincerity, where we are true to ourselves, to authenticity, where we are true to what calls us beyond ourselves. In Riding the Bull Home, we take the path to authenticity.

Questions for reflection

1. Where do you find yourself being called specifically to develop your intimacy with God?

2. What do you do to develop your rootedness? How did your perspective—your ways of imagining the world—become more broad and inclusive?

3. In what ways did you discover being more at home with yourself, with others and with God?

4. What manifestations of "otherness" still challenge you?

5. What were the consolations of your life at this time?

6. How did you experience yourself as uniquely loved? When you look over your whole life, can you recall specific instances of this devotion?

7. How did you manifest your growing rootedness in the world? The Ox-herding poem says, "Every act is a blessing and reveals the eternal blessings always present." How do you understand this line as applicable to your life?

7. The bull transcended

After a long struggle I find myself content,
Finally at home in this intimacy which roots me
Humbly to accept my lot in life and to celebrate
What is daily given, simply and joyfully.

Attention as complacency

As we become accustomed to living the path as mystery, and in our growing awareness of our kinship with everything, we become aware of being looked after, held in God's love, surrounded by the powers of good. We slowly stop worrying about whether we are doing God's will. The awareness of the omnipresent mercy of God transcends the anxieties that might arise about whether we are doing the right thing.

This deeper state of attentiveness allows us to be more intuitively in contact with God. We know at this stage that even if we make mistakes—though our care for the world stops us from being silly or imprudent—the basic concern of the Father is to transform all our mistakes into occasions for new life. We recall here that God saved us even when we were sinners and saves us even as we sin. This does not give us the license to sin. But it does give us the freedom to trust ourselves in God and be creative. We can do this because there is a felt sense of the constant presence of the relationship. It is like the artist who has perfected his technique so that when he picks up his brush, every stroke is a revelation. He no longer worries about what to do. He lets the brush speak, and trusts what it does.

The energies of our life have become coordinated with the energies of God and the good manifest in creation. We are filled with a sense of right relationships and with a sense of complacency in our path. We share the spirit of the Christ and a delight in what opens to us in our path.

This does not mean we cannot be troubled by the disorders of the world around us. It means we find ourselves so rooted in God's love, we cannot be shifted by the terrors of the times we live in. As Jeremiah, an Old Testament prophet who lived in a most difficult time, noted,

> Blessed are those who trust in the Lord, whose trust is the Lord. Each is like a tree planted by water, that sends out its roots by the stream, and does not fear when heat comes, for its leaves remain green, and is not anxious in the year of drought, for it does not cease to bear fruit. (Jeremiah 17:7-8)

This rootedness reaches up into our daily life and guides that life. Going with that flow, good things spontaneously happen. This is not coincidence, but is the result of the coming together of the ordered ego and the ground of our being. That dynamic shows itself, at this stage of attentiveness, when we do something spontaneously because it seems right. We go to the library and a book draws our attention to it; or we speak to a person to whom we have no reason to speak, except this urge suggests itself to us. We feel ourselves surrounded by love and protection. Athletes call this being in the "zone."

This state is characterized objectively by evaluative skills. The first of these is focus: the ability to remain centred on our primary relationship as stated in the first commandment in Matthew's gospel: "Love the Lord your God with all your heart and with all your soul and with all your mind" (Matthew 22:37). This dynamic focus sets goals, evaluates projects and accomplishes tasks. Because of this spontaneous interplay between the self and God at this level of attentiveness, we often think outside the box and in creative ways. The energies of the imagination are liberated to see and experience reality, unconstrained by the closed and broken myths that trap us in life-denying patterns of behaviour. The Examen is used to bring to light and to eliminate those negative tendencies and also to make sure the complacency we experience is distinguished from apathy. Complacency manifests itself in care; apathy shows itself in a lack of concern for others. Our rootedness in God's love makes us involved in creating and maintaining right relationships with the rest of creation.

This work can stimulate anxiety or stress or frustration, but the sense of focus and rootedness prevents us from being trapped or distracted or from becoming significantly de-energized by these factors. We are able to recognize and remain open to whatever possibilities emerge. This spirit of openness allows us to be attentive to what is actually present to us. In the midst of the struggle, we can enjoy what is delightful. In the midst of the struggle, we can be hopeful that what presents itself to us can be used to foster life. The result is an ease with what happens, and the ability to return to a balanced perspective and equanimity should we become upset. The discipline of remaining rooted allows us to avoid dissipating energy by feeding negative emotions and situations. Even if we are in very stressful situations, we maintain our boundaries and positive attitude and are not overcome by negativity.

One of the ways we can do this is by being prepared for times of trial. The habit of prayer exposes us, within the context of being held and loved, to aspects of the world that are damaging. When we encounter difficult situations, the stance we have cultivated in prayer enables us to be present to those situations without being overwhelmed.

The lived experience of being rooted is also prayer. Formal prayer may be a more heightened and self-conscious form of being in relationship, but this level of attention is prayer lived. We can say grace before meals. That is formal prayer. But we can eat the food gratefully and attentively and that is also prayer. Such attention finds and celebrates life in everything we do. Then our whole life is a prayer and our different relationships with everything are forms of prayer.

Operating here is the growing awareness of a level of dynamic relationships, which constantly exists among all aspects of creation beyond the ego's consciousness of those connections. It is as if we only begin to see when we stop forcing ourselves to see. Rather like viewing those stereograms that look like Jackson Pollock scribbles and seem like nonsense, when we let our eyes fall out of focus, three-dimensional figures emerge from the apparent chaos. We become aware we are an intrinsic part of a living organism that manifests itself through relationships, and we entrust ourselves to it. We tap into the intrinsic and underlying order of things, and this allows us to be more sensitive to the manifold dimensions of the extrinsic and surface nature of reality.

Lest we attach a false sense of importance to this reality and ignore its ordinariness, we might consider the difference between when we first started driving a car and our current experience. After years of driving, our instincts are honed and we do not think of being the driver when we drive. The driving is done through us.

Questions for reflection

1. Can you list the things you are so competent at that you forget yourself doing them?

2. Can you recall moments when you gave or received advice and became surprised at what you said or did? What happens when you just sit in the presence of God's love? What feelings, emotions, images, memories arise?

3. Have you ever found things happening to you at just the right moment?

4. How did creativity manifest itself through you at this stage of attentiveness?

5. You may have noted that the sixth Ox-herding poem is set in the evening; this seventh one is set in the dawn. What has happened in the night between these two states?

6. What happens when we start seeing with the eyes of Mystery and from the heart, rather than from the mind and the senses? What is the difference in understanding?

7. What is the "plot" that now holds the facts you observe in a coherent narrative?

8. Both bull and self transcended

Emptiness and the fullness of being. The same thing.
Deeper than love is intimacy. Deeper than intimacy, unity.
But from beyond both, and beyond language,
Saint and sinner, cosmos and each single drop of water,
Arise and disappear.

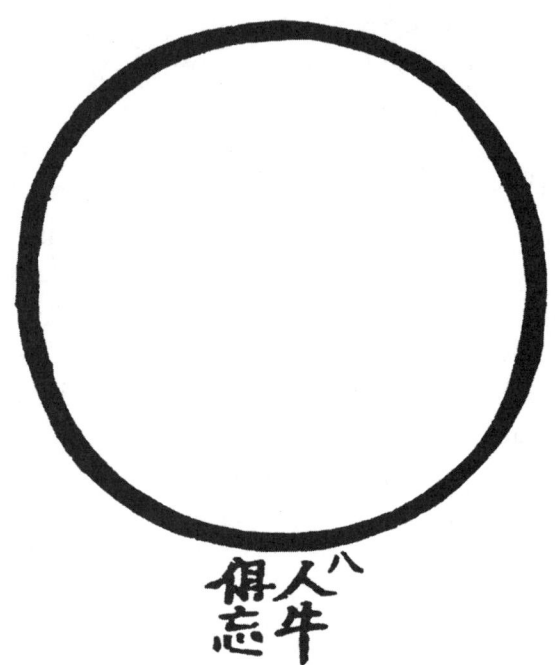

Attention as empty

Entrusting ourselves to the newly awakened sense of presence in us and surrounding us, we remain aware of ourselves. Only in developing the habit of living out of this trust do we slowly abandon the self-consciousness that, strangely enough, has brought us to this awareness of relationship. The previous state might be compared to a person who realizes he is not separated from anything in contact with him. There has been a movement from the sense of relationship between all things to the sense there is no self and other; there is just the awareness of oneness. This present state is different. There is not even the awareness of oneness. "Oneness" is a construct. It is maintained by a certain level of attention.

When we move beyond that level, there is only attention. Things just are. There is only emptiness. If the previous stage gave us a felt sense of union with the Son, the present stage gives us an unfelt sense of a deeper level: union with the Father. It reveals to us what our humanity rests on. We experience a radical poverty of spirit, which reveals to us in an unmediated manner how we are maintained by the mystery we call God. As Matthew's gospel puts it, "Blessed are the poor in spirit, theirs is the kingdom of God" (Matthew 5:3). Our rootedness seems to rest on no-thing, and that no-thingness permeates all that is. That no-thing-ness is not negativity. It is what the Buddhists describe as *sunyata*. It is both nothing and the fullness of being. But how do we experience ourselves as we enter this state of attention? At the level of greatest importance—that intrinsic sense of self—we first have the sense of being in free fall. We are not sure if we are rising or falling; we are not sure of direction. At the beginning of arriving at this state, any method by which we can place ourselves in relation to anything else evaporates. The sense of self slowly disappears.

The eighth Ox-herding picture describes this state of integrity where there is no other to be aware of and no self to be the subject of that awareness. There just IS. In his exercise on contemplating the Incarnation, St. Ignatius asks us to pray for the grace of intimacy, out of which flows love, out of which flows service. At first, this seems to be an odd grace to pray for, because normally we think of love developing into intimacy. But Ignatius sees it the other way around. Love always implies separation between lover and beloved. Intimacy is deeper than love, and is where the lover and the beloved become one. There is no separation. The love that manifests itself in grateful service flows from this unity at the depths of our being, where we cannot distinguish where we stop and God starts. This is not to say we are God. Rather, as human creatures we are unable to make the distinction. At that level of intimacy, there is no feeling, no conceptual world, no intuition, no awareness. There is No-Thing from a human perspective. To be sure, this level of relationship with the Divine always exists, but we cannot access it on an imaginative level directly and immediately. Though it supports the imagination and all its constructs, it goes beyond imagination. For some people, awareness of the nothingness we stand on can be received in a form of instant enlightenment. For others, the process is long and slow.

On one level, the progress to that sense of emptiness is quite liberating. On another level, it causes great anxiety, because there are now no longer any coordinates to say where we are or how we are. Kierkegaard once defined anxiety as the dizzying experience of freedom; the growing experience of emptiness creates anxiety because we want desperately to know where we belong and how. Living out of that emptiness erodes the remnants of the sense of self, which seeks such assurances. The final state is now not just a particular set of connections that is relationship. Now there is no relationship, because there are no connections. In Buddhism there is a set of aphorisms, the third of which might be applicable here.

Vision is mind.
Mind is empty.
Emptiness is clear light.
Clear light is union.
Union is great bliss.[20]

These aphorisms carry us to a certain realization. The first, "Vision is mind," states that we all live in imagined worlds, and we live in them as if they are real. The second aphorism, "Mind is empty," observes that those imagined worlds are constructs. They have no reality in themselves. This awareness illuminates for us that things, as they are, are impermanent. They emerge from emptiness and return to emptiness. That emptiness noted in the third aphorism is unpolluted by what arises from it and returns to it. The third aphorism, "Emptiness is clear light," leads to the fourth, "Clear light is union." This holds that we all share the emptiness from which all creatures emerge and into which they disappear. The fifth aphorism affirms that a lived awareness of such commonality is experienced as bliss.

The Ox-herding picture we are trying to open up is situated in the third aphorism. Emptiness is clear light. The realized experience of emptiness is one of clarity. This clarity transcends conceptual thought, and Cartesian dualism. To understand anything is complicated. There are many different ways of looking at a single thing. For instance, if we were to look up a word in a dictionary, its meaning is connected to other words, and those other words are linked to still more words. All of those words are contained in a dictionary, which uses a specific language. That language can be understood only in relationship to other languages, and those other languages are situated in cultures that have historical contexts. To understand something is not simple, and to try to construct the relationship between things is overwhelmingly complicated. It is complicated because a relationship is read in terms of structure, context, conceptual thinking, cultural perspectives, levels of intentionality and response. Relationships are operative within a historical framework of time and place. We do not have an absolute knowledge of those contexts to affirm what anything really is or means. This is not to say that we are relativists, but that we are relational. We exist in and through relationships. But more real and stable and rooted than those relationships is their basis. We experience it as emptiness. Out of that emptiness comes the excesses of overdetermination, so that things do not have single meanings but many, many meanings, depending on the relationships we subscribe to in trying to understand them. What we call a chair can be a piece of firewood, an antique, a work of art, something to sit on, a toy for a child, the subject of a painting, a cultural artifact, a tool a lion-tamer uses in a circus or a part of a set design. The values attached to those readings of a particular chair will vary from person to person and from context to context.

What does this mean? It means that identity, defined in terms of relationships, cannot be totally and fully expressed through concepts. But, beyond that, actual things exist because of actual relationships. I sit on a chair that sits on a floor as a part of a house situated in a neighbourhood of a city belonging to a nation defined as a geographical land mass, which is part of the surface of a planet in a solar system of a particular galaxy… and so on… until our situational skills become exhausted, and peter away in ignorance. Moreover, these relationships are in constant flux and so cannot be pinned down. And what then are those dynamic relationships apropos of the unceasing creativity of the Creator?

How is this emptiness to be read in a traditional Christian context? Emptiness is the state that exists beyond any human narrative. A Christian approach is to see the journey into emptiness as the journey of the Christian into the Third Week of the Ignatian Exercises when one contemplates the passion and death of the Christ. In his suffering and death, the Christ moves beyond those social and cultural narratives that give his life earthly significance. He is rendered bereft and abject. This stripping away leaves only one relationship intact. It is all one the Father has with him. In the light of this relationship that other relationships are seen and valued. We should observe the relationship Jesus on the cross has with the Father is different from the relationship the Father has with him. On the cross Jesus says, "Abba, Abba, why have you forsaken me?" He existentially feels an abandonment of his prime relationship. But his Abba enters the human Christ's very human death and brings that emptied awareness to a new level of humanity called resurrection.

For us the profound sense of emptiness allows us to see the relative value of all relationships, their contingency and their impermanent nature. We have the sense that there is nothing one can hold onto. Existential awareness at this stage is functional, because relationships at this stage are functional. This is a very powerful state of attentiveness to be in, as we are not swayed—or caught, or interested—in anything for its own sake. That awareness is like the warrior cutting through the knots of illusion.

There is a long journey into accepting and living out of this emptiness. Everything in us and around us posits a solidity of the self and of the world around us. It is only when we have fallen through the cracks of the world—say, by becoming unemployed or mentally ill, or by losing our country, family and friends, by experiencing the death of loved ones, thus losing all the relationships that construct and establish our identity, and so have no narrative within which to understand or share our experiences—that we have some sense of the pain and terror of that growing awareness of emptiness. Crisis or boundary situations bring our vulnerability to the fore point to that radical emptiness at the root of all of our experiences. It is an awareness hard to bear, and it challenges our easy understanding of what it means to be human.

In his novel *As I Lay Dying*, William Faulkner tells a tale of a family going to bury a mother. At one point, they look at a swollen river over which they have the impossible task of carrying the coffin. Two brothers, Cash and Darl, look at the quietly treacherous water and at each other "with long probing looks, looks that plunge unimpeded through one another's eyes and into the ultimate secret place where for an instant Cash and Darl crouch flagrant and unabashed in all the old terror and the old foreboding, alert and secret and without shame."[21] At that moment, which strips them of their masks, they share the sense of the terror of being human without defenses. They lose that "pride, that furious desire to hide that abject nakedness, that we bring here with us, carry with us into operating rooms, carry stubbornly and furiously with us into the earth again."[22] The mother is finally buried, but in the process the rest of the family, except for the errant father, lose themselves. That stripping radically challenges our notions of God and the familiar habitual structures around which we organize our lives. Looking back, it is as if, at this stage, the desire God has for us takes away even our understanding of God. We enter the dark night of the soul.

Encountering emptiness first strips us of all the defenses we have created to hide from our "poverty of spirit." It is little wonder that the world tries to ignore or repress that knowledge, or seeks—in vain, we might note—to fill up that emptiness with possessions or social status or other validations of our created ego. In emptiness, things stop making sense intellectually, or we get a sense of the radical inadequacy of what is taken for granted. Established positions and values seem empty or trite. We abandon even an earlier skepticism that posited a sense of a deeper awareness of how things should be, as opposed to how they appear. We give up the utopianism of a possible other world or the nostalgia for a previous world and the available ways of human existence not found in the present. We slowly give up the criteria for assessing whether something makes sense or not. It is a journey into confusion and out of confusion. It reminds me of someone who begins to suffer from Alzheimer's disease. First there is the dreadful anxiety and panic of losing the awareness of habitual understandings, but as the disease spreads and the person loses a sense of who and where they are, loses the sense of relationships and of their own history, a certain unforced calm descends. The person returns to what the Buddhists call "novice mind." This is an awareness freed from a fixation on preconceptions.

The awareness of emptiness slowly erodes even those feelings that are values refined to spontaneity. The person even moves away from the position of floating through a superficial world of value unconnected to their sense of self. As that sense of self disappears, so, too, does the particular sense of value connected with it. Emily Dickinson's poem captures the disappearance of that sense of self.

> *I felt a Funeral, in my Brain,*
> *And Mourners to and fro*
> *Kept treading—treading—till it seemed*
> *That Sense was breaking through—*
> *And when they all were seated,*
> *A Service, like a Drum—*
> *Kept beating—beating—till I thought*
> *My mind was going numb—*
> *And then I heard them lift a Box*
> *And creak across my Soul*
> *With those same Boots of Lead, again,*
> *Then Space—began to toll,*
> *As all the Heavens were a Bell,*
> *And Being, but an Ear,*
> *And I, and Silence, some strange Race*
> *Wrecked, solitary, here—*
> *And then a Plank in Reason, broke,*
> *And I dropped down, and down—*
> *And hit a World, at every plunge,*
> *Finished knowing—then—*[23]

The poem describes the movement beyond speech, and beyond knowing to a silence. This silence opens the reader to the context surrounding the act of reading. It moves us to the next Ox-herding picture. But in this present stage, what one attends to is that movement to an open space out of which "reality" emerges.

I imagine this passage to such emptiness could be compared to a manifestation of a psychotic break in slow motion. But this is not an existential angst endured by alienation wherein we have a heightened self-consciousness that collapses under the burden of too much awareness. Here the very constructions of self-consciousness are being erased in the context of us being loved and held by the Desire that offers us the fullness of life. Emptiness offers us the Fullness of Being. Indeed, while Nature abhors a vacuum, God, on the other hand, loves emptiness. At the height of this state of awareness, our emptiness and the felt sense of the presence of God come together.

Christians have a relationship of adoption by the Father similar to the sonship of Jesus that the gospel of John describes. Jesus prays that those who believe in him "May all be one, just as you, Father, are in me, and I in you, that they also may be in us" (John 17:21). The particular unity that Jesus, in his human nature, has with the Father is existentially reproduced in our own moments of transfiguration. In those experiences, the forms of self-consciousness that give us our felt sense of identity as otherness disappear. Admittedly, these are ecstatic moments and peak experiences.

But their reality continues to exert a force in our daily lives beyond the to and fro of our ego and its needs. We slowly appropriate that sense of emptiness as the first beatitude that Matthew talks about: "Blessed are the poor in spirit; theirs is the kingdom of God." Our radical poverty of spirit opens out onto our emptiness. Living that emptiness makes us aware we are protected and held and loved into the fullness of life at every moment of our lives. When we finally accept our emptiness, and become aware of it and accustomed to it, we realize it is a gift. It opens us to experience our communion with God in the ordinariness of our day.

The discernments we must make in the context of this level of awareness depend on where we are with regard to our emptiness. At the beginning, we are tempted to seek the comfort of the previous stage when we are aware we are held and loved. Then, as we grow into our awareness of emptiness, we are tempted to live in a form of detachment, holding everything to have equal value.

This is apathy masquerading as indifference. As we realize our emptiness more and more in our daily lives, we might be tempted to become spiritual snobs, affirmed in and by our awareness and thinking that everything is possible. Then we need to be attentive to the second temptation offered to Christ in the desert after his peak experience of being recognized as the "Beloved son" at his baptism by the Father.

> Then the devil took him to the holy city, and placed him on the pinnacle of the temple, saying to him, "If you are the Son of God, throw yourself down; for it is written, 'He will command his angels concerning you,' and 'on their hands they will bear you up, that you will not dash your foot against a stone.'" Jesus said to him, "Again it is written, 'You shall not put the Lord, your God, to the test.'" (Matthew 4:5-6)

We do not alienate ourselves from the Desire who holds us into being by setting ourselves apart from it and seeking to prove our identity to ourselves and others. To seek to prove it to ourselves implies a lack of trust in what is given as gift; to seek to prove it to others is a sin of spiritual pride. It says, "Look, see what I can make God do."

Living empty manifests itself in simplicity and humility. The desire for life coming through that emptiness is passionate and committed. It realizes creation is still being formed and our presence in the world is a symbol of that larger creation. Our identity is not within us but within a set of relationships, which make up creation, and within the relationship between Creator and creation. Emptiness is the realization of what grounds those relationships. Such realization, going beyond the realm of conceptual thinking, cannot cover the range and complexity of those relationships. As the end of John's gospel says, "There are also many other things that Jesus did, that if they were written one by one, I suppose that even the world itself could not contain the books that would be written. Amen" (John 21:25). The Word-made-flesh is not an incarnated concept. He is a human being. His kenosis as a human being reveals the relationship we have with God. Emptiness is our direct encounter with the Divine and the manifestation of that encounter. Out of that emptiness all forms of reality emerge and disappear. Forms cannot contain it; all the books in the world cannot exhaust it.

Questions for reflection

1. When you look back on your life, what were the times you felt stripped? How did that state affect your spiritual direction (if you were in spiritual direction at the time), your relationship with others, and your relationship with the world?

2. How does your emptiness allow you to remain in another's space without imposing your own agenda?

3. We can be constantly tempted to "fill our emptiness." What are the ways in which you are tempted and what are the ways in which you maintain your emptiness?

4. How does the world appear to you when you live out of your emptiness?

5. As you were enduring the process of "losing your life" (Luke 17:33), what were your concerns and attitudes? How did these change?

9. Reaching the Source

We come from God, and return to God. All paths lead to God.
What we sought for so long was always there, under our feet.
But now we know it, and now we see things as they are:
Each seeking God and each beloved by God.

Attention as source

The clarity emptiness allows shows us things as they are. It gives us the awareness we are creatures, still being formed by God. It makes us realize all of our life is handed over to forces beyond us, and at this stage we see all is gift. Often, though, how to open and use, share and celebrate this gift is also beyond us. But when good things happen, we can rejoice in what is given, and when bad things happen, we can mourn. We can offer them up to God to be transformed. A part of mourning is that sure knowledge of transformation. Being a creature means always participating in transformation. Nothing is permanent. Even our relationship with God changes; and, as we change, the way we experience God's relationship with us changes also. We, the world—indeed, all of creation—is on a pilgrimage. Along that path, things meet for a while and then separate. Meaning is created, and then circumstances and relationships change, so that constructed meaning changes. It is the nature of creation. It is impermanent.

The ninth Ox-herding picture offers a view of reality not distorted by bias. Reality simply is. It is not changed by our misconceptions. And we are a part of that reality. We change, the world changes, and creation is the product of the unceasing creativity we call God, or whatever name we care to name it. That Divine mystery and its workings, as Job discovers, is beyond our understanding. What we have been given to know is this Mystery desires all of creation, which includes us and every part of us, to receive the gift of the fullness of life. How and when this is to happen is part of God's providence. Our cooperation in its happening is our being attentive. Attention allows us to step into mystery, and when we are attentive, we walk a path that changes us and carries us through a changing world. We learn to accept this.

The awareness of impermanence gives us the freedom to delight in things as they come and go. In fact, this very coming and going is symbolic of emptiness. The Heart Sutra of Buddhism states that form is empty; emptiness is form. What we hold as reality emerges from the ground of being and returns to the ground of being. These are not two different states; they are the same. Form allows emptiness to be manifest, and emptiness allows form to manifest. As the passage in Ecclesiasticus puts it,

> To every thing there is a season, and a time to every purpose under the heaven:
> A time to be born, and a time to die;
> a time to plant, and a time to pluck up that which is planted;
> A time to kill, and a time to heal;
> a time to break down, and a time to build up;
> A time to weep, and a time to laugh;
> a time to mourn, and a time to dance;
> A time to cast away stones, and a time to gather stones together; a time to embrace, and a time to refrain from embracing;

A time to get, and a time to lose; a time to keep,
and a time to cast away;
A time to rend, and a time to sew;
a time to keep silence, and a time to speak;
A time to love, and a time to hate;
a time of war, and a time of peace.
(Ecclesiastes 3:1-8)

Heraclitus, the pre-Socratic Greek philosopher, says everything is flux: nothing remains the same and no person ever steps in the same river twice, for it is not the same river and that person is not the same.

Now all of this might sound very philosophical and esoteric, but it actually reveals a heightened state of spiritual attentiveness. For the most part, we tend to live our lives with a set of certainties. Only when we experience circumstances such as a death or an accident; the loss of a loved one, or a job, an illness, or even misplaced keys or wallet; or are victims of a burglary or have a crisis—things beyond our control—do we realize we live a fiction as if it is the truth. We have confused the habitual with the real. Habits of mind and behaviour have desensitized us to the mysteriousness of reality. When we become profoundly aware of that sense of mystery, we see things with the eyes of a child, with a sense of wonder. We see how constructed our understanding of things is. We also become aware of how limited our understanding is and, concretely, we can see some of the forces that make us "read" a thing in a certain manner. We realize our reading is conditioned, that we ourselves are conditioned, and so we do not accept our insights, interpretations and judgments as absolute. We are not so committed to our interpretations to exclude other interpretations. We begin to see things as they are against the background of emptiness rather than how we would like them to be for us. It was Wallace Stevens who wrote that description is interpretation. By this he means the way we put sense data together is through a system, and so we never see the world as it is, but always within a system of meaning.

The level of attentiveness that we are walking through now is not so dominated by the systems of meaning we use that we cannot intuitively grasp the reality of what is present to us. Our biases do not blind us from the sense of wonder and mystery that a thing shows forth, nor do we obscure the sense of its ordinariness. We come to a state in life when we do not have to argue a point, defend a position or rigidly indulge in binary oppositions. As T.S. Eliot says in *Four Quartets*,

> *We shall not cease from exploration*
> *And the end of all our exploring*
> *Will be to arrive where we started*
> *And know the place for the first time.*[24]

This is the perspective of the little boy in the fairy tale *The Emperor's New Clothes*. He sees things as they are. He knows the king is naked and is not wearing the delicate clothes that are supposedly discernible only by the elite. Ignatian indifference is one manifestation of this rootedness. St. Ignatius of Loyola, in his Spiritual Exercises, notes,

> It is necessary to make ourselves indifferent to all created things in all that is allowed to the choice of our free will and is not prohibited to it; so that, on our part, we want not health rather than sickness, riches rather than poverty, honor rather than dishonor, long rather than short life, and so in all the rest; desiring and choosing only what is most conducive for us to the end for which we are created. (#14)

Here Ignatian indifference operates on the level of choice, and that choice is dependent on the lived awareness of ourselves as creatures always in relationship with the Creator.

However, the awareness we are examining here operates at a more basic level: the level of perception that arises from a particular vision. The vision established at this stage of the spiritual path emerges from an orientation to the Divine, which sees God in all things, to use another Ignatian axiom. It sees all things open to God, and so can rest in any circumstance as an opening to the presence of God. It has the sense of the rootedness from which all things arise and to which all things go. It sees what is present as symbolic of that basic reality. For Christians this is understood quite simply as knowing nothing exists outside of God, and so we can be present to all things as a way of being present to God.

This is not to say that all things are God (pantheism), or that all things are in God (panentheism). It is simply to say not only are we present to every situation, but even more so is the Divine love present, and so we can be truly present to every situation as it is because the Divine love is there.

This level of awareness that allows situations to be is an indifference that is not apathy but is actually a passionate focus of our attention to life from the perspective of the Christ who talks about his oneness with the Father (John 10:30). He is simply aware creation is a manifestation of the creativity of his Father and the shared intimacy he has with the Father allows him to call on that creativity when it is needed to heal, celebrate and transform the worlds he encounters. The Christ sees things as they are. He sees that everything, even those most damaged by sin, can be transformed by the Father's love. He sees nothing as so fixed as to be separated from the love of God. This perspective is also available to those who are intimate with Jesus. As Paul writes,

> I am convinced that neither death nor life, neither angels nor demons, neither the present nor the future, nor any powers, neither height nor depth, nor anything else in all creation, will be able to separate us from the love of God that is in Christ Jesus our Lord. (Romans 8:38-39)

At this level of spiritual awareness, we do not have to maintain dogmatically an ideology or a particular tradition. Attentiveness comes out of a sense of being rooted, and our perceptions of reality arise from that rootedness.

There is a great deal of energy to be saved by being rooted and by living that rootedness in our life. We become like water. We can adapt to situations without losing our integrity. Out of that awareness emerges a sense of gratitude, wisdom, wonder and delight at the many different displays of life. There also arises a compassion for those who are not so aware, and so suffer and cause others to suffer because of their lack of awareness.

This is not a return to a position of naïveté, but rather an acceptance of a state of innocence, and of childlike wonder that the Buddhists call "novice mind." Picasso says it takes a long time to learn to paint like a child. It takes a long time as an adult to achieve the perspective of spiritual child. And as Jesus says, "Unless you become like a little child you shall not enter into the kingdom of heaven" (Matthew 18:3).

The little child does not live out of preconceptions. A child has a sense of immediacy. Adult life, on the other hand, is vastly mediated. The spiritual journey deconstructs those mediations. The intimate encounter with God facilitates those deconstructions so we are not caught up in false stories that stop us from seeing things as they are. We are creatures. We are the beloved of the Father, and we are held in the Father's love. We return to the source when we can live that awareness intimately and simply at all levels of our being, and not just intellectually or emotionally.

This is not a return to a lost Eden. There is still malice in the world, the brokenness of a fallen creation, and our own complicity in the dynamics of the disordered political, social and cultural systems in which we live. But what occurs at this level of attention is a delight in living, a sense of wonder at all we encounter and an engagement with life and with all the aspects of life available to us. That sense of wonder is a profoundly contemplative attitude. This is significantly different from the hermeneutics of suspicion that seeks to reduce the mystery of being and relationships to systems of meaning and control. Suspicion is grounded in power and insecurity; wonder emerges from rootedness and humility. Humility is open and seeks only the Father's will and the neighbour's good. Rootedness grounds us in a countercultural stance. Seeing things as they are does not offer the world a place of compromise. When we see things as they are, despite our lack of defense, we, like water, accommodate ourselves to our circumstances without losing integrity. This cannot be learned through politics or techniques on how to relate. It comes only after we have walked the spiritual path into emptiness through our poverty of spirit. Then we become simple and see life from a stance of gratitude. It allows our yes to be yes, and our no to be no.

We have discovered in that journey the creature's radical dependency on the Creator, and the interdependency all things have with one another. We discover how carefully we are looked after in spite of the destructive elements in this world. Seeing from a stance of being loved and loving gives us a discerning heart. It allows us to recognize the good present in everything, to affirm and celebrate it, to recognize the forces that seek to turn away from what is good and work towards transforming them. This gift of discernment is the realization of what needs to be done and what is possible to be done in a given situation. Reinhold Niebuhr's serenity prayer, adopted by Alcoholics Anonymous, is one such expression of the discerning heart:

> *God, grant me the serenity to accept the things I cannot change,*
> *the courage to change the things I can,*
> *and the wisdom to know the difference.*[25]

At this level of attention, the relationship between God and the journeying soul is such that the serenity requested in the prayer is given and realized.

Serenity allows us to live more fully in the present, knowing only God lives fully in the present. What is present to us is all we need to know at that moment. This is what it means to live as a person aware of being loved and cared for by God. It is to realize enlightenment is nothing special; it makes nothing happen—or nothing different. What has changed is the perspective of what we are present to in our lives.

We have become so attuned to the currents of life running through our existence, we have become one with them, and so we see life as that larger life sees it. We see what brings life and what takes life away. We get a sense of what is possible and a sense of some of the connections that make a thing what it is for us in its present manifestations. We see what is present as an invitation, a gift and a call to a greater celebration of life. Filled with that sense of wonder, we relax into life as we discover the Beloved offering the benefits of creation in each moment. Ignatius of Loyola would call this "finding God in all things." It is finding a path leading to the fullness of life in whatever we do. Finding that path means first being able to see it as a viable reality. The level of attention we are describing here is that state of being.

The temptation at this stage is to think we know it all. If we fall into that trap, we lose a sense of humility essential to every stage of the spiritual life. The assurance with which we see what is—and, to some extent, how, why and what it is—does not make us Godlike. The fullness of knowledge is God's alone; what is shared with us as we become one with life may make us prophetic in our ways of seeing, but that seeing is as a calling forth of life rather than a power play from a superior point of view.

The discernments we are required to make at this level of attentiveness stop us falling into the trap of a dogmatism claiming an outside authority about how things are and should be. That first temptation is internal. The second temptation is external. The second set of discernments, needed to refine our ability to distinguish between what is presented as true but is, in effect, false. Eve in the garden of Eden is tempted in this way. She sees and knows things as they are in her limited state, which is adequate for a life of right relationship with God, Adam and creation. Her temptation is to move from creature to Creator. She abandons her humility, hoping for a fullness of knowledge. What she loses is her immediate sense of rootedness in God. She and Adam then hide from God and from each other by covering up their nakedness. The ninth Ox-herding picture is about seeing reality nakedly.

We may be tempted to try to figure out whatever is hard to accept, but is in fact true, rather than leaving it to the mystery and the mercy of Divine Providence. The spirit of discernment given at this level of attention is spontaneously exercised by remaining rooted in the emptiness from which every form of attention springs. This allows us to see things as God wants us to see them.

Questions for reflection

1. How do we live our Ignatian indifference?

2. How do we daily experience life as a mystery?

3. What happens when we sit in, or allow ourselves to be embraced by, Mystery?

4. How does Mystery shape the way we see the world when we are attentive in this way?

5. What are the focuses in our circumstances that try to conscript us to false ways of seeing? How do we deal with each of them?

10. In the world

Poor of spirit, I celebrate life with those I meet on my path
In good times and in bad. I have no special powers
Yet, in that simplicity, the world is transformed;
Death becomes a door to resurrection.

Attention in the world

With the innocence of a child, we continue the journey. This journey never ends. It moves into the fullness of life, into the Trinity. We as creatures will never exhaust the depths of the love emerging from the Creator. Our fidelity to this journey contains our call to help others on the journey. Our concern for our neighbour as ourselves allows us to be most authentically ourselves. Our neighbour is us. We are all one. Our identity is not as an individual or one aspect of our personal life; our identity is contained in our relationship to all of creation, and of that creation in right relationship with God. Living out of that rootedness in our lives is a prophetic witness. Such witness does not call attention to itself but rather calls forth from those we encounter a level of attentiveness that enables them to become more and more truly themselves. We do this because we realize we are one body. We are the body of the resurrected humanity of Christ, and this body is gathering up all that exists to hand over to the Mystery we call the Father. About the end of this journey, St. Paul writes,

> The end will come, when [Christ] hands over the kingdom to God the Father after he has destroyed all dominion, authority and power.

> For he must reign until he has put all his enemies under his feet. ... When he has done this, then the Son himself will be made subject to him who put everything under him, so that God may be all in all. (1 Corinthians 15:24-26, 28)

The awareness of our identity, not as individuals but as community, calls us on the journey to see, know and love our neighbour as ourselves. We journey to manifest that love with all our heart and all our soul, with all of who we are, within the context of loving God, who never ceases to embrace us. This journey is the coming together of the lover and the Beloved, and at each stage of the journey the relationship becomes different.

In this last stage of the cycle, our identity is to manifest the presence of God's love in the world. Our fullness of identity is as creation in relationship to the Creator. The realization of that relationship carries us on the spiritual journey that has brought us to this moment. It is a journey into freedom, where freedom is understood as an authentic relationship with God. This authenticity manifests itself in indifference—not as apathy or ignorance, but as a passionate attention to God through service in the world. Everything one sees or values or does is within that passionate attention to God.

The last Ox-herding picture depicts an old person, vulnerable and rooted, a pilgrim in this world, joyfully accepting those he meets as kin. The witness of his life encourages others to leave behind the traps that take away from them the fullness of life he embodies.

The freedom of living passionately invites others to experience the freedom to which their present attention calls them. Such a level of simple service is the result of a deep level of self-acceptance and trust in divine providence. We live out of a sense of gratitude and joy for all that is given and with a sense of play that allows for creativity and the passing on of the spirit.

We are aware of our radical sense of being a creature, an awareness that we are not God or called to be God. We are aware in humility that being a creature is to be beloved by God. As the first beatitude of Matthew's gospel puts it, "Blessed are the poor in spirit; theirs is the kingdom of God." As we journey into love we become more and more aware of our poverty. But it is precisely in living out of this poverty that the energies of God are allowed expression. Then we become even more transparently living words of the Father. The service we render to the world is in and through joy. It is joy, and joy alone, that transforms the world.

We never come to the end of this journey into love. We never exhaust the infinity that is God. The gift given to us as creatures is that invitation to enter into an ever-growing knowledge and intimacy of love that does not end. The journey continues at a deeper cycle. Even the saints in paradise labour with the community of the Risen Lord to bring all back to the Father. The novice heart of the poor in spirit encounters always the love that calls us beyond the borders of what is known. We learn again and again the new asceticisms to develop and become at home in new relationships with the divine and the world. We allow the barriers and traumas that define our individuality and our sense of self to dissolve. We allow new anxieties of being to dissipate, and we discover at ever deeper levels the divine creativity manifesting itself through creation. We share the delight of that discovery with the world. Another cycle of the journey completes itself and opens us to yet an even deeper call to the fullness of life.

The temptation exists at every stage of the spiritual journey to think we have arrived. However, as creatures we are still a work in progress and we can honestly say no one fully arrives until all have arrived. Our work is to aid, in whatever way we can, that work in progress. This is not done by imposing onto others our ideologies or the limitations of whatever traditions we find ourselves in, but by living as creative words of the Father whose Mercy reaches out to all. In doing the same thing, we show that we are children of our Father in heaven. He makes his sun rise on people whether they are good or evil. He lets rain fall on them whether they are just or unjust (Matthew 5:45). Incarnating mercy creates community, because mercy does not condemn or alienate. Rather, the path of incarnation leads to the fullest embodiment of the Spirit. It moves beyond self to community and to greater and greater manifestations of community. This is the movement from tolerance to hospitality.

Our graciousness to everyone we meet and whatever we meet is not a form of condescension but a recognition in each encounter of an aspect of our very self. We are always coming home to ourselves in mercy: not in theatrical exuberance, but in simple ways. Always the path of what is to be done is ordinary and simple. It does not require magic or extraordinary power. It is beyond technique and yet, at times, seems unusual to others. The necessary words come in a given situation; what is at hand is all that is required, nothing more and nothing less. Each encounter gives, receives and celebrates life.

By being truly and simply present to others, putting aside our own agenda and concerns, life is passed on. That level of presence acknowledges the other in such a way that the person gazed at and engaged with experiences some sense of the love that surrounds and maintains everything. Then, what is given and received is the felt sense of being truly known and cared for in our genuine self. Love lived calls out love from the other. The harmony we live creates a harmony around us and establishes a resonance in those we meet. Like calls to like. Like creates and establishes like. The service we perform in the world is ordinary. It does not attract notice to itself. It gives people and things the space to become who they truly are.

Sometimes situations and people are difficult. They may bring out our aggression and we are tempted to respond to their violence with our own violence. Discernment at this level is how to behave in such a way that the aggression does not escalate. Gandhi advocated non-violence. Jesus talks about turning the other cheek.

The Buddha speaks of non-attachment. It is not possible to give some abstract principle for a concrete situation. That would be ideological. Nor do we have to be reactive. We can discern the most loving thing to do in each concrete situation, always aware of the broader contexts beyond the immediate in which we operate. Right action is a manifestation of right relationships and attitudes. What is ordinary and simple is the action of years of refinement of our attentiveness, which manifests the love between the Divine and each human.

Who knows how loving service to the world is to be manifest? It arises from a lived sense of intimacy where the Lover and the beloved come to a sense of what is important. They attend each other, and out of that attentiveness a path unfolds.

The journey into attention demands a discerning heart if we are to journey into love wherever we go. The call to love brings us to new areas of unredeemed life. We encounter new blocks and resistances and we struggle to overcome these. We reach new plateaus and integrate our experiences. From this new life we see things even more as they are, and share that life with others. The call and response of Desire to desire continues. In that call and response, life is created, is redeemed and becomes community.

Questions for reflection

1. How do we experience our lives now?

2. Where do we find ourselves on the journey as mapped out in the Ox-herding pictures?

3. How do we experience our relationship with the world?

4. Where have we discovered we have given life to others? What does it feel like to sit in the gratitude of being of service?

5. Where is our joy? Why do we at times give away our joy? How do we regain our joy?

Conclusion

If we look at the pattern underlying the journey through the Ox-herding pictures, we notice it is one of consolation leading to desolation leading to consolation. It is the nature of God's love always to seek us out, and our response to that love is to accept being affirmed, and so to move to a different and deeper stage of integration and intimacy. The affirmation gives us the courage and the energy to move out of the areas of comfort we have developed and into those new spaces and dimensions of our personal, social and spiritual life, which call out for conversion. There we endure the tensions of risk and conflicts with the forces that resist a higher integration. When those are resolved, we find ourselves becoming more integrated, more free and more joyful. We enter a period of consolidation that brings peace, calm and deeper rootedness. Only then do we begin to see there is more work to be done, and we set out again into the darkness.

The human journey to find, accept, use, share and celebrate love carries us out of the world only to return us to the world. Then we live on as passionate words of the Father called to continue the mission of Christ. Then we, too, incarnate the compassionate mercy of the One who desires for all the fullness of life. This journey ever deeper into the mystery of God's love and of our own awareness of what it means to be human, a creature beloved by God, never ends. We can never, as creatures, exhaust the love of God. St. Paul prays

> that you, being rooted and established in love, may have power, together with all the Lord's holy people, to grasp how wide and long and high and deep is the love of Christ, and to know this love that surpasses knowledge—that you may be filled to the measure of all the fullness of God. (Ephesians 3:16-19)

Part III

Ignatius's Rules
for Discernment
and Decision Making

Journeying into mystery requires discernment. In Part II, we looked at The Ten Ox-herding Pictures for a description of the spiritual path. These pictures offer profoundly human insights into the sequence of stances to be reached, examined and transcended by a seeker of truth on the path of enlightenment. The Buddha himself explicitly rejects a creator, refuses to endorse any views on creation and holds that questions on the origin of the world are simply speculation. In the traditions that follow and develop the Buddha's teachings, this is not the case. In Buddhist thought, the ox symbolizes the Mind (the true Self) and the herder symbolizes the seeker. My own reading of the Ox-herding pictures, from an admittedly Christian point of view, comes from the awareness of how helpful they are in understanding our own vocation to be spiritually intimate with the Divine. We are all mystics, and to accept that gift and self-understanding we need all the help we can get to avoid confusion. The Ox-herding pictures start off with the basic human experience of wonder, first felt as dissatisfaction and finally expressed as loving service. At the end of the modern era, we find ourselves culturally and spiritually dissatisfied. We long to live lives of grateful and creative service in a world torn apart by wars, political instability, economic turmoil and pandemics, and rendered more mysterious by new discoveries of science and technology.

Our present situation is not unlike that of the beginning of the modern era. The early sixteenth century in Europe was a time of cultural chaos and religious and political turmoil. It marked the beginning of modern science, with its focus on empirical science and of discovery based on exploration rather than on dogma. With that resurgence came the outpouring of an extraordinary body of literature. The imagination was liberated from doctrinal constraints but left to drift in the often conflicting currents of the times.

The Reformation challenged the Catholic Church in terms of doctrine, ethical behaviour and structure. The incursion of the Ottoman empire brought Muslim culture to a predominantly Christian ethos. The shift in social structures exacerbated the tensions between Church and state, and within the state itself the balance between nobility and monarchy was challenged. Western explorers redefined the maps of the world with new trade routes; astronomers displaced the Ptolemaic system of the earth as the centre of the universe with Copernicus's view of planets moving around a sun. The vernacular replaced Latin in terms of cultivated expression of speech and literature; the Bible was translated into the local idioms. The Black Death swept across Europe. It was a time of enormous confusion about whom and what to believe and what to do and how. A previously established world had crumbled and the emerging culture sought answers within the dynamics of human experience.

That culture asked the basic human questions: What does it mean to be human? How is one to behave in this new emerging configuration of reality? Where are God and salvation to be found? Those questions return today. The questions that shaped the Western world some 500 years ago at the beginning of the Modern Age now return in all their complexity at the end of that age today. We look for a way of discerning how to live, and to find a path that leads to the fullness of life.

To examine our present path through mystery, we turn to a figure who asked the same questions at the beginning of the modern age as we do today. He has been described as the master of discernment; some even see his emphasis on interiority as a forerunner of psychology. He is St. Ignatius of Loyola.

Ignatius of Loyola

Ignatius of Loyola emerged at a turbulent time, a figure of his times. He moved from being a worldly, venal, dissolute, pleasure-seeking son of minor nobility, intent on making his way in the world with the many skills at his disposal, to a person who surrendered his life totally to the disposition of God's desires. He did not do this through an act of the will, but by starting to pay attention not only to his own ego needs, but also to the callings of the Divine love, who used the occasions of Ignatius's life to carry him along the path of spiritual intimacy.

His life was driven by desire. This desire was shaped by the social, cultural and political forces of his day. We first encounter him as a soldier, ambitious for worldly honour, maintaining a siege at Pamplona against superior French forces. He is defiant against the enemy, rallies his comrades, but is wounded. His vainglory comes to naught, and instead, through his illness, he is forced back upon himself. He discovers his feelings are torn between fantasy and a deeper level of attentiveness that calls him beyond the ways he imagines the world.

Throughout his life, more and more subtle variations of that tension operate. First, he experiences the tension between courtly love and divine love. Then, on the path of divine love, the tension is between scruples, which focus on himself and his past, and a turning outwards, which results in extraordinary religious experiences. The dynamic of those experiences lead him to Jerusalem, where he discovers he is not to be physically grounded in the same geographical landscape as Jesus, and so he discards that fantasy. Intimacy with Jesus is not to be found in a specific, actual place, but in the imagination. He is moved to find God in all things, in all places, and in all peoples. The desire that called him in this manner leads him back to Europe, where he moves from a naïve preaching of the Word to studies in Paris. There he gathers around him some companions, the Society of Jesus. Some early ones to whom he gave the Exercises lose their way; out of this arises the need to create a way of being and belonging. Ignatius and his early companions formed the Jesuits as they are known today. In this journey against the narcissism of self-interest was posited a lover's abandonment to Divine Providence. Ignatius's last stance in this dialectic is contained in the Constitutions of the Jesuits. He constructed this document to facilitate the service of the religious order he founded to God through the Church.

In Ignatius's life, each step into a greater and greater intimacy with God was a refinement of the previous stage of attentiveness. In this way, Ignatius moved to a service of God in the world that was more and more symbolic of the Divine Love becoming incarnate.

He did this by paying attention to the movements of the spirits within him as he found himself in certain situations. He experienced himself as a desire for God, and he experienced God as manifesting His desire for him through the world he lived in. But he was aware that his narcissism at times misread his basic desire, so he would do the wrong thing. He also knew that the forces of the world that imposed themselves upon him do not necessarily come from God.

In a rapidly changing world, it is difficult to know what is the right thing to do. Many different and conflicting voices exercise authority. The matter is further confounded when our own awareness is inflected by the habits of a disordered life. How are we to find the truth? How are we to discover who we are? How are we to judge what is the best thing to do? These are the basic questions that provoked Ignatius, and they are the same questions that provoke us today.

Reading Feelings

What Ignatius left for us in his Spiritual Exercises is one way of discerning. He did this by paying attention to the movements of the spirit within him and to the effects those movements had on his life. He was aware that good feelings sometimes came from good and sometimes from bad things. Thus, we may feel good when we get a surprise gift from someone we love; but we may also feel good when someone we dislike is humiliated. He also realized that bad feelings sometimes came from good and sometimes from bad things. For instance, we may feel anxiety in the face of a necessary dental procedure, and feel sick at the abuse of children.

When bad things produce good feelings, those good feelings cannot be maintained, since their source is not in life, and so they are not long-lived. Thus the pleasure we may experience at putting down someone we dislike can fade and turn to self-disgust. Ignatius experienced this in his own life. He knew that feelings were not important in themselves, but that their source was. If he knew the source of those feelings, he could discern whether something was truly good.

But there was another problem. Why would good things produce bad feelings, and bad things produce good feelings? Ignatius came to understand that if one was facing God and going towards God by doing good things, then the path was affirmed through consolation; but if one was turned away from God, yet doing something good, there arose desolation, because one was working against a disordered orientation. Thus, if I am lazy and in a rut, the very idea of getting out of the rut and occupying myself with something worthwhile brings out feelings of anxiety and unease. But doing bad things when we are turned away from God brings feelings of satisfaction. The trouble with such self-indulgence is that it is addictive, and we need more and more bad things to feel the same level of satisfaction when we are turned away from God. We need to be constantly stimulated or distracted or narcotized. We feed this addiction from our own resources, and so become more and more self-absorbed. Then we start valuing only a fragment of our self, and we sacrifice other aspects of our self, as well as its move to wholeness and integration, to gain limited and limiting self-satisfaction.

Ignatius saw that the purpose of discernment was to be able to identify in particular contexts both the direction in which we are going, either towards God or away from God, and also to know the spiritual dynamics causing what we feel. Are we being moved to good or bad? Here Ignatius explored the semiotics of feeling. What is the feeling telling us about ourselves?

For Ignatius, awareness of feeling was important. Feelings are really values refined to spontaneity. Our feelings reveal to us what we value. If we have no feelings for something, it is not that we are indifferent, but we are apathetic. Encountering evil and submitting to it kills our feelings. We become hard-hearted. Then our range of feelings becomes more and more limited. We value less and less, and we become addicted to what we value, because we expect it to be an adequate substitute for God, who alone can satisfy all our desires.

On the other hand, the encounter with God increases our range of feelings. Feelings reveal to us the sensible spectrum of our identity as desire. We are created as desire for God. Every aspect of our being desires God. It is the nature of evil to suggest ways of satisfying that desire that frustrate our intimacy with God. We often succumb to those temptations because we have lost the gift of discernment. We lose touch with the vastness of our desire that calls us always to self-transcendence, spiritual freedom and a growing intimacy with God. Instead, we allow ourselves to follow paths that limit us and distort our relationships with God and the rest of creation. Inasmuch as we are in tune with the vastness that is our desire for God, the energies of our lives manifest themselves in the range and subtlety of our feelings.

Our sensitivities cover a broader spectrum of desire than the one constructed by the cultures we live in. We can care about someone who is ethnically different from us even if we both live in the same racist culture. In fact, at times our sensitivities can go against the cultures we live in. Ignatius is aware of this. While he sees a dominant culture advocating a path of riches leading to a social status that confirms our constructed ego, he also sees that being attentive to our deepest desire reveals both our poverty of spirit and God's constant care for us. Our deepest desire seeks only an intimacy with God. It is countercultural to live out of those values that do not support understanding ourselves solely as self-sufficient individuals or as purely social animals. We are first and foremost in relation to God as creature to Creator. We are desire created by Desire for Desire. The relationship between us as desire for God and a God who desires us is that of the Lover and the beloved. When we deny that love, we fall into desolation; when we accept that love, we find ourselves in consolation.

It is the nature of love to affirm what is loving and lovable. It is also the nature of love to seek to transform what is unloving and unlovable. When we walk the path to a greater and more encompassing love, we often find ourselves in places that cry out for life and conversion. Quite often those places are within ourselves, and so, when we walk the path to greater intimacy, we often find ourselves in places of desolation. We need to remain there until they are converted.

Becoming Attentive

Discernment is the work we do to understand what our feelings are telling us about ourselves. When we become attentive to ourselves, then, our feelings tell us something about ourselves and about the context in which they emerge. Each has a story to tell. But first, before we can hear that story, we need to be aware of our feelings: the positive ones, the negative ones, and a blend of both. We need to admit we have those feelings, rather than denying them or suppressing them or even misnaming them. After that we can question where they come from and what they are telling us about ourselves now. We can even do a journal dialogue with our feelings to find out what they can tell us about ourselves. Finally, we need to be aware that while our feelings are an expression of the relationship we have with God, we are more than our feelings. Our feelings reveal only the sensible range of our identity as an intimate relationship with God. They show us what God is calling us to be attentive to at the present moment.

Being attentive is a form of defamiliarization. We pay attention only to what is so different from our habitual state that it stands out. Being attentive presents itself in terms of consolation and desolation. These manifest themselves through our feelings, but what they mean must be discerned.

Each moment is an invitation to bring Christ into the world and an Annunciation to be accepted or denied. We do not have to do anything but accept the feeling as it is received. The desire of God that touches us and we receive as feeling is willing to work in and through us, should we, like Mary or the apostles, or any of the community of the beloved of God, say yes to that impulse. In admitting that feeling, we allow the dialogue God has with our whole being to continue. Such a dialogue carries us to greater and greater intimacy with God. Through desolation and consolation, we encounter what needs to be liberated and transformed. Through desolation and consolation, we discover what needs to be affirmed and celebrated. In this developing intimacy we find in ourselves an openness to the Father and a sharing in the gifts of the Spirit as the occasion requires.

In his small epic, "Milton," William Blake writes,

There is a Moment in each Day that Satan cannot find
Nor can his Watch Fiends find it, but the Industrious find
This Moment & it multiply, & when it once is found
It renovates every Moment of the Day if rightly placed[26]

For St. Ignatius, like for Blake, every moment presents an opportunity for growing more intimate with God. Ignatius is also aware every moment can be lost to that intimacy. For Ignatius, every moment of our awareness is the site of a battle between the forces of good and those inimical to our human nature. In his meditation on the Two Standards, which comes at the exact centre of his Spiritual Exercises, he makes this observation about how Satan works: "Consider how he summons innumerable demons, and scatters them, some to one city and some to another, throughout the whole world, so that no province, no place, no state of life, no individual is overlooked" (Sp. Ex. #141).

Ignatius's view is that at every moment we are caught in the tension between the Standard of Christ and the Standard of Satan. This struggle is not abstract or purely spiritual, but occupies every dimension of our being. Ignatius has created a way for us to become aware of that struggle in our ordinary lives and how to use it to transform our lives. He calls it the Examen.

The Examen of St. Ignatius

St. Ignatius explains the method of making the General Examination of Conscience using five points. How do we understand and use these five points? I want to explore three different models and how each shapes the practice of the Examen.

Ignatius states the procedure quite starkly in the following manner.

Method for Making the General Examen

The method contains five Points.

First Point. The first Point is to give thanks to God our Lord for the favours received.

Second Point. The second, to ask grace to know our sins and to rid myself of them.

Third Point. The third, to demand an account of our soul from the time of rising up to the present Examen hour by hour, or period by period: and first as to thoughts, and then as to words, and then as to acts, in the same order as was mentioned in the Particular Examen.

Fourth Point. The fourth, to ask pardon of God our Lord for the faults.

Fifth Point. The fifth will be to resolve to amend with the grace of God. Conclude with an Our Father. (Sp. Ex. #43)

This schematic presentation leaves out the dynamics of desire, which links the five points together, and as a result it is easy to "do" the Examen in a somewhat mechanistic and fragmented fashion and within the distorted perspective of our own traps and disorders. The mechanistic approach does not allow the development of interiority. It is objectivist, a grocery list approach to our personal history and does not use this form of prayer as a way of developing a greater intimacy with God or a greater clarity in our spiritual journey. Unless we approach the Examen in the context of a relationship with God and actually use the time of the Examen to be open to God and allow God to show us in love where and

143

how God is to be found, we end up using the Examen from an ego-centred, rather than a relational, point of view. Then we translate our lived experience into a list of faults understood from our distorted value system. For example, if we are perfectionists, or people pleasers, or self-righteous, we tend to evaluate our days in terms of that disorder. We would not be able to see that the perspective from which we evaluate ourselves is itself disordered. The result is that, instead of encountering God, we encounter only ourselves, and we damage ourselves. This form of introspection is deadly. It drains us of energy and makes us more closed in on ourselves.

But even assuming that we are in a loving relationship with God, the subtleties of our disordered nature often lead us to a form of abjection when we focus more on our sinfulness than on the loving relationship that roots our very being. When this happens, we see ourselves as loved sinners, rather than lovers who sin. In the first state, the sin defines us; in the second state, it is love that defines us.

The first model of doing the Examen is the willed step-by-step method often found in a traditional examination of conscience. This practice focuses on sin with an eye to understanding and changing our thoughts, words and actions with God's help. Ignatius gives a detailed way of dealing with unpacking our sinful dispositions by looking at our thoughts, words and actions. The way he does this suggests he is teaching a beginner, and indeed this first approach to the Examen is best suited to a beginner, who, like an athlete or a dancer or a musician, needs to know the basic steps and discipline before being allowed to trust a deeper and more open reading of the Examen. The danger of this is that we may become fixated at this primary level of reading ourselves.

A second model of doing the Examen is explained by George Aschenbenner.[27] Aschenbrenner fundamentally reorients the Examen as a "daily intensive exercise of discernment in a person's life." This reorientation is a move to interiority where the primary focus is on the subject and the underlying affective movements of the heart, and only secondarily on our thoughts, words and deeds. Aschenbrenner also sees the need to focus as much on the positive events in our lives as on the negative, so that "humble joyful

144

thanksgiving" might "gradually become an element of our abiding consciousness."[28] In this model, the Examen is a tool for discernment to facilitate an ongoing awareness of God's presence in daily life. This model highlights St. Ignatius's emphasis on discernment of spirits in our life.

A third model of doing the Examen would be as a contemplative exercise. This method focuses on the underlying dynamic of gazing at God in desire and inviting that God, who desires us, to a mutuality in the examination of our life. It is less a systematic, hour by hour review of life, and more a contemplative invitation for God to reveal what God wants us to see in the events of our daily life. This contemplative method functions much like Gospel contemplation, starting with a prelude of giving thanks as the context of the Examen, then asking for the grace, and finally entering into a contemplation led by God of events of our life. This method allows for a creative re-imaging of the events of the day through God's eyes. It moves the Examen out of the realm of memory, intellect and judgment and into the realm of imagination, affectivity and desire. This contemplative model differs from Aschenbrenner's model by giving room for the movement of God in prayer, rather than by using the Examen as a focused discernment of the movement of God during life. Some surprising revelations can emerge within this spirit of contemplation. For example, what was experienced as an affliction might be revealed as a graced moment, or what was first seen as a frivolous use of time may be seen as a joyful gift from God.

This contemplative model of the Examen is based on four things. First, we have the underlying dynamic of gratitude. Second, we have the third point of the Examen, where Ignatius suggests we "demand an account of our soul." (Here we note that Ignatius does not say we demand an account "by" our soul. It is not the soul who gives the account, but God. This indicates that God is the one leading the review, rather than us.) Third, we have the context of Gospel contemplation that forms the backbone of the Spiritual Exercises (Sp. Ex. #43). Fourth, we have the understanding of the Exercises as a path of spiritual intimacy in which our daily life becomes the site of that intimacy. This contemplative look at our life as an ever-deepening attentiveness between Lover and beloved sees the revealed blocks in loving as the invitation and site to an even deeper love, experienced in gratitude. We are grateful to have our blocks and disorders revealed, because their transformation means that we will be able to enter even more deeply into spiritual intimacy. We become more and more attuned and aligned to the Desire who desires us in and through the Examen. The time of the Examen becomes a special moment of experiencing spiritual intimacy. Awareness of sin then becomes the happy fault that allows a greater love to be discovered and expressed.

Is there then a correct model for doing the Examen? The better question is this: What method of Examen best gives life and best fits where we are in our spiritual journey, and our current style of prayer? Ultimately, our practice of the Examen must be judged on how it brings transformation, life and love to all we do. It is interesting to note that Ignatius ends the Examen with the Our Father. A prayerful contemplation of the Our Father carries us through the same dynamics of desire that the Examen does. The prayer admits our rootedness in a God who cares for us as a member of his immediate family. We ask God to look after us, to bring us closer to him through mutual forgiveness, and to protect and liberate us that we may celebrate the life he offers us.

Led by Gratitude

Let us now go through the Examen in the third way, as a journey led by gratitude into mystery.

The first point of the Examen is to thank God for favours received. Thanksgiving is a spiritual practice that unites us with God in a relationship of mutuality. "Eucharist"—the word used to describe the memorial of Christ's Last Supper—is Greek for thanksgiving. Thanksgiving is the lived expression of gratitude. Here gratitude arises from the recognition that we are radically dependent on God, and that God has not abandoned us but has invited us into a relationship that offers us life and the path to the fullness of life. Thanking God is more than words; it is a stance in the world, an attitude to be acknowledged and cultivated. It is a way of being. Thanksgiving arises from the awareness that we are rooted in God's love that gifts us, in individual ways, with what we need daily to live a full life.

St. Ignatius names his last contemplation in the Spiritual Exercises "The Contemplatio Ad Amorem": the contemplation leading to love. In it he suggests that we imagine ourselves surrounded by the love of God and all the good in creation, and imagine that love pouring into us. In effect this is what is happening at every moment of our lives, but we are too often unaware of it, caught up as we are by other things and concerns. Even that is all right. Love is content to do what it does unnoticed. It does not seek to draw attention to itself. The Examen allows us to notice that love by becoming attentive to it. In becoming attentive to it, we can accept it, open it, use it, share it and celebrate it. Thanksgiving is the celebration of that attentiveness to what God constantly gives us.

In this last contemplation, St. Ignatius suggests to us the grace to pray for: "Here it will be an intimate knowledge of the many blessings received, that filled with gratitude for all, I may in all things love and serve the Divine Majesty" (Sp. Ex. #233). That intimate knowledge includes the blessings of having been created and redeemed and whatever special favours we have received. It goes deeper into a realization that every fibre of our being, having been created by God, is destined to be satisfied by God, so much so that "God dwells in me ... and makes a temple of me" (Sp. Ex. #235). This profound indwelling of God makes me an intimate of the Christ who invites me to journey with him and labour with him to transform this world into a community of love. This is not due to any action on my part, but all this, and the grace to do it, is pure gift coming from God.

Resting in that first point of celebrating gratitude dynamically carries us to the second point. However, if God decides we need to stay with that first point, we should not move on. We will move on when God deems we are ready. In this, as in everything else, we allow ourselves to wait on God and for God.

The second point emerges from this awareness of being loved. One of the gifts of that love is to use it. It is the nature of love to affirm what is lovable and to seek to transform what is not yet love.

So that second point asks for the "grace to know our sins and to rid ourselves of them." This second stage of being held in love allows what is disordered in us to come to our awareness, and for us to be open to the grace that allows us to cooperate with God in ridding ourselves of what stops us from being loving. Since love does not force itself onto us, we must be willing to be open to its action in our lives. We ask for this grace. Our asking declares our willingness to receive it.

Held in love and rooted in love, we allow love to work its way into our depths and to the boundaries of our awareness. We allow God to show us those times and places and occasions in our day and in our lives that stop us from living life most fully. We also allow God to grace us by helping us get rid of them. Sometimes, just remaining in the presence of love is all the work we need to do to cooperate with God's desire for us. Sometimes the work being done occurs below the level of our analytical mind, and all we are conscious of is feelings of consolation and desolation. We can unpack those feelings to discover what values in specific situations are being affirmed or questioned. Here we recognize those feelings, admit them, investigate them and realize our identity is not limited to those feelings. We are more than those feelings. We are a relationship still being created, and those feelings do not define our identity, but only offer us a way of understanding where and how our relationship is at a given time.

Here we are given the grace we pray for in the first part of the second point: "to know my sins." But we also need the second part of that second point, the grace "to rid myself of them." The work of becoming human is the eradication of all that stops our growing intimacy with God. This is not a work we can do on our own. The Lover and the beloved cooperate to make the relationship better, so we can move to celebrating the path we walk. We can dispose ourselves to be changed by the one who loves us; we can dispose ourselves to incorporate the dynamics of change in our daily lives. We can even work, with our limited resources, to aid that change.

When we do this, we engage in the fourth and fifth points of the Examen. The fourth "asks pardon of God our Lord for my faults," and the fifth "will be to resolve to amend with the grace of God." Here we note that we do not pardon ourselves. We do not say, "I have been bad; I am sorry I have been bad." Like the tax collector in the parable (Luke 18:9-14), we stand in relationship with God in a humility that is not self-abjection, focused on self, but rather with our gaze turned towards God in trust, hope and delight in being loved so shamelessly. To seek pardon is to throw ourselves on the Compassionate Mercy that is God. It is an act of love in which we do not hide from God but allow God to be present to us as a healer and restorer and transformer of life. That love is given to all: as Christians, we know God's love is given to us even when we were sinners (Romans 5:8). God demonstrates his own love towards us: while we were still sinners, and even now when we still sin, Christ died for us. We do not kill God with our sins. We kill ourselves. Christ is willing to walk into our human deaths to bring us to a new life that celebrates life. Through the coming of the Christ in history and through the ongoing Incarnation in our lives, both personal and communal, we accept him in our annunciations of consolation and desolation. John's gospel tells us, "God did not send His Son into the world to condemn the world, but that the world through Him might be saved" (John 3:17). Pardon is the disposition to be saved. The Lover shares with us his gift, an intimacy with the Father, and we respond in love by accepting and living that gift. This response manifests itself concretely in our desire to live a more loving life. The gratitude that orients us to God runs through the Examen and manifests itself most fully in the way we actually live our lives.

The Examen affirms not only our relationship with God but also God's relationship with us. At the close of the Examen, we pray the Our Father. This prayer that Jesus gave us affirms our stance before God in the world. It is a prayer of petition and of acknowledged dependency. But it is a prayer that expects to be answered, because in the relationship of mutual love, God's response to that prayer causes gratitude to arise in us. Our felt relationship with God shapes the way we experience the Examen.

Thanksgiving

The Examen begins with an act of thanksgiving. This act makes conscious the relationship we have with the Father. Everything is gift. We, the poor of spirit, realize our radical dependency on God for everything good that happens to us. We might start our examen with the things we feel to be gift. But it is much more helpful to ask God to reveal to us the gifts that have been given. We do this because we might take certain gifts for granted. We might see them, but do not notice them as gifts. Or we may have no awareness that other things are gifts.

Thanksgiving is a form of celebration. It is the celebration of being loved and of acknowledging how love has been shown in real ways in our lives. There is a kind of hierarchy of recognition. Things are offered by God but they are not seen. They are taken for granted. We become conscious of the air we breathe only when we are drowning or asthmatic. We take our health for granted until we fall sick. We treat supportive relationships, and even our relationship with God, the same way. Only when we become adults do we realize the love our parents, flawed as they were, gave to us.

Then there are things offered by God—seen but not received. Like a tourist, we pass what gives life because we are on our way to somewhere else. Often we live our lives in the past, preoccupied with what has hurt us, or in the future, anxious about things we have little control over, and so we miss the present moment and the gift in the present moment. To be sure, only God lives fully in the present. In fact, for God, all is always present. But as we relax into love, we start appreciating the present more and more. We discover it is enough for the moment. We find ourselves engaged in different aspects of its multi-layered diversity. Our focus becomes less obsessive without becoming distracted. We become more and more attentive to things as they are, rather than restricting and evaluating them only for their usefulness to our present ego needs. That contemplative stance attunes us to the presence of life in our current situation.

When we become aware of these things, we might discover we choose not to accept some. Someone might tell us something. We say, "Thank you for telling me this thing, but I do not accept it." For example, someone has hurt us in the past. Now that person tells us that he or she is sorry. But we choose not to believe that statement. We choose to remain with our injured sensibility and the sense of identity that hurt gives us. Accepting a gift changes us. It declares our vulnerability and our interdependence. To accept a gift may make us feel indebted to the giver, and we would prefer not to be so. We do not feel thankful for the obligations the gift seems to impose upon us. Note here how the tendency to self-enclosure works against thanksgiving. We cannot be thankful because our world, and our ways of maintaining that world, are deconstructed by the gift. We prefer to maintain our view of the world rather than the liberation offered by the gift. God's gifts are never meant to trap us. If we are given a gift and feel entrapped by it, we might want to investigate the source of that feeling. It is helpful to discern every gift to see where it comes from and why. St. Paul says, "Test all things; hold fast that which is good" (1 Thessalonians 5:21). In the stance of thanksgiving, which gives us the entry into the Examen, we need to ask God to show us what to be thankful for. God's gifts open us up to love and to be more loving.

Some of God's gifts are opened but not used. There are stories of people who have had to move a parent to a nursing home and found in the wardrobes expensive shoes or perfumes given as presents at birthdays or anniversaries or at Christmas. These presents were opened and admired at the time of the giving. But they were put away and saved for some special occasion that never came. The perfumes dried out and the shoes became too small for feet now swollen with age. The same thing happens with God's gifts. We hear with each Eucharist that we are loved by God, and that we are God's beloved, but we find it hard to accept this. Our daily lives do not witness to that belief. We suffer from anxiety, doubt and a lived sense of alienation, when we are in fact surrounded at every moment by God's love and care. John's gospel tells us that our work is to believe, and it is work, because we have to struggle against those many forces in our world that make us feel as if God is separated from us. To use the gift of God's love is to live our life with a trust in Divine Providence. This trust allows us to risk by being creative and even to make mistakes, knowing this Love desiring us is stronger and more creative than any mistake we can make.

One of the mistakes we make is believing that God is sectarian and that God limits God's love to a chosen elect of whatever religious tradition or denomination. Luke's gospel presents us with a God who comes so that all can have the fullness of life, and we notice there that God does not limit love or life to an appropriate few or to the politically correct. Zacchaeus, the despised tax collector, encounters a love who invites himself into his house and shares his life with him. That sharing spills over in Zacchaeus's own newly discovered sense of being loved and he also abundantly gives of what he has taken to those he has cheated. Thanksgiving is a social act. It builds and maintains community. The gifts God gives us are to be shared and to be shared without proscription. God came to us while we were still sinners. God comes to us while we still sin. God comes not to judge or condemn us but to liberate us and to offer us all the fullness of life. Who are we to do differently? The outpouring of God's love is not to be dammed up by our closed and broken selves. Quite the opposite. God's love transforms those closed and broken selves in shared life.

Thanksgiving manifests itself in sharing life. I am often intrigued by the way in which street people or the very poor I know share the little they have. In some deep and profound way each of us is radically poor. We are totally dependent on God, and we are totally dependent on each other. When we realize this in ourselves and in each other, we can be moved to share what we have in a sense of community. That sharing is a form of thanksgiving. We give, grateful to be of help, and we receive, grateful that we are acknowledged.

Life is shared most fully when it is celebrated. That celebration might be a simple awareness of the delight in life welling up in and through us. Any expression of that delight, not contrived, hypocritical or sentimentalized, witnesses to and imitates the delight God has in his creation and in his creatures as they reach out to him and each other in love.

If attention is the principle and foundation of the spiritual life, thanksgiving is the basic stance of the pilgrim, which manifests the "praise, reverence and service" St. Ignatius says is our human vocation. Matthew's gospel has as the first beatitude, "Blessed are the poor in spirit, theirs is the kingdom of God." When we become aware of our radical poverty of spirit, we become aware of the overwhelming abundance of the goodness of God in our lives. We become aware that we live always in the Merciful Presence we call the kingdom of God. We become aware of how that Presence incarnates itself in our worlds, and invites us to journey with it to resurrection and a deeper union with the Father.

Thanksgiving opens us to the dynamic that carries us through the work of the four stages of the Spiritual Exercises of St. Ignatius. The Examen is the Exercises in daily life. Each of the four following points in the Examen parallels each of the four Weeks of the Exercises. The first point is dispositional. It situates us in relation to God as a lover accepting what the Beloved has given. The second point corresponds to the First Week of the Exercises. It examines how what has been given is ignored or misused. There we ask for the grace of the knowledge of our sins (see Sp. Ex. #56 & 63) and the grace to be rid of them. In the third point, we ask for an account of our soul and discover, as in the Two Standards of the Second Week, the ways in which we are drawn to God and the ways in which we are seduced by the evil spirit. In the fourth point, we ask pardon of God for our sins, and as in the Third Week, that pardon manifests itself in remaining in Jesus' presence as he returns to the Father by walking the path of his passion and death. The fifth point of resolution to amend with the grace of God carries us to the Fourth Week, when we seek to live transformed lives that work to transform creation into a community of love.[29] The Our Father, which concludes the Examen, appropriates and reinforces the work of the Examen as the growing awareness of our life as a radical dependence on the Father, who does not reject us but rather desires for us only the fullness of life.

The gratitude underpinning the Examen is existential. It manifests the desire we are for God and brings to the surface those actions, patterns and orientations in our life that turn us away from

God. It allows us to become aware that what we are not grateful for traps us in some way. We can bring these to the Father, who can transform every death into resurrection in ways beyond our imagining. The confidence we have in the Father allows us to entrust whatever disorders we have to that transforming love. Within this relationship we can see how our day has been constructed into moments of love and moments of self-absorption. We do not do the Examen by ourselves and with ourselves. In the Examen, we allow God to work in us, and God's disclosure of me to myself is liberating. It allows me to notice how the divine manifests itself to me and what my response is to the divine in terms of consolation and desolation in specific moments.

But the dynamics of love does not stop there. It seeks to repair what is broken or distorted by the lack of love. Asking pardon of God for our faults reveals several things. First, it shows our belief in a God who forgives. This is a God who has the ability to transform our perceptions and patterns of behaviour in such a way that community is created where before there has been alienation. To ask pardon is to submit to that transforming love, to accept it as gift, and to use, share and celebrate it in our lives. When we do that, we resolve to amend how we are present to ourselves and to others and to God. We accept how the path to a deeper intimacy with God opens up, and we follow it. The Examen is a site of intimacy. We open to God and God opens to us. We move to God through desire and God as desire moves towards us. In loving in this way, we learn to love. Loving makes us more loving. Avoiding love makes us less loving.

Ignatius is an existentialist. He is intentional about self-examination. If unexamined faults grow, they grow as weeds. Thus, there is the need to do the Examen every day and ask, "What are the weeds that are choking my garden?" We ask God, "What are the things that stop me from growing in love?" One of the common things that stop our growth is our self-image. It is helpful to consider if my self-image helps me to be in consolation, and if that self-image helps others to be in consolation. The Examen allows us to cooperate with God in changing a false self-image.

St. Ignatius suggests we pay attention to the Examen three times during the day (Sp. Ex. #24). First, immediately upon rising we recall what trait God shows us we need to work against. Second, after the noon meal, we can ask God to give us the awareness of when we have been trapped in the particular way we are prone to be caught, and ask for specific help. We are looking for particular strategies to overcome this unhealthy tendency. Third, after the evening meal is a general review of the day. But rather than becoming obsessed about the whens and hows and whys of the Examen, it is better to find out what times and methods work best for us to develop our intimacy with God. The object is a greater intimacy with God, not the use of particular techniques. The focus is on God and on that relationship with God, not on building up the disorder of being a perfectionist. We need to avoid the temptation for self-absorption and the distortions such narcissism brings. We need God to show us what to work on. We need God to give us the specifics of when we have been caught, because our distorted perspectives often cause us to miss those moments. Therefore, it is very important to let God tell our story for us, and then we can correct our story without maintaining the illusions of a false self or falling into despair.

The Transforming Power of Love

Ignatius firmly believes in the power of love to transform, and devises ways of becoming attentive to that transformation. He suggests we note the diminishing frequency in which we become trapped because of our real encounters with a real God. We can do this by looking at our history to check out if the encounter with God actually does work. For example, if we are prone to despair, we can see if a continual engagement with divine love actually diminishes the number of times we fall into despair, or reduces the severity of our despair. For Ignatius, grace, the presence of God's mercy in the world, is incarnate and effective. Touched by God, the blind see, the deaf hear and devils are cast out. From the scriptural contemplations selected for his Exercises, Ignatius does not present a Jesus who heals illnesses, but one who is an evangelical witness—a witness who brings us closer to the fullness of life as God offers it, rather than as we might fantasize. The Examen may not heal us of physical illness, though of course, if we are prone, for example, to gluttony or forms of despair, an encounter with God's love can find us living better over a period of time. Both gluttony and despair have physical manifestations. In fact, spiritual health promotes physical and emotional health. Stepping into mystery brings us closer and closer to the fullness of life. The effects are tangible.

In fact, if a particular examen is not effective, it is helpful to ask ourselves why it is not working. Are we approaching it from a self-help perspective? Are we indulging in forms of perfectionism? Is the approach the right one? Are we examining on the right matter? What particular fault might we need to deal with before we look at other ones? Some faults proceed from others; some faults are fed from others; some faults feed others. If there is no movement away from the fault, then you have probably chosen the wrong one to work with. Have you asked God which fault to work on? Have you chosen a fault around an issue of self-image connected with shame, and are you seeking a reconciliation with the values of the world rather than a deeper encounter with the God who has different values than the culture? In that case, the significant issue is self-acceptance, rather than change. God is not interested in conformity, but in conversion. He asks us to see, know and love ourselves as he sees, knows and loves us and all others. The Examen promotes this level of self-awareness and attentiveness.

As we move deeper and deeper into love, this level of self-awareness sharpens our ability to discern between good and evil. Evil tends to break down distinctions and to limit distinctions to pragmatic self-interest. Then we value only what interests us, and live life out of those limiting values. Such sin not only harms us and our relationship with community, it also moves beyond our personal relationships to infect the whole community. None of us is free of this. Each of us is somewhere on the continuum between selfishness and God, between narcissism and the fullness of community life found only in the Trinity. We discover in ourselves the tension between these two opposing drives. We are never purely one or the other, but a combination of both. What is important is not where we stand, but the direction we face.

Facing God

When we are facing God, the ordered aspects of our life resonate to God's desire for us, and we feel a sense of peace and joy, a sense of rootedness in God's love we can call consolation. But those disordered aspects of our life that do not know God, or have a false image of God, or even prefer to live an existence away from God, are challenged by the love we desire to unite with. We experience their reaction against that mutuality with feelings of apathy and anxiety, and with a distaste for the good.

Similarly, when we are trapped in our selfishness and we desire only to satisfy our narcissistic needs, that is when we are turned away from God. Our desire for God is felt as frustration and dissatisfaction. Those other desires that support our selfishness are pleasured and affirmed.

We need to know how to distinguish between the satisfactions given by encountering God and those that arise by being selfish. The satisfaction that arises from self-indulgence does not last. We become dissatisfied again soon after these desires are sated, because they do not tap into the source of life. They seek to be satisfied by what gives merely partial or inadequate life. It is only by being attentive to the past we can discover the repeated patterns arising from an urge to yield to both what tempts us and what liberates us to love. These differ in causes and effects, and show us that while the urgings of some desires feel the same, where they come from and where they end up differ. Experience can teach us to identify the subtle differences between urges as they seek to be fulfilled. We can learn to avoid certain contexts and situations because they promote selfishness. We may have a sense of unrest, but the context promotes an unhealthy way of satisfying that urge. Easy access to gossip, pornography or morbid introspection, for example, promotes an unhealthy unrest. But we do not have to be victims of a permissive context. We can adopt a hobby that brings us to a meditative, relaxed or creative state of awareness. We discover how important it is to have a project on hand—such as a good novel, gardening or a piece of needlework—that we can turn to easily to afford us ease and recreation. In our vulnerability, we can choose either something that gives life or something that is disrespectful of life.

Similarly, we can discover from experience how to distinguish between seemingly similar urges that have different results—some tending towards God, others tending towards selfishness. We learn from their effects. Selfishness tends to move us from the larger circles of community to more and more restricted forms of being alive. Addictions can separate us from a full social life, withdrawing us into alienation from friends, then family, and then even from other aspects of our very selves, until we are reduced to being enslaved to a soul-destroying compulsion we might hate but cannot free ourselves from. We become fragmented, and one fragmented aspect of ourselves controls the rest of our life.

We are created as desire for God. We do not have an identity within ourselves. Our identity comes only from God. In fact, our sense of self is basically empty. This is our radical poverty of spirit, and our human condition. It is the condition of every aspect of creation. We experience ourselves as a bundle of desires arising from an empty centre, which is also a manifestation of the desire we are for God. Actually, all our desires—the ones we sense and the one that we are—desire God. Disorder comes when some desires seek to fulfill themselves, independent of each other. The illusion they offer is that such fulfillment will fill up our emptiness. But the truth of the matter is only God can fill that emptiness. No one or nothing else can replace God.

The path of being attentive brings those disordered and separated energies into conformity with the Desire God is for us. In the spiritual life, this is done through asceticism. Its aim is precisely the integration of those energies into the forms of community that make up the self and society, and, still more, those larger and yet larger units of relationships that extend through creation. To practise asceticism is not to punish ourselves but to liberate ourselves into life and into relationship. The Examen is one way of doing that. In this it complements the aims of the Spiritual Exercises, the path of which carries us to greater forms of intimacy with God and integration with the community of all that is committed to the good.

When we step into Mystery, we need help not to get lost and we need some ways to understand the confusion that surrounds us. We need to be able to interpret the signs that present themselves to us as we walk our spiritual path. But we should note that we are dealing here with Mystery, and mystery is not susceptible to rules. Ignatius describes his rules for the discernment of spirits in the following manner: "Rules to Aid Us Towards Perceiving and then Understanding, at least to some Extent, the various Motions Which are Caused in the Soul" (Sp. Ex. #313). His rules are not a system; they are existential observations. They arise from his personal experience and show the attention he paid to his personal experience. While we may find his rules useful, we would also find it more useful to pay attention to our own experience and to become aware of the ways in which we are drawn towards God and what their signs are. We also need to know the forces that lead away from God and how these forces manifest themselves in our own lives. We need to be attentive.

Attention is the basis of the spiritual life, and in Ignatian spirituality God gets our attention through a process of defamiliarization. We notice what is unfamiliar to us. The felt range of Desire is our feelings, and what we notice on the feeling level is all that is different from our habitual, normal feelings. That difference can be noticed in terms of pleasure or pain. Ignatius describes the difference in terms of consolation or desolation.

While we are the desire for God, and the range of that desire extends towards God, what we experience as desire, in the forms of emotion and feelings, is usually a limited spectrum of that desire. God as Desire also desires us, and the way God gets our attention is by making us aware of how our desires encounter him as Desire. There are whole levels and dimensions of that encounter that go beyond the sensible. Indeed, God is always in contact with us, but we are not always aware of our contact with God. What we are aware of are our feelings. Our feelings are our values incarnate as body; our feelings as values reveal who we are in an existential and incarnate manner.

When those values encounter God, we feel either consolation or desolation.

Consolation and Desolation

Consolation is not necessarily feeling good or pleasant sensations. An awareness of our encounter with God can give us a sense of remorse for having been selfish or destructive. We can be in anguish over the violence in the world, dismayed at being trapped in occupations that destroy our integrity, and ashamed at the ways in which we have cooperated in exploiting the poor and powerless, and at our silence in the face of oppression. But consolation can also manifest in a sense of joy, peace, creativity. It shows itself in delight in life and in celebration of life with others. Similarly, desolation can be felt in the sense of pleasure and triumph we may experience at putting down the people we do not like. It can be the self-righteousness we enjoy because we are not trapped in certain shameful ways, like some others. It can be sensed in the melancholy we may endure because we are too refined for this world, or the license we relish in violence of anger. Desolation may also show itself in the anguish of loneliness, the anxiety of low self-esteem, the despair of the inconsolable.

So we need to be able to read our feelings and ask what they mean. What are they telling us about where we are in our relationship with God and God's relationship with us? These are two different things. God always loves us, but we do not always love God. God always speaks to us through our feelings, but we are not always aware of our feelings and are not always on speaking terms with God.

For the narcissist, feeling good is not a manifestation of Christian consolation. When the narcissist feels good, he is focused on his self-satisfactions. The narcissist's awareness of how God speaks to him comes in feelings of shame and confusion, remorse and the sting of conscience. God does not give good feelings to the self-centred, because that would just reinforce destructive behaviours. The evil spirit, on the other hand, tempts such a person with apparent delights. It is only when they have been sampled that this person finds these delights promised more than they delivered. Shakespeare's Sonnet 129 describes such an entrapment and deception:

160

The expense of spirit in a waste of shame
Is lust in action: and till action, lust
Is perjured, murderous, bloody, full of blame,
Savage, extreme, rude, cruel, not to trust;
Enjoyed no sooner but despised straight;
Past reason hunted; and no sooner had,
Past reason hated, as a swallowed bait,
On purpose laid to make the taker mad.
Mad in pursuit and in possession so;
Had, having, and in quest to have extreme;
A bliss in proof, and proved, a very woe;
Before, a joy proposed; behind a dream.
All this the world well knows; yet none knows well
To shun the heaven that leads men to this hell.[30]

Here the speaker is in the throes of uncontrolled lust and almost incoherent in his fragmented narrative. He realizes its destructive nature and can describe it and its results accurately, but that knowledge does not liberate him from the state of this present hell. The compulsion that dominates his life does not give him freedom, and the sonnet gives some clues about discerning. We see the difference between intensity and passion. Intensity focuses on ourselves and on our own needs. It reduces others to objects for our satisfaction. Intensity narrows the focus of our attention, and that narrowing of focus distorts, ignores or misrepresents the truth. What is achieved by this behaviour, which diminishes our humanity, does not satisfy our desire for God. It does not bring life. The promise offered by its seductions are illusory; its effects "a very woe." We are left frustrated by our course of action and, even though we realize it does not offer life, the entrapment by evil condemns us to repeat compulsively what we know does not give life. This is very much the case of the addict who regrets his destructive behaviour but is unable to stop it. In the spiritual life, when we are turned away from God, every self-destructive act promises satisfaction, but in effect fragments us more and more. This is what evil does to the self-centred.

Its effect on those who are seeking a path to the fullness of life is quite different. For those people, "it is the characteristic of the evil spirit to harass with anxiety, to afflict with sadness, to raise obstacles backed by false reasonings which disturb the soul" (Sp. Ex. #315). It attempts to turn our attention away from God, and from the Desire that draws us to God, towards ourselves, our inadequacies and the limitations of our resources. It urges us to draw false conclusions from the limited data it presents and our limited human perspective on what to do next and how to do it in order to live a fuller life. As we risk our lives, stepping into the unknown and wondering what to do next, we can encounter a sense of confusion that distresses us. Often the search for clarity does not lead us to self-transcendence but to paralysis. We do not have enough data or we have too much data, or we do not know how to read the data we have. So we do nothing. It is the nature of evil to freeze creativity. Then we stop in our tracks, unable to proceed on the path to life.

The desire that impels us and draws us to God manifests itself in our attention in a different way. We experience it as courage, consolation, inspiration, joy and peace. With the sense of being held and supported in love, things fall into place without much effort on our part. "Coincidences" happen. Our creative energies resonate with the creativity that comes from God and manifests itself in doing good.

The Dynamics of Consolation

As the Incarnation shows, God desires that all be redeemed. Grace not only affirms and supports what is spiritual, but also seeks out and transforms what is unspiritual. Consolation is not a static state of being. When we are ready, which is often before we know it, consolation carries us to places of desolation, and we are asked to remain there until they are transformed. We notice this in Matthew's description of what happens after Jesus' baptism in the Jordan. At the baptism Jesus is affirmed as the Beloved Son, and then the gospel continues, "he is driven by the Spirit into the desert." There he encounters a period of desolation. In that desolation he is given suggestions that, if he accepts, would deny his humanity, his mission and his identity. He would deny the Incarnation and thus his humanity if he turned the stones into bread by using his divinity.

He would deny his mission to bring the world back to the Father if he subscribed to the power of Satan. He would deny his human identity as radically dependent on God by provoking the Father to do what he wanted, rather than waiting on the Father. It is by patiently waiting on the Father in that state of desolation that the desolation is overcome. The gospel sequence states that after Jesus' temptations in the desert, "angels came and ministered to him."

When filled and affirmed by the spirit, experienced as consolation, we, too, are moved to those desert places that have no life in them. We are tempted to deal with the situations we find there in ways that spring from our selfishness, and thus deny our own humanity, mission and identity. We may seek to operate out of a sense of power, pragmatism or self-righteousness. Then we do not operate from a sense of relationship with God but from a sense of self. It is the nature of evil that, when we encounter it, we spontaneously close in ourselves, as if struck. We must resist the temptation to operate out of that withdrawal. If we can discipline ourselves not to react, we can reach a place of freedom that allows us to discern what is most life-giving for a particular situation. The spirit of life has led us into those circumstances and it will give us what we need to bring life to those circumstances. We need to be attentive to and hold onto the spirit of life that is always with us as gift. What is not life cannot maintain itself. Desolation is not the root of our being. The presence and the power of a life stronger than death and always active in our world uses those situations to bring out a greater good. What we have to do in those situations is to maintain our relationship with the forces of life available to us there. Otherwise, we may succumb, fall prey to desolation, and become destructive.

We are never asked to be destructive or self-destructive. If we find ourselves in those places, we should try to remove ourselves before we do greater harm to ourselves or to others. Often, when we are there, we deceive ourselves into thinking we are called to martyrdom, when in fact we have been so drained of life, we have no personal sense of life or any healthy relationship with God or with others. Blaise Pascal, the French philosopher (1623–1662), observes, "Men never do evil so completely and joyfully as when they do it from religious conviction."[31]

A false sense of life destroys us and others. We fall into despair or apathy, or malice, and misread where we actually are. We lose a sense of hope, and cannot see the good present to us even in little ways. At those times, we lose that sense of a bonded relationship with God in which we know that whatever happens, God is still somehow there. Then we lose a sense of our integrity and identity as a beloved of God, to such an extent we unwittingly cooperate with the forces of destruction in ourselves and in our relationships with others. When that happens, we are not being martyrs. A martyr is a witness to God's love by responding to that love in ways to withstand the forces of destruction in the world. A martyr does not cooperate with the forces of destruction. Continuing a destructive relationship or a self-destructive life path is not the witness of sanctity. It is the witness of despair.

The Dynamics of Desolation

When we are in desolation, we are not in despair; we are in temptation. We are in a state of vulnerability where we are assaulted and driven to the limits of our felt humanity. Desolation reveals a boundary state between being human and being less than human. It is a no-man's land, to use a military metaphor, needing to be reclaimed for humanity. We cannot do this on our own—maybe that is why the temptation to despair is there—but we can offer to God that space and those states causing this desolation and wait for God to enter them through us, and transform them. The most extreme example we have of this is death, and here we have the death of Christ as an example of how to live death. He endures death, and this allows resurrection to happen. Similarly, in our own lives there are those liminal states when we are suffering or have lost things or people or ways of being significant to our sense of self. We find ourselves in places and situations outside of our control. We discover our poverty of spirit and our radical dependence on the mercy of God. All we can do is wait for help to come. Our strength comes not from us, but as Ignatius says, "Let us find our strength in our Creator and Lord" (Sp. Ex. #324).

It is the nature of love not to leave us abandoned. Waiting in that darkness often takes away from us our many illusions about our own abilities and strengths, as well as the sense of who we are. Waiting also shows us the malign power of evil and the way such power attacks our weak points to undermine our integrity, our sense of being loved and lovable, and our call to live joyful lives in this world. We learn how to wait. We discover what does not help our waiting, and we discover for ourselves what does. The waiting opens our eyes to the presence of God already in the darkness, waiting for us.

The journey with God leads us from consolation to desolation and from that desolation to consolation again. As the journey continues, we are not asked to run from desolation but to see desolation as manifesting those places the love of God desires to reclaim and restore. When we find ourselves in such places, we are asked to cooperate with God through prayer, through the Examen, and by discovering ways going against the dynamics of that particular desolation. Perhaps this means being gentle with ourselves when we feel the aggression of our disordered energies, or treating ourselves to something ridiculous when we feel unworthy and unlovable. It might mean being firm in turning off those negative tapes that play through our awareness and distort the way we see ourselves and others when we become aware of them, rather than indulging in them.

When the sites of desolation are transformed, consolation replaces the desolation, and the consolation maintains, affirms and celebrates what was lost but has been found again. The consolation integrates those redirected energies into the larger weave of desires that is the community of the person. When such a healing is established and consolidated, the dynamic of reinforced love and desire reaches out once again to what has been separated, misdirected and felt as desolation.

What happens here on the individual level also happens on the larger levels of community. Paul talks about this in the first chapter in Ephesians. It is the process of creating community through integration. The dynamics of Desire that desires us, all of us, and every part of each of us and of all of creation, without any loss, weaves us together in a community of love. Paul asserts that God

> chose us in him before the creation of the world to be holy and blameless in his sight. In love God predestined us to be adopted ... through Jesus Christ, in accordance with his pleasure and will .... In him we have the forgiveness of sins, in accordance with the riches of God's grace that he lavished on us .... And he made known to us the mystery of his will according to his good pleasure, which he purposed in Christ, to be put into effect when the times will have reached their fulfillment—to bring all things in heaven and on earth together under one head, even Christ. (Ephesians 1:4-10)

Our spiritual journey is not completed until all are gathered in Christ and returned to the Father. We journey towards that fullness of consolation, and we are asked not to stop when we encounter desolation. Desolation is a necessary part of the journey.

Years ago I was giving a retreat in a large convent at Niagara Falls, Ontario. Part of the convent was rented out to a convention of teachers who were taking a day's workshop on dance therapy. The morning session was on theory. One of the teachers was in a wheelchair and his colleagues were worried that the afternoon part of the workshop, which would focus on the practical aspects, would be embarrassing for this man. So at lunch they suggested he not come to the afternoon session. During the coffee break in the afternoon, some were concerned about how he was doing and went to his room. As they approached it they heard a loud crash and then silence. They tried to open the door, but it was jammed shut. They called out and they heard him groaning. They wrenched the door open and found him sprawled on the floor, the wheelchair on top of him. He was laughing.

"What were you doing?" they asked.

"I was learning to dance," he said.

"And what have you learned?" they wondered, looking at him lying on the floor.

"I have learned ... I have learned that the fall is part of the dance."

In desolation we discover our fallenness. In consolation we discover the dance. As we step into Mystery, we learn to dance with God. It is a relationship defined by the movement of the spirits. Desolation is not necessarily a bad thing. It shows us the effects of the unredeemed in our lives. It shows us those places that God desires to transform. It shows us yet another space where we will experience the surprising effects of love.

It is the nature of evil not to want us to experience love. It desires that we remain trapped by fear, lies, pragmatic self-interest and a disgust for fallen creation. God's desire for us and our desire for God free us from those traps. We experience those traps in the stories we live out of, personally, socially, culturally. These stories frustrate our human desire for love by imposing upon us inadequate ways of seeing ourselves, others, God, and even the path to God.

Reading Our Contemporary World

Our contemporary world is driven by four basic narratives: security, meaning, liberty and belonging. God enters these four basic narratives and opens them to a path of radical inclusivity in which everything will be integrated in the love that is God. The entry of God into the human story is through desire.

The Stories of Our Times

Security

The chaos of our times has challenged us to our core. We have become destabilized by the rapid changes in our world. Ways of communicating have changed; borders have been redrawn and are in flux; our neighbours speak languages we did not grow up with; we have become suspicious of those in authority, be they secular or ecclesial. One can even regard the officials of law enforcement as just another gang. These are just a few obvious manifestations of the unstable world we find ourselves in. In the midst of this we are drawn by our basic and deep desire for security. Closed myths offer us security in these times. They dogmatically assert to us that their particular political or social or ecclesial ways of reading reality are the only true and divinely approved ones. In our vulnerable state we are often tempted and seduced into accepting their claims. But we need to be aware of how these closed myths operate. They exclude and demonize those others who do not agree with them. They maintain their authority by fear. Their orthodoxy and law is established by a centralized government using the politics of coercion to intimidate and suppress. Their stance is the narcissism of self-enclosure and self-righteousness based on the ideologies and the closed traditions of an institution. They do not give us freedom.

When we step into mystery walking towards God on the path of spiritual intimacy, we reject the security of such closed myths for a rootedness in God. Intimacy is found not in belonging to socially approved groups maintained by shame and guilt, but in the shameless and liberating embrace of God. Institutions offer us security and give us ways of reading the world and evaluating it. They offer us an ethic, but they cannot provide us with faith as a lived relationship with God. We experience the tension between narcissism and the community called Trinity in the desire we have for security. This security comforts us against the risk we experience living a rootedness in God who calls us always beyond ourselves.

Meaning

Our postmodern age has often been defined by a lack of, or the conflicting excesses of, systems of meaning. Many different incompatible points of view are available to us and each is supported with valid reasons. The search to understand what is going on, and for clarity and direction to overcome the confusion we feel and see around us, becomes an urgent concern today. Too often we are attracted to leaders who promise us such meaning. They offer us an authority to deal with the crises in our religious, social and political worlds. Often they claim their authority is from God. Yet we see their behaviour and their policies do not accord with our own awareness of how God operates.

The path of spiritual intimacy, which allows us to experience personally God's compassionate mercy, leads us not to clarity and systems of meaning but rather to mystery. Such intimacy creates real relationships. We are asked to live our relationship with the mystery we call God rather than in the clarity of systems. We are asked to place our trust first in God rather than in leaders. What such leaders want from us is orthodoxy, not our intimacy with God. To live in mystery does not mean we abandon meaning, institutions and those socialized forms of interaction that give us access to ourselves and each other. To live in mystery means we appreciate those ways of being as fingers pointing to the moon. Those fingers are not the moon. In fact, the moon illuminates the fingers pointing. It is mystery that gives those institutions their life. But it is wrong to equate the institution with the mystery. Institutions give us a socially approved way of living, but they avoid the deeper question of whether these ways of living are spiritually healthy. They offer us a clarity emerging from internal relations within their particular systems. They often forget the system itself is situated in a mystery bigger than what is intellectually available. Christ's reproach to the institutions of his day was that their systems justified ways of behaving that ignored the greater call of love. They displaced mystery with meaning, love with clarity, spirituality with religion. Their ethics was ultimately one of self-interest or of a truncated self-transcendence.

Liberty

Such a displacement leads to an ethical dead end. Too often in our contemporary worlds we confuse license, liberty and freedom. License is the social permission to behave in particular ways. These ways can be ethical or unethical. Liberty defines license. Institutions can grant us liberty, but our understanding of liberty is dependent on the institutions we adhere to. The quest today for liberty is often understood as the overthrow of oppression and victimization. But what is not understood is that the secular longing for liberty— personal, social or cultural—creates oppression for some other. Sweatshops in Asia give us the liberty to buy goods cheaply. Our civil liberty is maintained by the blood of others at war elsewhere, and in those wars the innocent become casualties. The cost of the liberty we desire is the enslavement of some other.

We need to distinguish very carefully between liberty and freedom. Christ in the Garden of Gethsemane gives up his liberty to maintain his freedom. Freedom is how spiritual intimacy manifests itself in the world. This intimacy declares that a right relationship with God is more human than the social constructions of liberty. Our freedom is as creations of God. Our freedom is not to be as gods. That deception was the one offered Eve in the Garden of Eden. A spiritual intimacy with God, on the other hand, would declare that sometimes, to be human, we give up our liberty to be free. When we abandon our freedom and seek liberty, we inflict violence in our world. This is not to say that we do not desire liberty, and that it is not a good thing. But the particular liberty we desire flows from freedom, not from enslaving others. The tension between liberty and freedom is shown in the use of power. Christ gives up his own power to be defined by the world, and so appears powerless in his passion. Yet it is because of his powerlessness that the power of the Father could manifest itself in its own way and its own time. Christ belongs first and foremost to the Father. We, too, belong equally so to the Father. Our freedom comes in living out of that relationship. Our liberty has value only in terms of that freedom. Our license, our actions, the choices we make within the context of our civil liberties are moral only when they maintain a right relationship with the Father.

Exclusivity

Often we define our freedom by myths of belonging. We demand to be free to worship and to live out our social and cultural identities of race, gender and creed. These identities create boundaries. If those boundaries are read as fixed and not porous, then those who fall outside our self-definitions are regarded as radically different from us. Those others become alien and are held as secondary to our primary values of self-determination. By doing this we place ourselves in a ghetto. But before we accept the definitions of ourselves as racial, or specifically gendered, or members of a cultural or religious tradition, we are human. In that humanity we are all creatures of God. Moreover, we are still being created. We do not know ourselves fully. We do not know what it is to be human. The mystery we are to ourselves deconstructs the rigidity of our self-definitions. Even when we define ourselves as Christians, what do we mean? We would claim to belong to the body of Christ, and claim that we are parts of the body of Christ. But Christ's resurrection extends our understanding of what it is to be human. Every human being is called to a spiritual intimacy with the Father. Each call is unique but of equal value. To abandon that call divides us into camps, ghettos and forms of exclusivity. By accepting our identity as defined by such, we deny or ignore a simple fact. We are creatures. We do not define ourselves. God defines us. We are unfinished business. We are open myths, and exclusivity of any sort traps us into accepting ourselves as closed myths. When we live this way, we use violence to assert who we are by destroying the other. There is a despair that is endemic in any form of exclusivity. It is a despair that abandons the invitation of the Other to help us reach a richer understanding of ourselves as community, and thus to reach a fuller way of living our lives.

Security, meaning, liberty and exclusivity are the plots of the stories we live by in our world today. These are not bad things in themselves. They become unhelpful when they replace or truncate a relationship with God. Then socially defined forms of orthodoxy replace spiritual intimacy. Then social acceptance betrays the deeper human desire for a rootedness in God, for a life lived in mystery, for freedom and for the drive to community where no one or nothing is excluded.

God Enters Our Closed and Broken Myths

Closed or broken myths freeze our growth into humanity. The gift of God's love for us enters into our closed and broken myths. It seeks to liberate us into seeing, knowing and loving ourselves as the Father sees, knows and loves us. We need to experience the power of that love in our own lives first before we can become aware of its presence in the world, not just some 2,000 years ago, but today, here and now. What happened in the Incarnation happens to us when God's love so enters into our personal lives and liberates us, we can live in our world in such a way others become liberated. The entry of God into our own brokenness is one we experience as a spiritual intimacy. Our journey with God as persons freed into love is a deepening of that intimacy. That path of intimacy carries us to, and beyond, the institutionalized boundaries of being human. It calls us even beyond how we imagine ourselves. It brings us to a creativity that builds up the community of love in which we are all intimately connected.

We all find ourselves somewhere along that continuum between narcissism and God. It manifests itself socially today in the tensions we experience between security and rootedness; meaning and mystery; liberty and freedom; exclusivity and community. We may even find that certain aspects of our lives are oriented towards one pole, while other aspects of our lives are directed to the opposite pole. In each of these aspects, there is the further tension between consolation and desolation, for we are never completely in one state or the other. As a result, we experience a complex of feelings arising from this confusion.

In discernment we need to be able to untangle those feelings and try to see where each comes from, and what each is saying to us. This may give us some knowledge and awareness of our present state of being, but we also need to know what to do. The difficulty in this life is how to discern in the midst of confusion. There are special times when we can withdraw from our normal surroundings and from some of the external forces that help create the confusion. We can go away on a retreat, for instance, to get in touch with our deeper selves and to find a heightened awareness of the presence of God in our lives. But most of us do not have the opportunity to do so. Most of us do not even have access to good spiritual direction to help us sort out the conflicting emotions that drive us. What are we to do then?

Discernment is not something we do alone. It is something we and God do together. Wherever and however we are, we can bring our complex sensibilities to God. We can desire to be attentive to God, and that desire to be attentive to God opens us to becoming aware how God is attentive to us. God announces his intentions through the longings we feel in our lives and through the situations in which we find ourselves. We can respond with a sense of humility acknowledging we do not know completely what to do. This makes us quite attentive to possible signs of what to do. But we are even more aware that God is also in the situations in which we find ourselves, and God desires only life to come from those situations. So we risk. We lean into the darkness. We depend on the mercy of God to help us, and we expect the relationship we have with God is such that things will work out all right. Sometimes God does not tell us what to do. But always God gives us experiences, and we discern what those experiences mean and what they offer as a path. He desires we trust ourselves the way he trusts us. Whatever we do will be all right. Our anxieties about not offending God may freeze us from the freedom God offers to us, and so God sometimes deliberately says nothing just so we do something. In our desire to be right and perfect, we give up the trust God has in us. This can lead to scruples, which is another form of narcissism.

The basis of discernment is not what we do, or what is to be done. The basis of discernment is the lived relationship with God. It was St. Augustine who famously said, "Love and do what you will." Love not only reveals to us what is possible, but shows us the path to make it real. A quotation attributed to Fr. Pedro Arrupe, a recent Father General of the Jesuits, says,

> *Nothing is more practical than finding God,*
> *that is, than falling in love*
> *in a quite absolute, final way.*
> *What you are in love with,*
> *what seizes your imagination,*
> *will affect everything.*
> *It will decide what will get you*
> *out of bed in the morning,*
> *what you will do with your evenings,*
> *how to spend your weekends,*
> *what you read, who you know,*
> *what breaks your heart,*
> *and what amazes you with joy and gratitude.*
> *Fall in love; stay in love,*
> *and it will decide everything.*[32]

When we fall in love, we do not choose between good and evil. In falling in love, our choices are always between two goods, to discern which is better.

Even here we can be deluded, because some things might seem good, but once we have started doing them we discover they are not good at all. At the beginning it is difficult, almost impossible, to distinguish between what is good and what seems to be good. The difference between the two is that what seems to be good is not rooted in the creativity of God and so cannot sustain its pretense of goodness when it is acted upon or lived out. The path of what seems to be good, but in fact is not, is seen by where it leads us. St. Ignatius points out, "love ought to manifest itself in deeds rather than in words" (Sp. Ex. #230:1). What happens is that, because it is unsupported by love, such a project turns into forms of destruction and self-destructiveness. As the gospel points out, "By their fruits you shall know them" (Matthew 7:16). For example, we might think it a good thing to spend our Saturdays working at a food bank. It starts off well, but after a few months we are so tired at the end of the weekend that our work during the week suffers, and we find ourselves withdrawing from our social world of friends and families to try to recover. What seemed a good idea turns out to take us away from the community that supports us.

Testing the Spirits

It is good, St. Paul says, to test every spirit (1 Thessalonians 5:19-22). One way of testing the spirits is seeing not only where they come from, but where they lead us. After we have reached a certain age, all of us will have had the experience of being deceived by what seems to be good but ended up badly. When that happens, we are weakened spiritually. We become anxious, or bitter, or find ourselves caught up in destructive situations. But such experiences are not without their value. They can teach us something about ourselves. We can reflect on those experiences to see if there is a pattern to be discovered in them. Because evil is not creative, we find ourselves tempted over and over again in the same ways. When we become attentive to that pattern, we become more quickly sensitized to the difference between what is good and what seems to be good. We can intuit what lies under the surface of the good urge. We can also become aware of how the pattern of our entrapment occurs. We become more attentive to our life. If we fail to do this, we repeat the same mistakes over and over again. As we step into mystery we do not need to be lost. Our life experience gives us material to help us on our path. The One who desires us and who accompanies us on our path does not abandon us to be deceived and led astray.

But there is a second way in which we can be deceived by what seems to be good. We need to be aware of the difference between being consoled and the after-effects of those consolations. When I am with the Beloved, I am deeply moved and caught in that intimacy. I desire nothing else and am content. But when that graced state of being rooted in love passes, I may still be so caught up in the effects and the sensations it stirs up in me that I may be tempted to do or commit myself to something that does not come from this intimacy I have experienced. Ignatius says, "A spiritual person who has received such a consolation must consider it very attentively and must cautiously distinguish the actual time of the consolation from the period which follows it" (Sp. Ex. #336). The suggestions arising in that afterglow may come from ourselves and not from the relationship. This can also happen if we promise something when we are caught up in the excitement of an occasion and lose our prudence through impulsiveness. Those seemingly good suggestions might come from the evil spirit, as in the case of Peter, who, upon confessing that Jesus is the Christ of God, advises Jesus that suffering and death are not the path of service for the Messiah. To that proposal Jesus replies, "Get behind me, Satan" (Matthew 16:23).

There is prudence in walking a spiritual path that is the result of humility and of having been deceived time and again by the evil spirits. Experience on the spiritual path comes when we have been caught in all the traps and been liberated by the compassionate mercy of God, and so we are attentive only to God and to the ways God is present in the world. We realize on the path to God just how easy it is to be trapped. The closer we are to God, the more we realize just how much of a sinner we are, and even more, just how much we are loved. This greater love stops us from falling in on ourselves. We realize the dynamics of disaster that run through our lives, but still more we experience the call to love that liberates us from destruction.

As we enter more and more deeply into Mystery, we become increasingly vulnerable. We learn to trust God more and more and so enter more easily the places in our lives and in our world that cry out for salvation. When we are vulnerable, we find ourselves torn between the forces in our life moving us to self-preservation and those moving us to an abandonment to Divine Providence. It is helpful to become aware how these opposing forces move us and to ask for the graces both to avoid the forces tempting us to narcissism and to cooperate with the ones moving us to self-transcendence (Sp. Ex. #139).

In his rules for discernment, Ignatius points out that the evil spirit acts like a coward before a show of strength and like a bully if he has his way (Sp. Ex. #325). It is the nature of evil to terrorize us with the trappings of power and authority, so we defensively withdraw into ourselves and are caught by our own addictions and compulsions. This dynamic reduces us to seek security, conformity or other debilitating social patterns of self-understanding or expression. Then we remain trapped in a world turned away from God, and we succumb to the self-justification such a world offers. Ignatius talks about our drive to covet riches so as to gain the approval of the world and thus reinforce our pride. These riches may not be just economic. Any form of giftedness can make us rich. It could be physical beauty, intellectual acumen or power. We can use any of these to establish and maintain social status, and we can deceive ourselves that our identity is to be found solely in those ways of self-understanding. This is not to say that these things are wrong in themselves. They are wrong when they displace the relationship with God as the source of our being and identity. So it is very useful to examine how we perform when we find ourselves in vulnerable situations, and to ask ourselves why we do what we do when we find ourselves in those situations. This is one way of being attentive to ourselves. We note these tendencies so we do not become unwittingly trapped by them. They are present in our lives;

the more aware we are of them and the more we turn towards God for help not to be mastered by them, the less impact they have on our journey towards the fullness of life.

To do this it is helpful to look at our past, to notice how we were trapped, and so found ourselves alienated from what is good in life. But we can also seek to discover the patterns of behaviour in ourselves and in the culture we live in that foster that alienation. We might find we have a low self-image, which prevents us from enjoying our life because we think we are not worthy. We might then compare our "miserable" lives with those fashionable ones projected by the rich and the famous. Then we live by the values of the world. Or we may accept this false image and justify ourselves by claiming to live an abjected life, the way we think the saints and the martyrs did. We project in those ideological and non-Incarnational depictions of sanctity, which deny our human nature and are presented in certain falsely pious hagiographies of the saints, a way of being countercultural we emulate to justify ourselves. It is always important when we do something like this to ask ourselves, "Does God want this?" "Does this fit into the pattern of liberation, or of self-deception in our lives?" "Am I offering to God something God has asked for, or am I offering to God something that I think is good and so God should want it?" By looking at the patterns in our life we get some sense of how we can be self-deceived. We need to remember that saints live human nature to the full, in imitation of Jesus Christ.

Another and deeper drive exists in our life: the desire we are for God. This desire permeates our whole being, constantly calling us out of our known and established selves into the Mystery of being desired by God. Our God desires all of us and every part of all of us. Saints realize that desire.

Becoming More Ourselves

In our living out of that call, we must constantly give up our self-images, especially those that have fulfilled their function of bringing us to a certain stage of attention. The journey ever deeper into love reveals a pattern of coming to a self-understanding, being established in it, and then leaving it behind as we are called further beyond our selves. It is the nature of the spiritual person to be such a pilgrim. We journey into the depths of God, and that journey never ends. We are always leaving things behind, and the freedom we are invited to live out of calls us to that disassembling of the constructs we consider to be identity.

To live that way gives us a sense of our poverty of spirit, and we find ourselves imitating the path of Jesus in Philippians 2:5-8. Our attitude then is

the same as that of Christ Jesus:
Who, being in very nature God,
did not consider equality with God something to be grasped,
but made himself nothing,
taking the very nature of a servant,
being made in human likeness.
And being found in appearance as a man,
he humbled himself
and became obedient to death—
even death on a cross!

This attitude of identification with Jesus manifests itself not in the approval of the world, but rather in its opposite, in desiring only to do what the Father wishes even if it means bearing the displeasure of the world or being overlooked by it. Our identification with Jesus and in Jesus gives us a relationship of absolute dependence on the Father. This humility is right relationship and it is a relationship of disposition where we wait on, and are attentive to, the Father.

We do this by being attentive to the consolations and the desolations in our life. These are the ways in which the Father guides us.

Through being attentive to these consolations and desolations we can make good choices. We note that, while such choices reinforce our relationship with God, they do not necessarily give us success in the world, affirm our ego or satisfy our cravings. Good choices carry us to a fullness of life, for God did not create us to be miserable or self-destructive, or to alienate us from others. Good choices are made for intimacy with God and are maintained through intimacy with God. We can make a good choice in a long and care-filled process of discernment. But, after making that choice, we can withdraw from that relationship with God in which the commitment was made. Then we later find ourselves in difficulties and wonder if we made the right choice. We have abandoned the relationship that gives the choice its energy, support and direction. Rather than changing the decision, we need to re-establish the relationship. The Examen is one way of maintaining and developing a relationship with God. We can make good discernments only when we put on the heart and mind of God, and when we see things from God's perspective. Otherwise, we confuse our perspectives with God's.

Making Choices

When we have God's perspective, the ordinary occasions of our life do not require an overt process of discernment. But there are times when we must make a major decision. At such times, we often find ourselves torn between two goods and enter a state of confusion. In this state we are vulnerable, and the self-serving dynamics of our desire for what is good struggles with the drive we are for a fuller life. We do not know what to do. Each choice has its good and bad points, and we cannot evaluate and count up the worth of those points. However, we can pray about each of the choices we have to make for a period of time and see if we move to a stable state of consolation or desolation about that particular choice. As we do this, the context of prayer brings us into a conscious intimacy with God. This intimacy evaluates our choice and lets us know if we are to follow it or not by leaving us in consolation or desolation. We need to do this over time because sometimes the choices we face are difficult ones, and even thinking about them can bring us to a state of anxiety, fear or doubt. We must let the choice sink into the depths of our being, where we encounter God, before we know what to do.

One way of choosing is by the way of emptiness. We admit all the desires, but as we sit, conscious of our poverty of spirit, we allow ourselves to sink into that emptiness. Lesser desires drift away until only the important one supported by the emptiness, and manifesting it, remains. Similarly, the thought of a particular choice can bring us delight. We need to sit with it in prayer to see if the choice does indeed connect us to the creativity of God and so is a good choice, or whether it merely satisfies some aspects of our self-interest, but is not really life-giving.

We can also look to our past and see if we can discern when we have made good decisions and how we have done them. We can look at the times when we have made bad decisions and how those came about. Sometimes the pattern of bad decisions is more easily seen, since evil is not creative and the pattern tends to repeat itself. God, on the other hand, being creative, surprises us by moving us out of such patterns, and so there is the element of defamiliarization in good decisions. It is not that we look for novelty if we are afraid of boredom. But if we have a pattern of looking for novelty in making decisions, we can ask if the presence of novelty, and the desire for novelty, leads us to make good or bad decisions. If we are comfortable with repeating ourselves, we should ask if such a pattern liberates or traps. Repetition can lead to a deepening of our spirit or to its deadening. Discernment depends on the self-knowledge of how we operate and of our habits and our focus. It also shows us how the temptations to which we are prone operate on us. But while self-knowledge is important, a lived intimacy with God is even more important.

Lived intimacy lets us trust God will not allow us to be deceived when we try our best to find out what is the right thing to do. Lived intimacy also allows us to risk as we discern. We do not have absolute certainty when we discern. To be sure, we can always be deceived. But we trust in a God whose creativity can transform any disaster into new life. Resurrection is the transformation of the disaster of death into the entry into a new creation. We believe in a God who creates, redeems and favours us by offering us the life of the resurrected.

This God holds us to life. Our lived awareness of our rootedness in God gives us our identity and our sense of self. From that intimate knowledge flows our creativity, which builds up and celebrates community. When we walk into mystery, we walk into fuller and fuller dimensions of how we are community. Our desire for God and God's desire for us carries us to this lived reality. Yet in our lives we also experience the opposite pull, which denies our rootedness in God. Then, instead of experiencing ourselves as content, affirmed and held in God's love, we experience ourselves as anxious and plagued by existential doubt. We seek to assuage that doubt by conforming to the dominant norms that surround us, and so succumb to peer pressure and forms of cultural and institutional exclusivity. Then we see the other not as invitation, but as threat.

Our discernments thus are caught between the tensions of rootedness and anxiety; complacency and self-doubt; creativity and conformity; community and exclusivity. When we try to make decisions, we are often not aware of these deeper dynamics operating in how we make choices. In his Spiritual Exercises, Saint Ignatius offers us a way of looking at the tensions in our life and at how these opposing forces can affect us.[33] Often, what has contributed to forming those forces occurs quite early in our lives. An inconsistent primary caregiver, domineering parents, an oppressive family or severe schooling reinforce the path of anxiety, self-doubt, conformity and exclusivity. Unless transformed, this destructive early patterning repeats itself in later life. Instead of intimacy, we are more comfortable with ideologies, which manifest themselves in forms of dogmatism rather than pluralism. These dogmatic positions, which freeze our creativity, maintain a self-interest that denies the integrity of our humanity as members of an all-encompassing community for whom we are responsible. Then, instead of celebrating life, we become cynical and mistrustful. We close down, and in closing down we transform the Spirit's movement in our own lives and in the life of our communities into closed myths. The decisions we make emerge from our life or death in the Spirit.

The way we make decisions operates from many different layers of our being. These range from the physical and emotional to the intellectual, intuitive, social and spiritual. In each there is a tension between consolation and desolation, and among the different levels there are diverse relationships that move from harmony to dissonance. An awareness of those different layers and how they affect us helps us to avoid making bad choices. We might discover that we do not make good decisions if we are hungry, though we may also discover that fasting helps give us the spiritual clarity to see what is important. Also, we may discover that we need some distance from our habitual social environment to make enlightened choices freely; but we can also discover we need the input of those close to us to give us necessary data for significant choices. We may never have the perfect conditions—whatever those may be—for the choices we make. But then again we never have the perfect conditions to live a full life. Rather than obsessing about these, we must make do with what we have. In that messiness of imperfection God came as the Incarnate one; in that messiness of imperfection, God journeys with us. That lived awareness is all we need for discernment.

With this lived awareness we need spiritual help so as not to succumb to our negative tendencies. We certainly can pray for this help, and the prayer can be more effective if we are aware of and focused on what we need. It is one thing to pray to God for help, and another to pray to God for a specific help. Focus brings the level of attention to a desired effect. It cooperates with grace. Similarly, it is helpful to pray towards the true life we desire—for example, intimacy rather than ideology—by maintaining this positive focus and by disposing ourselves to receive it. The intention to make a good decision manifests itself in how we dispose ourselves to make that decision. We can prepare by putting ourselves consciously in God's presence. Then we ask the Spirit to help us in our decision making, and after that we can ask for the specific grace we need, be it wisdom, courage, patience or freedom to make the right choices.

When we have to make choices, we find ourselves in a vulnerable situation, and often our demons come out. So it is very helpful to be aware of how the tensions in our life play out in concrete situations. This allows us to distinguish what appears to feel good from what is really good. If we find ourselves being moved in one way and then in another, it is good to stay with that flux until we settle down emotionally. After a while, one thing appears most stable and it gives us consolation. But before that, we oscillate between consolation and desolation, and must wait prayerfully for those emotional swings to settle down into a steady state. If that final state is consoling, we have made the right decision; if that state leads us to desolation, we have made the wrong one. We also know there are times when we must make a decision and we are not moved one way or the other. We feel becalmed. Then we have to find ways of getting out of this impasse.

Because evil is never creative, habitual patterns of illusion appear when we try to make a decision. Once we know those patterns, we are less likely to succumb to them—less likely, but not always. Ultimately, we trust the compassionate mercy of God to aid us in making good decisions and to protect us from making bad decisions. We cannot be so frozen by the fear of making bad decisions that we refuse to make a decision. Even that refusal is a decision, and being made out of fear rather than freedom, is a bad choice. Indeed, we cannot make good choices when we are trapped in disorder. Since the pattern of disorder is rooted deep in our constructed selves and shapes even the ways we perceive, understand and act, we can do destructive things even when we are in love.

We cannot be frozen by the real fear that even in freedom we can make bad choices. We cannot be so caught up in scruples, wondering whether we are making good choices, that we revisit the decision-making process over and over again, second-guessing ourselves. To be sure, stepping into mystery requires prudence and care, but risk and uncertainty are unavoidable. We can risk in love, knowing that the Love who loves us can transform any mistakes we make into new life. That Love also desires the fullness of life for us and so aids us on the path to fullness of life.

Thus when Francis of Assisi wanted to make a choice, he prayed, and then, with his eyes closed, opened the Bible at random and pointed to a place on a page. What he read there he took as a command from the Divine. We have in the Scriptures elements of such risk taking. After the death of Judas, who had betrayed Jesus, the apostles prayed and drew lots for someone to replace Judas. In both these instances, the context is one of prayer or of an intimate relationship with God. Secondly, there is the question of intentionality. Both approaches focus on what needs to be answered. Finally, Francis and the apostles do not second-guess themselves. In decision making, we need to dispose ourselves and allow things to happen. We walk into mystery one step at a time, aware of a loving God who actively creates us as an ongoing project so we may experience God's love and care.

This does not mean we can be careless and silly. The project is a mutual one, and so we need to be as attentive to our lives as we can. Discernment does not necessarily give us a blueprint for action or a twelve-step plan. What it does give us is a perspective that allows us to see out of God's eyes and heart.

When It Is Difficult to Know the Right Thing to Do

Often, for whatever reason, we do not have such a disposition. The two possible goods we must decide between seem equally useful for the glory of God and for our own spiritual growth. In such a state, some techniques that would dispose us to attaining clarity are helpful.

St. Ignatius suggests two ways of getting out of the impasse. The first is by weighing the options in the context of prayer and within the lived awareness we are creatures designed by and for God. Weighing the options is empirical. The second approach is more statistical. We imagine ourselves in several different basic situations and imagine what choice we would make in those options (Sp. Ex. #178-188).

The First Way

The first way of proceeding consists of six steps. All centre on a focused intentionality. We want to make a decision. We are not postponing this decision for any reason—say, out of fear of consequences. To make this decision, we must be clear about what we are trying to decide. Such clarity is supported by making only one decision, rather than considering "a" or "b" or "c" simultaneously. When we must make a choice from several options, we need to deal with each option separately. We need to ask ourselves: "Do I choose 'a' or not?" When we do this, we eliminate any distractions from this simple choice and so we find ourselves in a position of focused clarity.

Ambiguity and confusion give the destructive forces in our lives room to work. Sometimes to get that necessary focus, we need to distract ourselves from our daily preoccupations. We might find another place where there is quiet and a change of lifestyle. But if that is not possible, or if we are intense people, we can subvert our intensity—which is a form of self-preoccupation—by taking up a hobby, such as going to the movies, painting or exercising. These activities allow the deeper work to be done by distracting us from the habitual, and they maintain our focus. Some people find it helpful to consider the choice before going to sleep. In sleep our conscious preoccupations are suspended while the energies underlying those preoccupations, which shape our lives, manifest themselves in dream work. Whether we can recall our dreams or not, positions are worked out, options explored, and the drive to God, present also there, moves us to a choice. In all of this, an alignment of energies creates a perspective in which a decision becomes apparent.

To facilitate that alignment, we must also be very attentive to ourselves as the desire for God, and of God as desiring us. We need to work on our side of that mutuality so all we desire is God. This manifests itself in our becoming disposed—almost in that state of wise passivity Wordsworth talks about, or the negative capability that Keats describes—which allows us to be receptive to what God desires for us, without any interference on our part. Keats describes this disposition as "being in uncertainties, Mysteries, doubts, without any irritable reaching after fact &. reason".[34] For Wordsworth,

"*The eye—it cannot choose but see;*
We cannot bid the ear be still;
Our bodies feel, where'er they be,
Against or with our will.
"*Nor less I deem that there are Powers*
Which of themselves our minds impress;
That we can feed this mind of ours
In a wise passiveness."[35]

For both poets, the creative act occurs when we are open to Mystery in a focused way.

In this state of focused desire, Ignatius says we should pray for God to move us in such a way that we know what he desires, and out of that stance, we use our reasoning to produce the pros and cons of the decision to do *and* not to do the thing. To facilitate this process, he enjoins us to consider the advantages and disadvantages "solely for the praise of God and the salvation of my soul" (Sp. Ex. #181). It has been my experience that people who use this technique generally set down the advantages and disadvantages without this explicit criteria. This approach flushes out all sorts of concerns and effects. Having done this, it is even more helpful to cross out those points lacking the motives of praising God and saving our soul. We should note here that while some motives might praise God, in our particular circumstances they might not bring us closer to the fullness of life. Similarly, we might consider some reasons that could allow us to live a fuller life but would not necessarily praise God. Both these qualities need to be brought to bear on the considerations at hand. It is helpful to do this exercise this way because it flushes out and brings to explicit awareness the complexity of the divided heart we bring to most decisions. The exercise carries us to a greater freedom in looking at our motives and submits us to a greater sense of abandonment to the Divine Providence.

The technique consists of looking at the pros and cons of doing something and of not doing that thing.

The four columns are drawn up this way.

Should I do X?			
I will do X		I will not do X	
reasons for	reasons against	reasons for	reasons against

Abstractly, it might seem that the columns duplicate each other, but the existential work in writing down the reasons brings all sorts of questions and issues to the surface.

The best way of understanding this is to consider the process like a court case. We have the prosecution and the defense. Both sides want to make the best case for their argument, and both sides realize that they must refute the arguments of the opposition. The biases of both sides are exposed in this technique. This technique is also helpful in group discernments when one brainstorms for each of the columns and then also works to eliminate what is not for the greater glory of God or the good of the community.

The process of surfacing reasons for and against a proposal does not attach values to any one reason. Some reasons might be more cogent than others. But after looking at all that have arisen, one then chooses the prospect that seems more reasonable. Ignatius notes, "After I have gone over and pondered in this way every aspect of the matter under question, I will consider which alternative appears more reasonable" (Sp. Ex. #182). Ignatius does not speak of which alternative "is" more reasonable, but uses the word "appears." He knows that one can be deceived even after employing this process, and that is why he insists that a verification process is imperative.

The discernment is not complete until we bring the decision to prayer and maintain that prayer to see whether, in the presence of God over time, we are consoled or in desolation. The consolation would assure us that the energies of the decision resonate with the creativity of the Father. If we make decisions in the context of a retreat, we see if confirmation is given by God by the way the retreat goes after the decision has been brought to prayer.

If we do not have the time or the opportunity to bring our major decisions to a retreat setting or even to an extended period of prayer, it is important to allow our community of believers to check out the decision. Such a community would not necessarily mean a group of our friends or allies, for they would share a common bias. Nor would it be an authority figure, because we have been socialized to view authority as the giver of truth rather than truth as the giver of authority. No: we desire to situate the discernment in a community of truth seekers whose lives actively witness to their beliefs.

When we walk into mystery, we are not left alone. We discover people who also walk through mystery. It is to those people we inquire about our decisions. They have a lived intimacy with God, they have experienced the ways of the world without being trapped by those ways, and they offer each other that openness through which God enters into the world as companions on the journey.

As we walk into mystery, we open ourselves to that community. This community extends through time and space, cultures and traditions. We are all interconnected, and the decisions we make, big or small, bring us into a closer relationship or separate us from that sense of belonging that is the mission of the Christ.

The decisions we make either accord with love or they do not. Loving people make loving decisions and make love more manifest in the world. People who do not love create chaos and division. Their false sense of order destroys community, while every good decision builds up community.

A Second Way

Ignatius offers a second way of making a discernment when we experience an impasse. He starts with a basic insight: love does not act against itself. Our love for a thing is either in concord with our love for the Creator and the Creator's love for us, or it is not. What we seek to do is to be an expression of spiritual intimacy. This intimacy determines the level of attachment we have to the matter under consideration. We desire to act solely out of our love for God. What we are discerning to do is simply a gesture to show that love. We are grateful to be able to make such a gesture, for we know God does not need us. Rather, God wants us and desires us.

We ask, "Does this gesture build up or destroy the community of love that God calls us to?" Ignatius suggests that when we experience ourselves as loving, but do not know what to do, we should imagine ourselves advising someone else whom we love and would like to see reaching the fullness of life, and then follow the advice we give to that person ourselves. There can be practical variations on this technique. We can ask someone we trust, someone who truly cares for us and who is not caught up in our situation, to suggest what to do. A community can help an individual make the same discernment.

Behind all three directives is a common stance of the lover communicating with the beloved. Ignatius expects that, when we have to make a decision, we are not only in love with God and with our neighbour, but we are also in love with ourselves. We are actually moving away from narcissism to a greater involvement in creation-as-community, and we see ourselves as a work in progress. Too often we can be trapped by notions of our personal inadequacy, and so we do not see and love ourselves as God sees and loves us. We find it difficult to believe that we are lovable and can love. We need others to affirm this in us, and we need a growing sense of our best selves to bring our habitual selves to this freedom.

The technique we have just explored gives us a possible answer regarding what to do. The second technique Ignatius suggests in this sequence gives us a way of proceeding to find such an answer. Once again he asks us to engage in an imaginative composition. We are on our deathbed. We have nothing left to lose, and after death we desire to be caught up fully in the love of God. Here Ignatius does not ask what we wished we had done, but asks rather what would have been the best method to make the present decision. The focus here is on how we could have made a good choice. Sometimes we can make choices by deliberately ignoring key sources of input, or we can go about things the wrong way to get the ends we desire. Our deathbed gives us some imaginative freedom from such disorders. It makes us indifferent. This is very much like the medieval contemplations on death, the *memento mori*, which confront us squarely with the reality of the transitory nature of all creatures and the reality of our death. Death puts our life in perspective, for, as the psalmist tells us, the Lord

knows how we are formed,
he remembers that we are dust.
As for us, our days are like grass,
we flourish like a flower of the field;
the wind blows over it and it is gone,
and its place remembers it no more. (Psalm 103:14-16)

The lived awareness of this existential reality can take much nonsense from our lives. It frees us to ask the questions of how best to use our lives, and what is the best way to discover how to do this.

We may discover our helplessness after reaching such an awareness, and then we might turn more desperately to God to find an answer to our questions. The austere awareness of our radical poverty and our radical dependence on the compassionate mercy of God moves us, like a beggar, to seek help wherever it may be found. Such humility promotes indifference and brings us into contact with a God who always offers us a path to life. God would not deny us that path if we are open to seeing it. In this state of openness, we expect that such a path will be given. That gift is for our use. In using it we discover what to do.

The third imaginative exercise Ignatius offers is to imagine ourselves not in life or on our deathbed, but in the third stage of our human journey. Now we are dead, and in the presence of the God who judges us lovable and capable of loving. This is the God who has loved us even when we sinned, and who so loves us that, even when we were sinners, God missioned his Son, the Christ, to come and defeat the forces of evil turning us away from Love. That Son comes to show us our true identity as the Beloved of the Father. After death we find ourselves consciously in the presence of that Love still loving us. This Love is not a passive thing but a dynamic activity reaching into the very depths of our being, allowing every aspect of our created self to encounter what will bring it to the fullness of life. We are asked to imagine the realized eschatology of our lives, which is already present even now, though we are not aware of it with our present burdened consciousness.

While the previous method presented us with the limitations of our not yet realized identity, this position takes the opposite stance. But it, too, asks, "In that state of acknowledged intimacy, what decision would we make about the present matter? How would our 'Yes' to love incarnate itself in our present condition?" The decision we make in this state of grace we should carry out in our present life so that when we do die, our orientation towards love will be satisfied.

All three steps—viewing the decision from the perspective of life, death, and after death—move us towards an ever closer encounter with the Father. The beginning, the middle and the end of our discernment process should yield the same result and point in the same direction. There should be no dissonance between the results we have arrived at.

As in the first method of discerning, using the four columns, the results of this second method also need to be brought into prayer using consolations and desolations to gain light and understanding of what we are to do. We bring the results to prayer and see if, over a period of time, we find ourselves in consolation or desolation about our decision. The period of time is crucial, because the spirit of deception, unlike the spirit of truth, cannot maintain a state of consolation in a person. Our plan encounters in this continual prayer the desire God has for us. This meeting creates either a resonance or a dissonance in us. We are shown in this way whether we are cooperating with God or not. So, praying over the decision for a time gives us some assurance of how it sits with God and the fullness of life that is our destiny.

Opening up to Life

Not only do those big decisions define our path—so also do those small, everyday choices we make almost unconsciously. Our habitual actions become normal to us and we often confuse normal with natural, defining natural as the way things are, as real. But God's encounter with us in our daily lives challenges this view of reality. We are unfinished business and still being created. We will continue to be created until the fullness of life is reached when God is all in all. Until then, we are on a spiritual journey, walking into Mystery. The awareness of the presence of that Mystery in our daily lives brings with it a sense of wonder and awe. We become contemplatives. Everything fascinates us. Like children we become vulnerable to the world as we explore it. We find in it an encounter with the divine that touches the depths of our being, and we discover the pain and destructiveness of all that corrupts God's ongoing creativity. We find both this glory and this horror within ourselves, within our families and communities, within our societies, within our cultures, within the world, and even within the immense dimensions of creation, the multi-universes of which we are a part. All of this is present in our daily life, and so, as we walk ever deeper into that Mystery, our discernments include the choices we make every day.

It helps to take some time daily to acknowledge this mystery so as to bring to consciousness what is blessed and to acknowledge what is not. We can also ask that Mystery which of our habitual actions do not bring us closer to God or make us more celebratory of our lives. We might think we already know the answer, but often how we see our lives and how God sees our lives are quite different. We might want to break a bad habit out of our sense of perfectionism or because of cultural conditioning, but God would rather we focused on correcting something different. It is very helpful to ask God what in our daily lives we can adjust, and how to do it, and then see if it works. God might desire us to be kinder to ourselves, or to discover the moments of gratitude in our day we overlook because we focus on what is to be done rather than on what has been done. Becoming aware of these things and accepting them slowly changes the way we see ourselves and the world and the presence of God in our world. Then we discover the ongoing work of the Incarnation in, through and around us. We discover the world is not as we had imagined it, and we not as we had imagined ourselves. Such daily work changes us as much as the major decisions we make change us. Both carry us into the realm of mystery and closer to God. When we do this work, we enter the process of redeeming the time.

Part IV

Redeeming the Time

Introduction

As we journey into mystery, we discover we are constantly entering into one story and leaving another. We live our lives in stories. They shape our lives, our responses to life, our expectations about life, and even our look back on our lives. Conversion changes the stories of our lives. As we lean into the darkness of the mystery surrounding us and try to discern how to walk through that darkness, or how to wait in it, we find ourselves re-evaluating those stories. These stories come from our personal experience, from our family circumstances, from the society we find ourselves in, and from the cultural senses of time and place establishing our identity. But the stories we live out of also come from the way God sees and knows and loves us. Sometimes the stories we live out of are supported and reinforced by the story that is God's story for us. At other times those two stories conflict. As we journey into mystery, this conflict becomes more apparent, and we find ourselves caught up in a life-or-death struggle to embrace the path to the fullness of life we are offered daily. Then we are asked to abandon the limiting stories we have lived by and to enter more fully the story that God creates for and with us.

Past, Present and Future

Nowhere is that tension most clearly available to us than when we consider our past, our present and our future. These are not three separate aspects of our life in time: our past shapes our present and our future; our present shapes our past and our future; and our future shapes our present and our past. Each shapes the way we read the others. All together they give us some awareness of how we understand ourselves and how we value what we are given. But my self-understanding is not me. I am more than how I see and understand myself. I am more than a construction of time. I am a construction of God. But as a construction of God in time, I am still being created, and so still subject to forces, both benign and malignant, affecting my life.

It is our Christian belief that all of time—itself a creation—is held in God's care, and that creation finds its fulfillment only in relationship to the Creator who loves it into being. Each of us is held in time, but each of us is also held in the timelessness of God's love. Our journey into mystery is often one we do not pay overt attention to, caught as we are in our daily living. But that does not mean Mystery is equally indifferent to us. The Desire who loves us and invites us to the fullness of life is always attentive to us. We, in turn, can become attentive to God, as a lover is attentive to the beloved, when we start noticing how our stories of our past, our present and our future are in constant dialogue with God. Such awareness brings us to the intersection between time and eternity where, with a sense of wonder, humility and gratitude, we perceive how we are being loved into being.

The presence of God is always around us, not as one thing among others, but as the very ground of our being. Like a fish in water, we take that grounding for granted. We become aware of our radical dependence on God only in times of crisis and vulnerability, when we experience our fragility as creatures. At those times, the stories we live by are tested by our suffering or our joy. Then we discover the limits of the stories we hold as beliefs.

When we pray, we place ourselves in that same ultimate context in a self-conscious manner. We allow ourselves to be held by God as God is for us and not how we want God to be. When this happens, we find what is good in us is affirmed, and what opposes the path to life is challenged and deconstructed. The Love who loves us has created us as lovable, capable of loving and of being loved. That Love desires for us the fullness of life and unceasingly works to bring us closer to our identity as the beloved of God. To pray is to spend time in that presence as beloved to lover. In the presence of such love, all that is less than love—untruth, shame and all that does not celebrate life—is transformed. Then we can look and allow ourselves to be looked at in a gaze that affirms our life.

Often when we pray we are conscious only of ourselves, our needs, our anxieties and our concerns. They fill our consciousness, and we see life only through that perspective. We might have an overview of ourselves as a victim, or of not belonging. We might see life as a constant struggle for justice or freedom. We might even be possessed by a sense of emptiness, holding life has no meaning or purpose. Out of these senses we build up a limiting image of ourselves, an idea of who God is and how God operates in the world, and even how the world is run. The oppression we find ourselves constructed by alienates us from life, and we become ashamed of who we are, wanting to be different from how we understand ourselves and find ourselves in the world.

Moments of Incarnation

The encounter with God allows a moment of Incarnation to happen. God enters into our felt narratives, however they are constructed, to change those life-denying aspects and to affirm those that bring us closer to our true nature. These narratives might seem to be intellectual concepts, but in fact they are rooted more basically in our lived and felt experience. Often our learned theologies and catechisms present us with an image of God to which we give intellectual assent, but our felt experience of God—and the one we operate out of spontaneously—does not coincide with that image. So, when we are at prayer, our image of God changes. The encounter is personal and mysterious, and does not subscribe to any ideologies. Indeed, when the energies of God enter any damaged situation, they restore the situation to a right relationship with God and allow it to be open to mystery, rather than leaving it trapped in circumscribed formulas. What is true of that situation is also true of us. In prayer we allow ourselves to be touched and opened by God, at times beyond even the boundaries of our imagination.

In prayer, however it is constructed, there is an encounter of two desires. Our desire for God meets God's desire for us. Our desire for God may be thwarted by other desires, and so the meeting in prayer is shaped not only by how open we are at that time, but also by how God desires to treat our qualified response to his loving. We open to a God who desires for us the fullness of life. God does not seek to destroy us, and so we can learn to trust ourselves in his presence, and allow ourselves to be looked at by him in a loving and shameless manner. Often we feel, "If God really knew me the way I know myself, God would not love me." This is quite common, and quite wrong. God does really know us, and in fact God knows us better than we know ourselves. Prayer allows us to know ourselves the way God knows us. As we discover this, we discover our feelings towards God changing. We open ourselves to wonder and awe, gratitude and humility. We discover we are loved even when we sin. We discover a God who desires to heal our hurts, celebrate our joys, and cover us with a transforming love. Only by resting in this love do we find the affirmation of our life allowing us to look at the dark sides of our human existence and to offer them up for transformation.

Part of the spiritual journey is first to discover we are loved. This love allows us to bring to light those aspects of our life that are trapped by shame and disorder and do not yet celebrate the gift of spiritual intimacy. Being accepted and loved burns the shame out of our lives. Being accepted and loved establishes our self-esteem, liberates our creativity and diffuses our anxiety of living.

When we sit in the presence of God's love we allow God to transform us. We read our past differently, we live our present more gracefully and we accept the gift of our future as an opening to the fullness of life. All we have to do is to sit in that love. Nothing more. If we stay with that, we are transformed.

As an exercise, we can sit in the presence of God's love. We can imagine ourselves as in a warm bath surrounded by that love. Or we can breathe in that love and breathe out that love. In our breathing in and out, we allow that love to enter every fibre of our being, healing, comforting and celebrating our life.

Our Redeemed Past

In the first book written in English by a woman, Julian of Norwich, the 14th-century mystic, talks of her experience with God.

> He showed me a little thing, the quantity of a hazelnut, lying in the palm of my hand, and to my understanding it was round as any ball. I looked upon it and thought: What may this be? And I was answered generally this way: It is all that is made. I marveled how it might last, for I thought it might fall into nothing because of its littleness. And I was answered in my understanding: It lasts and always shall, for God loves it; and so all things have being through the love of God.[36]

All creation is held in God's love. Julian describes that experience of love: "He is our clothing. In his love he wraps and holds us. He enfolds us for love and will never let us go."[37]

All of us, and every aspect of each of us, both in time and space, are held in God's love. What is good and what is bad are equally held in God's love. Our past, what is good in it and what is bad in it, is held in that love. We can acknowledge the gift of that love when we reflect on our past.

First, we can become aware that creation is intended as a gift from God to us, and, as such, time is a gift. We can think of the patience of God as time. The parable of the wheat and the tares (Matthew 13:24-30) and the whole question of forgiving our neighbours seventy-seven times seven (Matthew 18:22) gives us a clue about how God treats us in time. God uses time to allow us to discover we are loved.

This is so unlike the agents of destruction who manipulate time for their own ends. They want to end life because they do not want life. There are wars and forms of violence fostering apocalypses now. Fundamentalisms encourage such a perspective. What is not in keeping with certain points of view must be destroyed so the pure may exist uncorrupted. This is not God's way. God invites us to be patient with ourselves and others the way God is patient with us. If we look at Matthew's genealogy of Jesus, we discover God making use of a prostitute, an adulterer and a con artist, among others, to bring God's living word into the world. We notice that God chooses a people who are unfaithful and devious and corrupt to be his own. If we look closely at our own lives, we notice as well that he has chosen us and cares for us, even when we are destructive and self-deluded.

God is patient with us and for us. He loves us and hopes for the best. Sitting in prayer offers us a chance to be patient with ourselves and others the way God is patient with us.

We are invited to be patient with our past. What it fully means is not revealed as yet, and we are still being created. Our interpretation of the past is limited, and sometimes only years later do we discover how aspects of that somewhat distant time fit into our spiritual path.

When we look at our past, we discover what has been good for us and has affirmed our sense of life and joy, and discover moments that were quite the opposite. It is helpful to remember first of all what we have discovered to be good in our past. Those moments fill us with gratitude and with a sense of purpose and life and belonging. Often we do not remember those moments. We take them for granted. We all suffer from a perfectionism that makes us remember only the bad. We see only out of our hurts, and this shapes how we live our lives, either focusing on or reacting against the negativity we endure. We forget a simple thing: we are here because of the good in our life. That good has brought us to life, kept us alive, and shared life with us often in simple, quiet, daily ways that do not demand to be noticed. Among them are the air we breathe, the food we eat, the water we drink, the health we still have, the network of friends, family, acquaintances and colleagues who acknowledge us and weave us into a social fabric that supports our identity. These are among the many things we unthinkingly take for granted. They make up our lives, and we notice them only when they are troubled or not functioning as they should. It is useful occasionally to take some time to jot these down, just so we can become aware of them. We can then be alert to just how much of our lives is out of our control and how we are not destroyed by our radical interdependence on others, both in the natural and social world.

When we take things for granted, we do not feel grateful for them, so in this exercise of gratitude it is important to start off with what we actually feel grateful for, and to stay with that sense of gratitude and let it reveal to us the things that have so touched our lives and shaped them. As we sit in the presence of God, we ask God to show us these aspects of our redeemed past. As they arise, we discover a sense of rootedness, a sense of interconnectedness, of security, belonging, focus, joy, self-worth. It is important to stay with what is given, and to relish what is given. We let it show us how it has made our life good. We discover that, as one moment reveals itself, it recalls to mind other such graced moments. As we open these gifts, we discover we are opened by them. It is the nature of gift to create, and re-create, us because such gifts affirm us as we are in the eyes of God. We get some sense of how we are loved and cherished, not in some abstract theological formula, but in a real, intimate and uniquely personal manner.

When we pay attention to our past in this manner, we open ourselves to receive what has actually and already been given. We need to accept it as it is, rather than relying on our version of it as seen through the distortions of our hurts. Those hurts tend to eliminate the memory of all the good things that have happened to us. Our prayer here, of resting in the good of our past, works to deconstruct the biases we spontaneously operate out of. When we accept the good in our past, we find we can be more hopeful and less anxious about our lives. The awareness of those good things in our past allows us to be more creative and communal in what we do, and so we can celebrate the path we walk upon. In opening us, the gift allows us to participate more self-consciously in the ongoing work of creation and redemption.

What changes is not the past, but our limited awareness of the past and our biased interpretations of the past we remember. Our histories are not our past, but merely interpretations of that past. As Jesus does with the disciples on the road to Emmaus, our own encounter with the compassionate and redemptive mercy of God will give us another reading of our past. That encounter allows us to see what is present to us in a new way. When we sit with the gratitude that arises from acknowledging our redeemed past, we find we are led on a journey of redeeming the time.

We step into mystery as we step into the past. At first, that journey carries us to the places of overt consolation and affirmation, but as we journey on, we come to those places and moments we did not experience as gratitude when they were happening. At that time they did not seem like a gift. In fact, it seemed then as if our life had come to an end, and we could find no way forward.

I remember such a time when, against my parents' wishes, I entered religious life. After six months I was expelled from the novitiate. I thought my life had come to an end. I had given up a full scholarship with the promise of a job to follow my studies. It happened one day when the novices were playing soccer with the novice master. One novice missed the ball and kicked another by mistake. He said that famous four-letter word and the novice master expelled him on the spot. Being naïve, I met with the master of novices and reminded him that people were not only saying this word all over the place, but in 1966, at the height of the hippie revolution, in Western Europe, were also doing it all over the place. Thereupon he expelled me, too. I was put on an early train the very next day.

It was an extremely difficult time for me; only years later did I realize the gift I had been given. I suspect that if I had stayed, I would never have been free to be singularly committed to God. The Society of Jesus would have been an idol for me. That freedom allowed me to re-enter the Jesuits and to remain a Jesuit in good times and in hard times, because I had the lived knowledge that God was looking after me and would not let me be destroyed, even when I was willing to destroy myself. As a Jesuit, I do not see the

Society of Jesus as God, but rather as an imperfect though graced instrument of God, and I cherish it as such. No more, no less. Being expelled allowed me to become a good Jesuit rather than an institutionalized one. Being expelled gave me the freedom to be passionate for the God who desires every part of all of us in an exclusive way.

The knowledge that everything can be taken away and we can emerge freer and more joyful than before—even though it takes a long time—is very liberating. It reveals a God who takes care of us, who can enter the death of our selves and bring us to a new life. It also reveals a God who does not let anything hinder the embrace of the lover with the beloved, no matter how good it is.

I imagine we all have experienced such moments when they reached a dead end and then were liberated in ways beyond their control. Looking back, we can ask ourselves these questions: What was taken away that I mistakenly believed I needed? What was given to me that I now realize was more valuable? How did this come about? What have I learned from those moments of my history?

One thing we learn from hard experiences is we are not in control. None of us consciously sets out to destroy the life we work to maintain; when that life is destroyed, we find ourselves helpless and without a narrative to make sense of what is going on at the moment. We have fallen through the cracks of the conventional world we have made our home, and now we find ourselves homeless and lost. It is at such times we experience the "abject nakedness"—to use William Faulkner's phrase in *As I Lay Dying*—of our humanity.[38] Shakespeare's King Lear himself experiences this radical displacement. He comes to understand that "The thing itself:/ unaccommodated man is no more but such a poor bare, forked animal ...."[39]

From this radical poverty, in time we realize the empty promises of the world, and stop trusting them. But we also come to realize that, unlike the characters in those two tragedies, we are not abandoned to an indifferent creation and a soul-denying life. We are not destroyed but carried in time to places of healing and transformation. We see we have been saved in spite of ourselves and by a love with the power and the desire to do this. We discover we are loved even when the forces of death surround us with malignant intent. We discover even though we walk through the valley of the shadow of death, we need not fear its evil. We discover we are held in a love stronger than death. Remembering such death-into-new-life experiences not only confirms for us our relationship with God, but also assures us what has happened in the past continues into the present and for the future. We are not saved to be destroyed. As the prophet Jeremiah pronounces, "I know the plans that I have for you, declares the Lord. They are plans for peace and not disaster, plans to give you a future filled with hope" (Jeremiah 29:11).

Covenant Moments

Each of us has had such covenant moments when God has shown himself in our personal history and has done the impossible. We need to remember those covenant moments of call, crisis and salvation. They counteract the always oppressive claims of doubt when the uncertainty about the future raises a question: Why should the future be like the past?

But our assurance is not with the future. It is with the knowledge we are loved and cared for by a God who desires only our well-being.

These covenant moments are our personal Passovers and Easters. Passover is a defining moment in the identity of the people of God in the Old Testament. The transformation from slavery—where a people's identity is constructed by an oppressive secular power—to a sense of self constructed by God and manifest in the giving of the Law occurs in the Exodus story. That Passover story can be read on several levels: personal, social and cultural. Dante, in his letter to Cangrande della Scala, gives us four levels of reading: The Literal, The Allegorical, The Moral, and The Anagogical.[40] The literal represents the most obvious reading. It states what actually happened. The allegorical tends to understand the literal set of actions as being symbolic of certain other principles. The moral draws ethical principles from the literal action. The anagogical applies those principles to the final state of the believer. At the literal level, in the Passover, a people passes from slavery over the Red Sea. On the allegorical level, Passover symbolizes our redemption in Christ, while the moral level views Passover as depicting the conversion from sin to salvation. The anagogical level is concerned with an eschatalogical state, and reads Passover as our final entry into the bliss of the New Jerusalem at the end of time. Our covenant moments can be read on these four levels also. Something good has happened to us. It shows us God's love for us by freeing us from a closed myth, and symbolizes a moment in the fullness of life he offers to us and to all.

Each of our covenant moments has given us an experience of life as God desires it. That experience not only grounds and re-translates all of our other experiences but places them in a belief system established by our "passovers." Moreover, covenant moments verify other such moments in that same belief. Covenant moments coalesce and flesh out the sense of God's relationship with us as one of creation, redemption and celebration. When we experience rising from death to new life, we can see the power of God in this world.

Such covenant moments are celebrated liturgically. In the Jewish calendar there is Passover; in the Christian dispensation there is Easter. When we pray our covenant moments, we first recall them and then enter them so the gift they are for us can enter more deeply into our lives. This is especially important at moments of crisis or at times of greater vulnerability in our lives when we need to be aware that we are rooted in God's love.

Remembering is a covenant moment in itself. It re-enacts the passage of the event with the convictions gained at the end of the event. Here we see the past from the point of view of the present. With that perspective, we can now see the presence of God in those times when we did not experience that presence. We get a different sense of how God is present.

There are times we neither feel nor understand his presence. At those moments we have reached the limits of our knowing and we go beyond them. Then the terrors of a fallen creation overwhelm us. We find ourselves in a space and a time alien to our familiar notions and habits. Our constructed world is taken away and we are bereft. All our fears, anxieties and demons, both personal and collective, rise to the surface of our awareness and run rampant through our lives, creating havoc and despair. We are powerless against them and they have their way. We experience a sickness even unto death, as Kierkegaard names it.[41] It takes a long time to acknowledge and accept this very real aspect of the human condition. In the Book of Exodus, the Israelites wandered in the desert for 40 years until they could be sufficiently freed from the destructive forces they carried within themselves and enter the Promised Land. Psalms 78 and 106 give voice to that history.

But amazingly, the Israelite people were not destroyed. Equally amazing is that, in our own covenant story, we are not destroyed. Transformed, yes; bearing the scars of our wounds, yes; but so it is also for the risen Christ after his crucifixion. We bring to our new life the memory of having survived—and not by our own will or doing. Like the disciples on the road to Emmaus, our new life allows us to reread the incidents of our past life in a different light. We see darkness as another way through which God brings us into a deeper intimacy with him.

Remembering a covenant moment is itself a covenant moment. A covenant establishes, deepens and renews a relationship between God and us, where we experience the compassionate mercy of the One who desires us and who offers to bring us to the fullness of life. We can live our days forgetful of God. Busyness takes over, or we become complacent and distracted. Forgetfulness fosters a lack of gratitude, and limits our appreciation and celebration of life. We fall into uncreative patterns of behaviour because the fear of risk, change and possible loss traps us. But when we remember God, our day becomes restructured, and a different set of values comes into play. We focus on and become intentionally conscious of our spiritual relationship, and this opens us up to behaving in more loving and compassionate ways.

As the first experience of covenant shows, I am a product of God's personal intervention in history and in my own history. The second experience of covenant, remembering the covenant, allows that intervention to continue, since I operate not out of my own will and self-protection, but out of a sense of that relationship.

We realize in doing this that covenant is not a moment fixed in time, but a dynamic that occurs in and through time. To be sure, we have covenant moments, but just as significantly we have covenanted lives. Covenant roots and orients our life. If acknowledged, it permeates our conscious living. This is a further level of the gift of our redeemed covenant history. We have accepted the gift, opened it and are using it.

In living our covenanted history, and in bringing that past into the present, we become living witnesses of redeemed history. Our very presence allows the outpouring of God's love in our lives to pass through us and thus to touch the world we live in. We give life to others by living our own redeemed life. In this way we share the gift that has been given to us and that has become us. This sharing, unrestricted by gender, colour, creed, tradition, age or nation, celebrates the life offered to all. It is a manifestation of the kingdom of God among us. It brings us to know we are among the company of saints, through time and space, who celebrate their spiritual intimacy with God by sharing what has been given to them freely and creatively. In their union with each other in God, they build up the Body of Christ by labouring with that same Christ in transforming creation into right relationship with the Father. Our work in praying our redeemed history is part of that ongoing transformation.

You may remember that the Eucharist is a form of remembering. It is called anamnesis. The Eucharist remembers the Passover in the Christian tradition by celebrating through the Paschal meal the life, death and resurrection of Jesus the Messiah. Jesus celebrates that transformation in the Last Supper where he says, "Do this in memory of me." In the Divine Liturgy of Saint John Chrysostom, the anamnesis begins with these words:

> Remembering, therefore, this command of the Saviour [i.e., to eat and drink in remembrance of him] and all that came to pass for our sake, the cross, the tomb, the resurrection on the third day, the ascension into heaven, the enthronement at the right hand of the Father and the second, glorious coming ....[42]

Christ's symbolic act in transforming the bread and wine into his body and blood picks up the significance of the Passover and opens it into an eschatalogical state where all will be restored within the compassionate mercy of the Father. When we pray our covenant moments, we participate in that divine transformation. The personal redemption we have experienced is one of the effects of the saving power of the Compassionate Mercy who desires all come to the fullness of life.

Praying our redeemed history aligns us to the powers of good existing through time and space. We join the presence of the company of the blessed. We discover even more we are loved and are capable of loving in such a way that the community creation is meant to be is established, affirmed and celebrated. Praying our covenant moments lets our awareness sink to the roots of our being where we and creation are one and are held in God's love. Like breathing in, we sink to the depths; breathing out, we offer to the world the gift of that goodness who has loved us into being.

Unredeemed History

Praying our past, we discover there moments where we have not experienced redemption. We find those moments have taken life away from us, diminished our self-esteem and trapped us in forms of alienation. We are unable to grasp how they fit into the story God is telling to the world with our lives.

Here it is helpful to consider three stories. First is the story of Joseph, which concludes the book of Genesis (chapters 37 to 50); then there is the story in Luke's gospel of the disciples meeting Jesus on the road to Emmaus (Luke 24:13-35); and finally there are the two genealogies of Jesus in the gospel (Matthew 1:1-17 and Luke 3:23-38).

In the Joseph story we have a narrative of ups and downs. Joseph is the spoiled youngest son of his father. According to Old Testament law, youngest sons had no or few rights. (Yet the Bible is filled with younger sons who usurped the claims of the older, or whom God chose over older sons, starting with Abel, son of Adam and Eve, and also Jacob (over Esau), David (over his many older brothers), and in this story Joseph, who is his father's favourite. The desire of God here runs counter to the cultural traditions of the times. The pattern is biblical. What is despised by the world is chosen by God to transform that world. God favours the *anawim*—the little ones; the pattern continues in the New Testament when Jesus, the cornerstone rejected, becomes the basis for redemption for all, as Joseph had done for Israel. In this, Joseph, like Jesus, fulfills the insight of the Psalmist: "The stone that the builders rejected has become the chief cornerstone. This was the Lord's doing; it is marvelous in our eyes" (Psalm 118:22-23).

This insight is important for living with our unredeemed history. All that is unredeemed in our eyes becomes, in God's plan, the means of a closer intimacy with the Father. This path towards that intimacy runs precisely through the pain of what is rejected, either by us or by the world we live in. This does not happen overnight. It takes time, that gift of God given to us, for our help and salvation.

In the Joseph story, we see this growth to intimacy and conversion through a series of misfortunes and reversals. Joseph, the favoured son, missioned by the Father, is captured and sold into slavery to the Egyptians. He loses his favoured status but works his way up to becoming an overseer of his master. He loses this privileged position when he is falsely charged with trying to rape his master's wife. Joseph is thrown into prison, where he prophetically interprets the dreams of two fellow prisoners. After several years, the Pharaoh himself has a dream he does not understand. News of Joseph's gift reaches the Pharaoh, and Joseph translates the dream. Pharaoh appoints him to implement the dream, which saves Egypt from a famine. Once again, Joseph rises to the top and becomes installed in the royal court. From there he rescues his family and his Israelite nation from famine. The book of Genesis ends with the Israelites going to Egypt under Joseph's protection. Ironically, their salvation brings them into slavery. The next book in the Bible, Exodus, discusses their subsequent captivity, their release in the Passover and their receiving the Law that establishes their covenant relationship with God. In that ongoing story, we find a similar pattern with both Moses and the Israelites. They are favoured, then fall from grace, and then are favoured again.

Joseph's journey through time, that of like Moses and the Israelite people, is a pattern of consolation leading to desolation leading to consolation and then back again. Our own path through time is similar. We enter into larger and larger patterns of integration, and those larger patterns are established by the deconstructions of the earlier patterns. Our own reading of our unredeemed history falls into that pattern. Good comes out of bad, even though our limited imaginations cannot conceive how this can possibly happen. But it is the nature of God to be stronger than evil, and more creative and compassionate. It is God's desire that everyone and everything be saved, and that this happen in and through time. The Incarnation, resurrection and Pentecost are not otherworldly events. They do not occur outside of time. Indeed, in all three, God enters time in a new way and transforms the meaning of time. It is in time and through time we encounter God. In our dark moments we do not experience God, but God is there.

Martin Buber recounts a very odd story in *Tales of the Hasidim*. In the midst of the persecution of his people, a holy one prays to find out why evil exists. One night he has a dream in which his master appears to him. The rabbi cries out, "Why are you silent in such dreadful need?" He is answered, "In Heaven we see that all that seems evil to you is a work of mercy."[43] This is a very hard saying to understand. How do we explain violence and brutality, the abuse of innocents, malice and arrogant power, stupidity and selfishness? How do we reconcile these with the Compassionate Mercy that is God? How do we deal with the silence of God in these situations?

As creatures, we always encounter the question of evil. In the Scriptures, the book of Job provides one answer: we see from a limited perspective, and so are not privileged to have the stance to see the absolute context in which everything is placed. That stance is God's alone. The gospel of Matthew gives us a refinement on this position. In that parable of the wheat and the tares (13:23-30), a farmer plants his field with wheat. Someone sows tares (weeds) in the same field. Both are members of the grass family, and look similar shortly after germination. But as soon as wheat begins to form grains, the difference becomes obvious. The tares take valuable nutrients away from wheat and are vulnerable to parasites, which can destroy the whole crop. It would seem correct to pull out the tares before they do more damage. But the owner of the field forbids this. He waits until harvest time to separate them.

The issue here is one of discernment. First, how do we know what is evil and what is good? Sometimes the two cannot be distinguished. Evil may look like good; and good can look like evil. Also, what seems evil to some in one cultural context may be good to others operating out of a different context. For instance, who defines who is a terrorist and who is a freedom fighter? Second, as we have seen from our covenant moments, the gift of time allows what seemed to us to be evil to be converted into good. A greater good comes out of the destruction of something cherished. At the Easter Vigil, we hear these words sung in the "Exultet":

> *O happy fault,*
> *O necessary sin of Adam,*
> *which gained for us so great a Redeemer!*

According to the Christian dispensation, Christ entered the world as Saviour because of the primal sin of Adam and Eve, and Christ makes us into his body of the resurrected humanity. Third, since only God is absolute, evil is not absolute and is ultimately under the power of God. The issue then is not why there is evil, but how to live with it. What are we to do when we are infected and surrounded by the forces of destruction? These tend to destroy our faith, that intimate relationship of trust in God. This corruption raises an even more basic question: How do we live with our unredeemed history?

Christian eschatology tells us that our salvation is at the same time now and not yet. We are saved, but our salvation is not fully realized yet. Like the disciples on the road to Emmaus, we, too, journey with God, but we do not recognize that intimacy because we are trapped in our unredeemed histories. In Luke's account, the two disciples celebrated Passover in Jerusalem when Jesus was killed. They are returning home, downcast by the destruction of their messianic hopes, when they encounter a stranger. He translates their history for them, and with their new understanding of their past, they are able to recognize the one who travelled with them. It is the Christ. If we see redemption as a realized intimacy with God, then the promised kingdom is not some otherworldly timeless state but the ever more profound awareness of the presence of Christ in our midst. That presence and our awareness do not form an abstract perfection divorced from the struggles of life. It is the living awareness of the indissoluble bond between Christ and us that Paul talks about in his letter to the Romans:

> Who shall separate us from the love of Christ? Shall tribulation, or distress, or persecution, or famine, or nakedness, or peril, or sword? As it is written, For thy sake we are killed all the day long; we are accounted as sheep for the slaughter. Nay, in all these things we are more than conquerors through him that loved us. For I am persuaded, that neither death, nor life, nor angels, nor principalities, nor powers, nor things present, nor things to come, nor height, nor depth, nor any other creature, shall be able to separate us from the love of God, which is in Christ Jesus our Lord. (Romans 8:35-39)

But despite the assurances of Paul, and despite our own awareness of our covenant moments, there are aspects of our past we experience as unredeemed. These reveal themselves to us in our lack of gratitude for them. They have made us closed in on ourselves, fearful, cynical, suspicious, filled with shame and regret, and wishing these past moments were otherwise. Those aspects are not just individual but also familial, social and cultural. Every aspect of inhumanity degrades us personally, even if it happened to someone else at another time and in another part of the world. We find ourselves trapped or complicit in this degradation. We cannot help ourselves.

In this situation we have two choices. We can despair and allow the situation to eat away at the remains of our well-being, or we can, even though we might not believe its efficacy, develop the habit of handing it over to God and whatever dispositions God puts in our path for our growth in our spiritual well-being. These may include therapy, support groups, spiritual direction, social justice involvement, and changes in lifestyle and environment. We may not be able to do much ourselves—in fact, we may be able to do very little, and that little could be exhausted at the level of personal maintenance. Because of that unredeemed past, we might experience depression, when even the basics of living use up resources we do not have. We can end up only with a sense of abandonment to Divine Providence. Just that sense in itself is a prayer. It holds onto a relationship with God. We may have little or no sense of God's presence in our life at this time. We pray in desperation, like the father of the epileptic boy prays to Jesus, "Lord, I believe. Help my unbelief" (Mark 9:24).

The healing and transformation of memories comes through a process of mourning. Mourning is quite different from grieving. In mourning, we hold our dead up to the Father. In mourning, we acknowledge the presence of the dead in our lives, as well as the effect of the dead. The power of the dead draws life away from us, and so we must find ways to be separated from the dead. If we do not, we are overtaken by grief, and grief can kill. First, we recognize what we are feeling and admit it. After admitting to having these negative feelings, we start investigating where they come from and what stories they tell us. We allow ourselves to ask not only how truthful they are, but what we get from them, what price we pay for holding onto them. We investigate the power they have over us in shaping how we look at ourselves, others, God and the world. We try to find out what these stories conceal from us, and how they stop us from seeing or experiencing the good, which is also part of our heritage. Finally, we see we do not need to identify with our feelings. Our feelings are simply one limited way of knowing who we are. The dynamic range of our identity extends beyond the boundary feelings of consolation and desolation. Just as light goes beyond the colour spectrum, so, too, our identity as desire for God, and God's desire for us, goes beyond any felt sense of self. One of the deceptions of evil is it limits our self-awareness of our identity. We can become blind or hardened, and we end up living in a series of patterns restricting our well-being.

Our dead is whatever removes from us a sense of gratitude for life. These are usually disturbed relationships, diminishing our joy, creativity and appreciation of others. They cause us to turn in on ourselves. We cannot see in them the possibilities of change or conversion. They so freeze our understanding of creation that we hold God's creativity as finished and the forms of reality we perceive as the only way things could be. When we do this, we lose sight of the fact creation is ongoing, because God's creativity never ends and cannot be stopped. Things change, and our sense of things also changes. What we hold in our past as unredeemed is not fixed. When we hold those moments up to the Father, we dispose ourselves to allowing their power over us to be broken or transformed. The moments might not change, but our experience and our understanding of those moments can and do change. We might still bear the scars from those moments, just as Christ after his resurrection still bears the scars of the crucifixion. How the experience or the understanding of those moments change, or will change, is not for us to know, because our perspective is still trapped in our disorder. Like prisoners, our fantasies of freedom differ from the reality we will be given.

We may never discover why something has happened, but with liberation we discover how to use what we have endured for the good of others. Our suffering allows us to empathize with other people's suffering. Our unredeemed past, offered to God, can stop us from handing on the heritage of such violence to others. Inasmuch as we can find ways of dealing gracefully with that past, even though we cannot yet understand why it happened, we can share those insights with others who are similarly trapped and are caught deeper than we are. Those insights, because they are not sentimental wishful thinking or abstractions from some ideological stance unconnected to personal reality, are genuinely helpful. The ideologue would say, "'Love your enemies, do good to those who hate you'; that is what the scripture says." But for those who have suffered, one knows there is a huge difference between loving our enemies and thinking we have to like them. Loving our enemies does not require us to expose ourselves to their ongoing destructiveness. Loving our enemies does not mean allowing them to continue to do what they have done. Loving our enemies does not mean giving up those boundaries protecting us from such violence.

We are asked to love our neighbour as ourselves. We cannot love our neighbour if we do not love ourselves. Good spirituality is very practical. It is not theoretical, or abstract, or ideological. It emerges from lived experience. It is a science of interrelationship and as such cannot be systematized. Living with our unredeemed past does not mean we have to be retraumatized by exposing ourselves for ideological reasons to the states it creates. Even Christ, after his resurrection and before his ascension, does not appear to his enemies. But the gospels written in the spirit of the resurrected Christ offer us a way of dealing with our unredeemed histories.

We ask God to enter those histories, and we pray for the grace to see the presence of God in those histories, or at least feel the effects of that presence. We let God do the work of redemption. It may seem dreadfully pious to say we can offer our unredeemed histories over to Jesus who carries them to the Father. We can ask, very practically, how this can be done. We do so through prayer, in that living contact with Jesus, who is always disposed to the Father. We also do it through all the other means at our disposal to live a healthy life. These can include counselling, therapy, spiritual direction, group support and direction, art, and body work. Those means are manifestations of a creator God's concern for us. We know Christ on the cross brings the broken of the world to the Father when they ask. Think of the good thief crucified with him, and Jesus' promise that this man will be in paradise with him. We know that the Father, throughout history, transforms brokenness into forms of life and creativity. How we experience our brokenness, and how God intends to dispose of us and our brokenness, are two different things. In Isaiah, God speaks to the people who are trapped in servitude and who have lost a sense of their identity. God tells them,

"You are my servant,
Israel, in whom I will be glorified."
But I said, "I have laboured in vain,
I have spent my strength for nothing and vanity;
yet surely my cause is with the Lord,
and my reward with my God."
And now the Lord says,

who formed me in the womb to be his servant,
to bring Jacob back to him,
and that Israel might be gathered to him,
for I am honoured in the sight of the Lord,
and my God has become my strength—
he says,
"It is too light a thing that you should be my servant
to raise up the tribes of Jacob
and to restore the survivors of Israel;
I will give you as a light to the nations,
that my salvation may reach to the end of the earth."
(Isaiah 49:3-6)

We do not know when and how that transformation will take place, but we are invited to live in that hope and out of that imagined reality as best we can and from where we actually are. Jesus says in Mark's gospel, "Therefore I tell you, whatever you ask for in prayer, believe that you have received it, and it will be yours" (Mark 11:24). That actual living out beyond ourselves is walking in the darkness of the mystery ever drawing us to a fuller life. It calls us to risk because we cannot see the future we are invited to explore. From our present perspective, such a risk seems doomed to failure simply because we cannot see how it would work. If we do not risk, we live with a bad faith and in our unredeemed imaginations. Only when we seem to have nothing left to lose do we make that journey out of ourselves. This is what happened to the woman in the gospels who suffered from an unstoppable hemorrhage for twelve years.

> She had suffered a great deal under the care of many doctors and had spent all she had, yet instead of getting better she grew worse. When she heard about Jesus, she came up behind him in the crowd and touched his cloak, because she thought, "If I just touch his clothes, I will be healed." Immediately her bleeding stopped and she felt in her body that she was freed from her suffering. (Mark 5:26-9)

We try everything before we try God. The woman in the gospel story (as Luke 8:43 tells us) has spent all her money on physicians, but none have helped. She is driven by her need to do the unthinkable. Even though she is ritually unclean, she goes beyond her shame and appears in public, and even more shocking, she touches a man in that unclean state. This would make him unclean also. But Jesus does not rebuke her. Instead, he says her faith has brought her healing. Her desperate need brings her to risk. She does not know what the result will be. But we do. The story is told in a gospel aimed at unbelievers.

Our unredeemed histories tend to make unbelievers of us. We have been hurt by the world we live in and this closes us down. We do not understand why God could make such things happen. Our hurt creates a theology of unbelief and indifference. Against that abstraction we are invited to a living experience of encounter, where our real lives meet a real God. Praying our unredeemed history invites such an encounter. We do not have to journey through life with the violence done to ourselves in the way the world suggests. The world deals with our pain by saying suck it up, move on, get on with life. Grow up! That is the way the world operates. It is pragmatic and uncaring. Such a stance is toxic. After a while, the poisons we have sucked up and moved on with destroy our integrity, our sense of life and joy, and our trust in God or others. We become spiritually crippled, and only God can heal us of that infirmity. Our unredeemed history always and everywhere points out our need for God. We can go to God and pray for liberation, healing and acceptance. We are still being created, and our unredeemed history is part of the chaos over which the Spirit of God moves. It transforms that chaos into community—a place where we can be at home.

Our unredeemed history is part of our spiritual path. At times the trauma of that history can block our spiritual path and stop our journey ever deeper into love. We can become frozen or, worse, we can become destructive and turn away from God and from our deepest desire for the fullness of life. But we cannot tolerate the frustration of such unfulfilled desire, and so we seek to alleviate it in compulsive and destructive behaviours. When we dare to examine how the dynamics of our unredeemed history affect us, we discover the need to experience forgiveness, reconciliation and conversion.

We discover we cannot find these things on our own. We need others and we need God. But how can we get what we need? Neither God nor any other is here at our command. Their presence to us is a gift. We can only dispose ourselves to be open to receiving that gift. For that to happen, we also need to find out how to be so disposed to recognize the gift when it is presented to us. What we can do is first to become conscious that we are always in God's love. We then invite that love to enter more deeply into our lives. We can breathe in that love, and feel its spirit go to those places in our body it desires to cherish. We can breathe out our anxiety and the blocks that manifest themselves in our body. We can rest in this growing sense of ease and liberation. But we can also be more intentional, believing for ourselves what Jesus said to the leper.

> When Jesus came down from the mountain, great crowds followed, then a leper approached, did him homage, and said, "Lord, if you wish, you can make me clean." He stretched out his hand, touched him, and said, "I do want to. Be made clean." His leprosy was cleansed immediately. (Matthew 8:1-4)

The leper disposes himself to God and asks for a specific healing. It is granted. We can dispose ourselves to God and ask for that healing of our unredeemed history. We allow God to do the healing in his own time, and in his own way, and at his own pace. We can breathe in the love and feel it going to broken places of our life. We can breathe out the love with our breath and let it go to those people, places and situations that take away life from us. We can stay in that exercise and we can repeat it whenever we want. The daily exercise is rather like weeding a garden. It lets things grow. It opens our spiritual path.

Forgiveness

When we do this, we engage in the work of forgiveness. Forgiveness establishes right relationships among people and between disparate aspects of ourselves. In forgiveness we move to acceptance and transformation leading to integration and community. Sin, on the other hand, leads to fragmentation and to forms of conformity to a disordered aspect of our self or community. For example, the addict subsumes a whole life under a particular compulsion; a tyrant imposes an individual ideology onto a people and its communities. This is quite different from the Christian notion of community, in which there are different gifts but one Spirit. These gifts are the manifestations of the Spirit. They are there not for themselves but for a service of God in the world. Uniformity does not create community or intimacy. How we dispose ourselves is not to satisfy one particular drive, person or ideology, but to maintain the relationship of spiritual intimacy that God enjoys with us as community. Christ came into the world precisely to effect that intimacy. Forgiveness allows intimacy to be established and to flourish. When we say Christ came to forgive sins, we mean something quite concrete. We mean our unredeemed history is capable of being transformed. We also mean we are invited to cooperate with that process of conversion. Christ does say, "Whenever you forgive sins, they are forgiven. Whenever you don't forgive them, they are not forgiven" (John 20:23). We do this not only for others but for ourselves. In fact, it is impossible to forgive others, if we do not first have the experience of God forgiving us so we can then learn how to forgive ourselves. We need to learn to cooperate with God in these healings. The process of forgiveness is more than just saying "I forgive you" to others or to ourselves. Forgiveness is a creative existential act. It is performative. It does something.

There are several steps in the process. The first step is recognizing the areas that cry out for forgiveness. One of the difficulties in living in a violent world is becoming so habituated to violence, it becomes acceptable, normal, unnoticed. Then we pass along violence as a way of living and of being with others. We become blind to the destruction we cause ourselves and others. But we experience its effects in our daily sense of loneliness, alienation and suffering. To figure out what needs forgiveness, we can ask ourselves, "Where do I not celebrate life?"

It is one thing to ask that question and another thing to accept the answer. We can be so overwhelmed by what is given, we can despair. But as we travel ever deeper into the spiritual life, we become more sensitive to the immediate need of God's mercy in the world. We discover in real ways our radical poverty of spirit and our helplessness in the face of the destruction we find in ourselves, in our families and communities, and in our world. There is humility in accepting this state of affairs, in seeing how limited we are and how enormous the task of reconciliation is. We hardly know where to start. We start off where we are and with the little we have. We might be dreadfully limited in what we can do, but we do not have to despair and we do not have to do nothing. We can hand over to the Father the violence in which we are complicit. We can watch the news as a form of contemplative prayer. We can pray that the compassionate mercy of God enter into those places of destruction and transform them. We remind ourselves it is God's world and God alone can do something about the situations we observe. We do not have to despair or close ourselves down. We can give voice to what we hope for. We can become agents for change. We can discern what to do.

We can live beyond ourselves, in a hope that has nothing to do with optimism, or in a perseverance that refuses to see the present constructions of reality as a final solution. This perseverance—like the patient endurance all those years of Simeon and Anna outside the temple in the midst of foreign occupation, religious despotism, and the conflicts of different political factions—takes away much illusion about the nature of the world and about our own ability to change certain things. But because *we* cannot change them does not mean they cannot or will not be changed. We can live in the promise for change given by God and experienced in covenant moments. Simeon's and Anna's patient witness is rewarded, according to Luke's gospel. They see the infant Jesus when he is brought to the temple at the ritual purification of Mary, 40 days after his birth. Their desire for God has been similarly purified, and this allows them to see the presence of Christ in their midst when everyone else sees a poor family with a firstborn child. Waiting is witness.

Anna Akhmatova tells of waiting for her son Lev outside a Stalinist prison. She writes in the preface to her poem "Requiem":

In the terrible years of the Yezhov terror I spent 17 months waiting in line outside the prison in Leningrad. One day somebody in the crowd identified me. Standing behind was a young woman, with lips blue from the cold, who had of course never heard me called by name before. Now she started out of the torpor common to us all and asked me in a whisper (everyone whispered there), "Can you describe this?" And I said, "I can." Then something like a smile passed over what had once been her face.[44]

Her gifts shape her waiting, and this endurance has power for other people. How we wait in our unredeemed histories depends on the gifts we have. One of those gifts is memory. We can remember the good in our past life when we realize that we have been cherished by God. Memory also holds our unredeemed history and this memory can turn us to God and away from false images of God. Who is this God who allows such things to happen? It is a God who risks us in this world, as he risked his Son. That son walked through the destructiveness of this world, showing us the way through such deaths, back to the Father. Each of our lives is also a walk through death back to the Father. We cannot avoid death and its many dimensions we experience in this world. How we walk through the pain, malice and suffering attendant on our lives witnesses to others. Anna Akhmatova's gift was to write a poetry of witness to the Stalinist cruelties of the previous century. She lost a husband and then a son to those purges. In the dedication to "Requiem" she writes,

> *Mountains fall before this grief,*
> *A mighty river stops its flow,*
> *But prison doors stay firmly bolted*
> *Shutting off the convict burrows*
> *And an anguish close to death.*
> *Fresh winds softly blow for someone,*
> *Gentle sunsets warm them through; we don't know this,*
> *We are everywhere the same, listening*
> *To the scrape and turn of hateful keys*
> *And the heavy tread of marching soldiers.*
> *Waking early, as if for early mass,*
> *Walking through the capital run wild, gone to seed,*
> *We'd meet – the dead, lifeless; the sun,*
> *Lower every day.*[45]

We, too, are everywhere the same. We suffer, endure dreadful loss, find ourselves in a world that is brutal, violent and uncaring. As the Buddha's First Noble Truth points out, "Everyone suffers." In the face of that suffering, we can turn away from God. This is the risk God takes with us. He knows us better than we know ourselves, but he also knows we can frustrate the desire we are for the fullness of life by turning away from the path leading to that life, for it carries us into death and to a dying beyond our control. Yet how we live is how we die. In life we can be faithful to that Desire who calls us beyond ourselves. We learn to step into Mystery, constantly risking ourselves to the Father and to the constant dying of the selves we know. We endure the darkness in which we find ourselves, and seek to walk a path through that darkness. In that darkness, the Father finds us.

In the darkness of our unredeemed histories, the path lies through forgiveness. The beginning of forgiveness is to recognize evil for what it is. Akhmatova's poetry names what she is forced to endure, and she goes further. She admits the effects it has on her: anguish, pain, desolation, the desire even for death. She writes to death:

You will come anyway – so why not now?
I wait for you; things have become too hard.
I have turned out the lights and opened the door
For you, so simple and so wonderful.
Assume whatever shape you wish.[46]

There is an honesty in this poetry. It names the human condition in all of its abject nakedness. It is the abject nakedness of Christ on the cross, waiting to be resurrected.

Forgiveness, that movement towards resurrection, not only recognizes and admits the painful realities of our lives, it also investigates that pain. Where does it come from? What does it do to my life now? What are the stories it incarnates? What is the value and meaning of those stories?

The pain we experience is often the collective effect of a series of different perceptions. Our present unhappiness emerges from past wrongs not corrected. It could manifest itself as a combination of alienation, sadness, injustice, oppression, helplessness, and disempowerment. If we can allow ourselves to be present to that pain without increasing our trauma, we can allow that pain to speak to us. We need to find a safe environment for that to happen. We can sit in prayer, conscious of being held in God's love, and ask God to be present to that pain and to show us where it came from and how it affects us. We might imagine ourselves in a room with three chairs. In one chair is the pain; in another is God; and in the third, us. We can speak to the pain and we can speak to God; we can let the pain speak to us and to God; we can let God speak to us and to the pain. We can let each of the three ask questions, tell the others what it needs, listen to what the others say. This imaginative exercise allows the blocks in our spiritual path to be observed and deconstructed.

Often our present unhappiness is the result of past experiences; these shape the way we look at life, since we often see out of our hurts. Those hurts can turn us in on ourselves. The exercise in the paragraph above offers one way out of that impasse. But the pain might be so compacted, all we can do is ask to be held by God, and to experience that holding as a form of healing. Such healing takes time, as the love who holds us slowly removes the poison from our unredeemed past that makes us unable to live fully in the present and hopefully towards the future. Such holding allows us to present ourselves to the gift forgiveness offers.

Sometimes the pain trapping us is so powerful we cannot forgive ourselves or others. The mourning, which invites us to hand over our losses to the mercy of God, still leaves us grieving, trapped in our own worlds of wanting justice as we see it, community as we desire it, and a meaning making sense to us. With a sense of horror, we discover we are unable to be freed. We cry out for conversion from the anger, despair and self-righteousness that possess us.

We discover we cannot forgive or experience forgiveness. It is beyond us. We discover then only God can forgive. Christ on the cross does not tell those who have brought him to this suffering he forgives them. Rather, he says, "Father, forgive them, they do not know what they do" (Luke 23:34). Sometimes we can only ask the Father to forgive because we cannot. In this act of humility we realize we are not God. The most we can do is to offer up to God our pain and the people and situations that have caused that pain. We do not hold them but offer them to God. We let God deal with those situations at God's own time and pace. We wait in hope to see what happens.

It is tempting to think Christ's experience on the cross is only about his own business. A human being dying alone. This is simply not true, either for him or for us in our anguish. His mission was to bring creation back to the Father. When we say he takes the sins of the world upon himself, one meaning we attach to this is that his human person incorporates all of creation. On the way to the Father, he carries with him all the aspects of disorder the Father transforms into resurrection. Our unredeemed history is not a closed book. It is being transformed even though we do not realize it. Our own pain and anguish over continuing to be trapped does not tell the whole story. That story is with Jesus. That story *is* Jesus. Our suffering is—as the body of Christ and as the corporate body of Christ, with the ongoing work of the resurrection—to bring all to the fullness of life. We are not alone. We are not abandoned. We bear in our lives the sufferings of Christ because we are part of the humanity of Christ. That is the gift of the Father to us. God adopts us as his children, even though we do not have the divine nature of his Messiah.

We can ask Jesus to enter the pain of our unredeemed histories because he has already done so. When we give the pain of our past over to Jesus, we are bringing to our awareness, as best we can, the truth of our lives. That truth is multiple. It is the reality of our entrapment and our inability to rescue ourselves. It is the reality that we are not alone, but a part of the body of Christ, and this presently suffering and abused body is drawn by the desire the Father has for us and for all creation. This reality calling beyond ourselves is towards the fullness of life, envisioned by the author of the book of Revelation as

> a new heaven and a new earth: for the first heaven and the first earth were passed away; and there was no more sea.

And I John saw the holy city, new Jerusalem, coming down from God out of heaven, prepared as a bride adorned for her husband.

And I heard a great voice out of heaven saying, Behold, the tabernacle of God is with humans, and he will dwell with them, and they shall be his people, and God himself shall be with them, and be their God.

And God shall wipe away all tears from their eyes; and there shall be no more death, neither sorrow, nor crying, neither shall there be any more pain: for the former things are passed away.

And he that sat upon the throne said, Behold, I make all things new. And he said unto me, Write: for these words are true and faithful.

And he said unto me, It is done. I am Alpha and Omega, the beginning and the end. I will give to the one that is thirsty of the fountain of the water of life freely.

All who win the victory will be given these blessings. I will be their God, and they will be my people. (Revelation 21:1-7)

The mission of Jesus is to transform suffering into celebration. Our cooperation with Jesus in this mission is to ask him to take our pain and all our unredeemed history and hold them up to the Father. Like Jesus, we wait on the Father to manifest his compassionate mercy; like Jesus in his earthly life, we wait on the Father to give us the grace to forgive ourselves and others. This does not reduce us to passivity or apathy. With Jesus we try to live out of our desire for the fullness of life; with Jesus we lean into the Father's love.

This approach has several dimensions. We strive as best we can not to do things or encourage thoughts and habits that work against leaning into love or against accepting it. We struggle not to live unredeemed lives, and we wrestle with the identity our destructive background has engendered in us. This is hard work and daily work, and is why the examination of consciousness described in Part III is so crucial in our walking through mystery. These examinations allow us to resist the forces of destruction seeded in us by our past. But we can also live as if we have received the graces of redemption. In Mark's gospel, Jesus tells us, "Whatever you ask for in prayer, believe that you have received it already, and it will be yours" (Mark 11:24). This does not mean we project an ideal world from our brokenness and then pretend it is real. Such a stance is also destructive. Because we are blinded by those elements in our past, we need the help of spiritual direction to point out how our biases distort our perceptions.

We can also practise spiritual exercises in which we imagine Christ taking our brokenness because he loves us—the way we take on the brokenness of those we love—and holding that brokenness up to the Father for healing. As a form of prayer, we can imagine the Father accepting our broken humanity, and then wait in prayer to see what happens next. Here the imagination becomes the meeting ground between us and God. We cannot force the prayer to an outcome we prearrange. We enter the prayer with an invitation for God to open our imagination to seeing him at work there. The work in this exercise is not escapist fantasy or projection. An opened imagination allows God to work in our lives, for we live out of our vision, created by that humanized imagination. It shapes what we perceive and what we incarnate as value.

Imagination Incarnate

Our vision is embodied imagination. God encounters us in and through our imagination. The work we let God do in imaginative prayer is transformative. In therapeutic clinics, visualization is used to create states of well-being and to facilitate transformation. In the spiritual life, visualization is more powerful, because we allow God to become engaged in restructuring our life. The Spiritual Exercises of St. Ignatius is based on the work done on the imagination in prayer. Prayer using the imagination transforms our life.

Our unredeemed histories can be transformed by allowing God to enter into them. In the narrative that unfolds, we can enter the scene in which Jesus hands our unredeemed histories to the

Father. We can contemplate what God does with what is given to him. We can see God give the transformed story back to Jesus. Just as the Father transforms Jesus' death into resurrection, so, too, God transforms the history of Jesus' passion and suffering into one of redemption for all. We can ask for the grace to see how our own past of passion and suffering are offered a new and different life as well as a new story. We can see Jesus handing us back that new story, the same way he handed their story back to the disciples as they returned home to Emmaus after the Passover in Jerusalem. As they received that gift, it opened and transformed them. They became bearers of the Good News. They did not enter paradise on earth. They still belonged to a divided Jewish religious establishment under Roman occupation. But how they lived their lives was different. They were able to live more fully in the present because they experienced a transformed past, liberating them.

The work we do in enabling Jesus to liberate us from our unredeemed pasts indicates to God our desire for such a freedom. This gift is offered to us in God's own time and in God's own way. We pray for the ability to recognize this gift, to accept and use it as it is given. It may not come in ways we accept easily, and we may desire a form of innocence satisfying only our individual needs. But what comes to us comes for the building up of community. We pray to remember we are a corporate body and that no one is fully saved until all are fully saved. This process takes time and involves the ongoing mercy of God. Praying our unredeemed histories puts us on the path to the fullness of life for all, which is our inheritance.

The path to fullness of life is forgiveness. We experience this forgiveness when we have a sense of the way forward and of stepping into the darkness beyond the discomfort of our present sense of self. Forgiveness is a journey. It comes to an end only when everyone and everything has been redeemed. How or when that will happen is beyond our knowing. What we do know is that whatever we do to further that state of reconciliation in our own lives and in the lives of others builds up the kingdom of God. Then we act as peacemakers in this world.

In continuing the mission of Jesus in our times, our stance as peacemaker is the result of walking a spiritual path that first accepts our poverty of spirit. When we discover how radically limited we are, even spiritually, we can take stock of those forces using our limitations to trap us in destructive ways of living and of seeing ourselves. Becoming aware of some of those traps and of our own inability to be freed from them brings us to our need to deal with the anger these stir up. That aggression turned outward in violence, or inward in depression or addiction, is destructive. We cry out to be freed from that aggression, which seems woven into our very being. We cry out to be converted. Even though our destructive instincts do not disappear, we find we can discipline ourselves not to indulge them. Then we try to be merciful to others as we ourselves desire mercy. Such mercy comes only when all our actions are focused on seeking and doing the will of God. Discernment in action purifies our heart, and those who strive to live out of a purity of heart become peacemakers. They accept the path of giving and receiving forgiveness. They hand on the gift that they themselves have received. They can only give what they have been given and have received and integrated into their lives. When we pray our unredeemed histories, we enter the path of the beatitudes to become peacemakers. The God who desires each part of us to live in a passionate communal freedom enters into every aspect of our lives to bring us all together into the fullness of life.

When we pray with our unredeemed histories, we can breathe in this love that heals, consoles and transforms. It goes to those areas that cry out for liberation. When we breathe out love, we can become the open door through which the mercy of God enters into the damaged and violent dimensions of the world. We can breathe in love and breathe out love. When we do this, our unredeemed histories are transformed. Then, we live more fully and joyfully in the present.

Living the Present

The Redeemed Present

Each of us is scripture in that God always speaks in and through our lives. In Scripture, we find people encountering God and people turning away from God or searching for God. We find the same thing in the history of our lives. The occasions of our lives are always in the presence of God, and there is no moment when God is not present. But while God is always present to us, we are not always present to God. This does not necessarily mean being conscious of God as God, but, more likely, being conscious of what gives us life. Sometimes we turn away from life and our difficulties. Then the violence in the world brings out our own aggression, hatred and ignorance. When we turn away from a path that leads to life, we turn away from God.

Turned from God, we live in a limited and distorted present. It restricts us and traps us in disorder. Often this view of the present is shaped by our past. When the past is not redeemed, it is brought into the present and we live the past in our present lives. Old hurts and patterns of behaviour and response are played out over and over again with the same results, reinforcing our entrapment. A story is told of Heraclitus, the pre-Socratic Greek philosopher. While walking along a beach, he came across some boys fishing. When he asked them what they had caught, they replied, "What we have caught and killed we leave behind. What we have not caught we carry with us." The answer to this riddle, which stumped the philosopher, is "lice." Our unredeemed history is, at best, like lice. The damaged past brought into the present irritates, causes unnecessary discomfort and spoils our delight in living.

When the past is redeemed, we can see and live in the present in a much more real fashion. We can be more present to the present in all of its complexity. It is very difficult to live fully in the present. In fact, only God lives fully in the present, because God is the abiding present. The rest of us, being creatures, live in a continuum called time. Our present is the meeting place of past and future. Sometimes the past dominates our present; at other times the future dominates. We do not consciously live this way. Often our lives are unreflective states formed by habits and anxieties. This is why the awareness examen is so important if we want to step intentionally into mystery.

Here we are trying to live the present mindfully. The Buddhists say if we can drink a glass of water mindfully, the world will be saved. But to drink such a glass of water, we must be fully present to the water. A seemingly insignificant act is often absorbed by other concerns and goes by unnoticed. Or we may be thirsty and become aware only of satisfying our need. This applies to everything else. We can reduce our identity to our needs, and reduce our needs to the immediate. We focus on ego wants. What satisfies these is important only in terms of ourselves. The same thing happens in prayer. The God we pray to becomes the projection of our answer to our desires. In this case, like the glass of water, we do not experience the thing in itself, with all of its connections and interdependencies. To do that we must become attentive; when we are inattentive, we do not experience God as God. Only God can be present to all those connections and levels of interdependency situating our life. Only God can be fully present to us in ways we are not even present to ourselves. Only God lives fully in the present.

On the way to God, our becoming mindful in the present requires a certain discipline with which we can be aware of what is actually present to us. That level of awareness comes at the stage portrayed in the ninth Ox-herding picture (see Part II). We need a sense of self aware of, but not caught by, ego needs. For most of us, this level of consciousness is intermittent. St. Ignatius calls it "indifference." When we are indifferent, we see and value everything only in relationship with God. We cannot will indifference, for this only intensifies our projections onto the world. Our habits and patterns of existence stop us from living simply in the present by creating expectations of the future. These habits are creations of the past, and often we think they constitute our identity. Then we confuse the habitual with the real. But it is not the past that makes us who we are. It is what we do with the past in the present that reveals to us and others who we are.

We can use the past to free us to live in the present, and we can use the present to free us to live in the future. As a student over the years, I met my fair share of bad teachers. I found it helpful not to dismiss those bad teachers, but instead to ask why they were bad. What did they show me about how not to teach? Beyond being professionally competent, good teachers do not teach subjects; they teach people. They enter the world of their students and incarnate their own lived insights of the material they present in that world. Self-forgetfulness is crucial in teaching, and the effectiveness of instruction can be judged by the dynamics of self-transcendence the students manifest. They discover themselves and they discover a path carrying them beyond themselves. What happens here is symbolic of what happens in the spiritual life. Encountering God in the present allows us to discover ourselves and to be carried beyond ourselves.

The Gift of the Present

But how do we live in the present as freely as possible? Working with our redeemed and unredeemed past and praying the beatitudes as a spiritual path create an openness, allowing us to see the gift given to us at every moment of our lives. My mother opened and saved all the perfumes and Italian leather shoes we gave her for Christmas. When it was time for her to move, her wardrobe was filled with these unused gifts. The perfumes had dried up in their bottles and the soft Italian shoes had become brittle and cracked from lack of use. She loved them and was saving them for a day when they would come in handy. That day never came, and the perfume bottles and the shoes were thrown away. Similarly, living rooms in some houses are never used. There are certain people whose lives are like that: unused or lived elsewhere from where they are.

If some exist in a state of deferred pleasures, others seek to hold onto the joys of the present moment. They try to freeze time. It is like the beginning of the Buddha's spiritual journey. His father did not want him to see human suffering and so kept him in an enclosed palace compound from which the sick, the old and the damaged were removed. Instead he was surrounded by beauty, sensuality and pleasure. But in spite of all that care, he encountered an old man, then a sick person, and after that a corpse. He saw change, decay and death. He encountered impermanence, which was the beginning of his spiritual quest to find an answer to human suffering. That quest led him to the insight that everyone suffers. None of us can avoid suffering; trying to hold on to the joys of the present creates more suffering.

Yet we can still enjoy the joys of the present. A Zen story illustrates this point. One day while walking up the side of a steep mountain, a man looked up and saw a tiger coming down the path to him. He turned around, but saw the tiger's mate climbing up the path behind him. Desperate to save himself, he climbed down over the cliff holding onto a vine. As he hung there, two mice appeared from a hole in the cliff and began gnawing on the vine. As it was about to break, he noticed two ripe strawberries growing within arm's reach. He plucked them. How sweet they were!

While we cannot truly hold on to what is impermanent, we can enjoy it as it passes. We can eat the ice cream cone on a hot day before it melts. We deny our humanity if we think, well, the ice cream will melt and be gone in a few minutes anyway, so why bother? We do not stop living because one day we will die. In fact, our very living is how we die. Similarly, we cannot hold our breath because every time we breathe out we are one breath closer to death. We do not leave the ice cream cone uneaten because once we have eaten it, the ice cream cone will be gone. The way we celebrate what passes is to accept its coming, its staying and its going.

The book of Ecclesiastes bemoans the works of humans caught in the passage of time. It declares, "All is vanity." But the author of that Old Testament book had not experienced the Incarnation, where God does enter into time and transforms every moment of time into a passage to eternity. William Blake writes, "Eternity is in love with the productions of time."[47] The aspects of present time that give life can be celebrated; the gift of the present time is that it offers the site for finding and discovering ourselves found by God. God can only find us where we are, not where we are not. The Sufi mystics tell the story of a drunk man looking for the keys to his house under a street light. The watchmen making the rounds decide to help him, but find nothing. They ask him where he dropped his keys. He points into the darkness. "Then why are you searching here?" they ask. "Because," he says, "here is where the light is."[48]

If we want to see where the gifts of the present are, we must live in the present. Too often we live away from the present in a space we impose on it, and so we do not see the present for what it offers. Instead, we suffer needlessly, because it does not offer what we desire. To see the present we need to bring an openness to it, so that its possibilities reveal themselves to us. Blake wrote, "If the doors of perception were cleansed every thing would appear to man as it is, infinite. For man has closed himself up, till he sees all things thru' narrow chinks of his cavern."[49] Our biases narrow our perception of what exists or is possible. Our biases transform our sense of wonder and our ability to live in mystery into egocentric concerns reducing our wonder to apathy or self-serving ends, and our life to pragmatic and utilitarian causes. Then the present becomes a project of creating and maintaining certain forms of our self. It stops being seen as an invitation to enter into and celebrate the Mystery holding all of our life.

The freedom we gain by praying our past affects the way we see and live in the present. We do not have to be trapped by our anxieties and fears. To be sure, it is human to experience these, but we do not have to be paralyzed by them. When we are trapped by them, we try to exercise control, and often that control is more destructive of our well-being. The fear we might feel in a dentist's chair tightens up our body. That rigidity heightens our susceptibility to pain. We tense up in a defensive position to avoid the pain, and instead we feel it even more keenly.

Many things beyond our control can render our life very problematic: accidents, illnesses, the death of people dear to us, family crises, the sudden loss of a job, or financial insecurity. All of these are common in our world. We might think they happen only to other people, but they can and do happen to us. We might refuse to consider these possibilities because thinking about them does us no good. But we can also consider that all the things beyond our control are held in God's Providence. This Providence cares for us. The Jesus of Luke's gospel tells us,

> "I tell you, do not worry about your life, what you will eat, or about your body, what you will wear. For life is more

than food, and the body more than clothing. Consider the ravens: they neither sow nor reap, they have neither storehouse nor barn, and yet God feeds them. Of how much more value are you than the birds!" (Luke 12:22-24)

The writer of Paul's letter to the Romans is even more emphatic about this care. He writes,

"I am convinced that neither death, nor life, neither angels nor demons, … neither the present nor the future, nor any powers, neither height nor depth, nor anything else in all creation, will be able to separate us from the love of God that is in Christ Jesus our Lord." (Romans 8:38-39)

God, who looks after us in ways we do not see or understand, loves us more than we love ourselves. As God's Beloved, we are cared for and cherished.

With that confidence in God we can live mindfully in the present. This does not mean we escape into prayer. When bad things happen, pious people tend to seek an escape into prayer. Saying prayers can be used as a form of therapy or as a self-soother, but real prayer allows us to be in communion with God. This communion helps us to deal with the issues that surround us. Intimacy with God does not wipe away problems or anesthetize us from pain. Instead, this intimacy gives us the spiritual consolation and tools to deal with what causes our suffering. Consolation may come in the form of an emotional distance allowing us a bigger perspective on what is troubling us; or it may come in the form of insights into how not to be trapped; or we get a breathing space to recover some of our drained energies; or we might have the sense of being supported in our very being.

Praying opens us to a mutual encounter with God, and rather than expressing our needs to an idealized projection, brings us into a present more encompassing than our own. Prayer opens ourselves to a community of the Trinity and to all the forces of good in creation. Our problems are not just our own. They belong to that larger community of which we are a part. We are helped in ways and by others we may not even be aware of. We do not have to run from our problems, nor remain isolated by our problems. A bishop in one of the most difficult dioceses in Canada once became increasingly harassed by the complexity of the issues he had to face. He was almost on the brink of a nervous collapse when he received an insight. At prayer he said to God, "You know I am slow and stupid, so if you want me to do anything, you must tell me clearly and simply in ways I can understand. I will do nothing until you tell me what to do." The bishop realized that it was God's world, not his. He was merely God's servant. Then he stopped worrying. And then he started to notice the things that needed to be done got done. Some things just fell into place. Finally, he discovered the way in which he and God communicated with each other. He discovered how to be more present to himself, to others and to God in life-giving ways.

Living in the present is learning to let go. This allows the gifts of the present to appear. We can be so filled with anxieties or lessons from the past that we never can appreciate what is given to us. When I was a child, my family went off on a holiday to Barbados, and there I caught double pneumonia and nearly died. The incident so frightened my mother that we never went on another family holiday again. Every year one would be planned; my mother would agree; and on the day before we were to set off, she would simply refuse to go. This continued until all the children had left home, and it was only when we were grown up that she allowed herself to go on vacations with my father and youngest sister, then an adult. She could never avail herself of that gift of enjoying what the present had to offer, and to be honest, that suspicion of holidays has been passed down to the children. To this day, going on holidays is something we rarely do, even though when we do, we have a really good time.

The present as a gift needs to be received and accepted, opened, used, shared and celebrated. But how do we do this? The first thing is to ask what is the gift of the present time given to me. How does it reveal itself? Place yourself in a prayerful state and then ask for the gift of being able to recognize what is being given. You might ask the Spirit to help you in your desire. See what emerges in prayer and list how that gift manifests itself. Even the sense of gratitude and peace you find yourself in is part of the gift. You might find yourself sitting with the felt sense that all is gift, even though an intellectual awareness questions that felt state. The awareness that all is gift comes from a deeper place within us—from that place where God touches us and we touch God. Pierre Teilhard de Chardin writes of that place,

> And so, for the first time in my life perhaps (although I am supposed to meditate everyday!) I took the lamp, and leaving the zone of everyday occupations and relationship where everything seems clear, I went down into my inmost self, to the deep abyss whence I feel simply that my power of action emanates. But as I moved further and further from the conventional certainties by which social life is superficially illuminated, I became aware that I was losing contact with myself. At each step of the descent a new person was disclosed within me of whose name I was no longer sure, and who no longer obeyed me. And when I had to stop my exploration because the path faded from beneath my steps, I found a bottomless abyss at my feet, and out of it came; arising I know not whence; the current which I dare to call my life.[50]

The current of life emerging from the felt emptiness grounding our being gives us a sense of rootedness, and witnesses to our being sustained by God. It arises through the mysterious layers of our self into our social and personal lives, revealing the gift of life given at those levels. We can sit with that sense of connection and the healing work it does in consoling and celebrating our lives. In addition, should we be so moved, we can jot down the things we are presently grateful for. Writing them down usually brings up more and more things—some we take for granted, some we had forgotten, and some surprise us because we were never aware of them. We contemplate these things with a sense of gratitude.

Resting in gratitude transforms us, especially if we have become accustomed to seeing out of the hurts blocking us from appreciating the good given daily. When we see and live out of our hurts, we live out of a distorted image of ourselves, often that of a victim, and such a life reinforces the distortion and contributes to the building of bigger prisons of entrapment. Seeing and celebrating the good in our lives liberates us to enjoy life more, and as the Scripture says, "to the one who has more will be given, and that person will have an abundance, while the one who has not even what he has will be taken away" (Matthew 25:29). The parable of the unused talent, from which this existential insight is taken, examines the use or neglect of the gifts given to all. The gifts of the present moment are how the lover acknowledges the beloved. Those gifts tell us we are loved, we are lovable, we can love. They also tell us something about the One who loves us and what that One desires for us, even as we find ourselves surrounded by troubles. The gifts assure us we are loved, cherished, cared for, watched over and desired in the most intimate and absurd ways.

The Story of the Body

When we are present to gratitude, we become aware of our bodies. Our bodies make us immediately present to the world and to ourselves. They provide us with our felt sense of the presence of God. Sitting in gratitude attunes our bodies, and we may experience physical sensations in this prayerful state. Because I had double pneumonia as a young child, my lungs are badly damaged. I recall going to a reputable reflexologist in Kuala Lumpur. As the soles of my feet were kneaded and massaged, I felt this warmth in my lungs. I asked what was happening and was told that the massage releases blocked energies, even deep-seated blocked energies from illnesses or traumas. The same thing happens when we sit prayerfully in gratitude for the present. The body responds to the love it experiences and accepts. As the physical expressions of any love are felt in the body—think even of the joy experienced at a Eureka moment of insight—so, too, the embrace of God can be experienced in and through the body. The scripture of our life can be read through the body, which holds both the narrative and the text of our lives. Our bodies incarnate our lives. Any act of becoming present to ourselves and of becoming aware of the present is felt in the body.

A prayer of presence can start with becoming aware of every part of our body. We can become aware of the soles of our feet, then our toes, the top of the feet, the ankles, calves, knees, thighs, pelvic area, stomach, solar plexus, lungs and the breaths we take, throat, arms, hands, fingers, neck, face, mouth, nose, eyes, forehead and the top of our head. We can go up the front of our body, and down the backbone, buttocks, and back down to the soles of our feet again. We simply note the body, the sensations contained at each part, and the feelings and stories each evokes. We can sit with our body in a sense of wonder and mystery, experiencing the expansiveness and connectedness such a contemplation evokes. We can become aware of the breath entering the body as gift, being accepted by the body as gift, being used and celebrated in the body as gift. We can also become aware of breathing out as the gift of ourselves to our surroundings and to those to whom we are connected. We do not evaluate what we experience to be either good or bad, acceptable or not. We do not close ourselves off from what is already present in the now. Instead, we use the exercise to open and reveal us to ourselves. We become aware of our mood, and of the way the space around us—the air, the light, the ground, the sky—all shape how we are now. We stay with that awareness as it expands to present to us people and places called to mind. We become aware of those people and places being connected to us. We experience that connection not just in our minds and memories, but in our bodies. The sense of those connections expands beyond what is felt. We slowly settle into the knowledge we are connected and interrelated to everything. We are not alone. We have never been alone. God is connected to us and we are connected to each other. The gift of the present moment is always this. Each moment offers an entry into the kingdom of God. It realizes the covenant Christ made to be with us always, even to the end of time (Matthew 28:20).

The assurance of this relationship remains, no matter how often we lose sight of it and live disconnected from ourselves, others and God. Living in this assurance changes our lives, grounding and guiding us, and relieving our anxieties. It makes us aware of the Divine Providence upholding our very existence. Jesus tells a parable of a rich landowner who hires labourers early in the morning, mid-morning, at noon, mid-afternoon and late afternoon. They are all paid the same, and those who worked hard all or most of the day complain that their salary was the same as those who did very little work. On the level of economic justice their complaint seems valid. But they have had the assurance all day of being paid and of being able to afford to buy food for their families, while those without a job suffered the anxiety all day of not knowing how or where to earn the money they need to live on. The labourers chosen early were able to live the gift of the present. Living the gift of the present allows us to celebrate our lives no matter how hard they are.

We may not have the ability to experience this at every moment of our daily lives, caught up as most of us are in our daily routines. Those daily routines define who we are, and the habitual becomes for us the real. Then we forget who we are and what it is to be human. To be human is to be spiritual. Our growth in realizing our humanity is a movement to living our lives in right relationship with God and to the awareness of our interconnectedness with the rest of creation. Matthew's gospel puts it quite simply. Jesus says, "'Love the Lord your God with all your heart and with all your soul and with all your mind.' This is the first and greatest commandment. And the second is like it: 'Love your neighbour as yourself'" (Matthew 22:37-39). We journey into this love, and we do so by becoming attentive to where we are at the present moment, and to what this present moment opens us out to. Being attentive carries us to God. But being attentive also makes us aware of how God searches for us, finds us and comes to us. Each moment offers an entry into the sacred and an encounter with it. This is not passive. The energies that we are are always dynamic. We are made in the image and likeness of God, and God is not an idea or a concept or a thing. God manifests God's self as the constant giving of life through the creativity making, sustaining and fulfilling creation. The energies we are, as well as the energies manifesting God's presence, come together to form the present moment.

Finding God in All Things

To find God in this present moment is part of the Ignatian project summed up in the phrase "finding God in all things." To find God in all things is to find life in all things. When we look at our present life, we can ask where we find life in our here and now. God is the giver of life, but often when we think of God, we do not think of life. We take life for granted and we think of God as absent, or only available in special and dramatic ways. So we miss the ways in which God is quite commonplace and accessible. Anything that gives life is a gift from God and a witness to God's presence in our lives. But finding God in all things is the end of a long process. It usually begins, as the Ox-herding picture tells us, with us looking for ourselves, and this leads us to look for a God who will satisfy us. This can translate to looking for a path and values giving us life, meaning and joy. We look and look until we are found by God. We experience being found in the consolations we are given. These lead us to a sense of who we are in relationship to God. Every circumstance then becomes an occasion for dialogue with God, and out of this dialogue emerges a sense of our identity in relationship with God. We start seeing and understanding all things in the light of that relationship, and, through that relationship, we discover a path that gives life. We find our call. After finding our call, we start discovering the specifics of that call. We discover how to live our vocation, and in living our vocation, we learn to live more and more in the present. We discover the presence of God in all things and the particular gifts of God in everything. Living this way focuses and energizes us. We know what we have to do; we know what we can do, and we do what we can. We leave the rest to God. When we find God, we weave our energies into the flow of energies coming from God, having a sense of being rooted, alive and creative no matter what we do or where we are. The lived sense of relationship carries us further beyond ourselves into ever greater awareness of community on personal, social and cultural levels. It is the nature of evil to cause disconnection and fragmentation, while being grounded in God's love carries us to right relationships with all of creation.

Now, because we are still being created and still suffer the effects of living in a disordered universe, we find in ourselves a tension between the forces moving us to community and the forces drawing us back into forms of narcissism. The work of redeeming the present first involves seeing the ways tension operates in our lives. Today that tension manifests itself in four major dialectical narratives that shape our contemporary world. Each of us finds ourselves somewhere along the continuum between security and rootedness, meaning and mystery, liberty and freedom, narcissism and community.

Given the nature of reality today—with conflicting perspectives, truths, modes of operation, and values—unless we want to live second-hand lives that lack personal integrity, we are each forced into being spiritually attentive to discover who we are and what we are to do. A relationship with God always calls us beyond ourselves into the fullness of life, but that drive to self-transcendence can be frustrated by the securities we substitute for it.

Security is not a bad thing, but it becomes limiting when it prevents us from a spiritual intimacy addressing all of our being. We are attracted to security because it seemingly protects us from the vulnerability of being human. In every present moment we are vulnerable. We can choose either to depend radically on God, or we can turn towards institutions, projects or people to give us the comfort of an established identity.

Similarly, we may choose forms of meaning and seek to understand the reality we live in in terms of ideologies denying or truncating the Mystery who desires us in—but also beyond—the meta-narratives of our times. Being human, we do not know everything and we cannot control all the implications and allusions of the narratives out of which we live. We are vulnerable. Yet the desire for complete closed systems of meaning to explain everything carries us to idolatry. On the contrary, true systems of meaning are characterized by openness and point us to an awareness of the mystery of life. Then questioning carries us to wonder and awe, and the search for meaning brings us to the silence and emptiness out of which all meaning arises.

For us human beings, meaning is institutionalized. We are born into familial, social, cultural, ethnic and religious systems of meaning. These narratives situate us, but, at times, they can also limit and distort our humanity. Like the priest and the Levite in the Parable of the Good Samaritan, we may ignore our neighbour because the social constructions of ourselves do not accommodate what is defined as "other." When this happens, we live in ghetto mentalities. We see the "other" as alien rather than as an invitation. We limit our relationships and deny the call to community where the fullness of life is available for all.

When we live in ghettos, we accept the social liberties those enclosed forms of society engender. They are sanctioned by the norms of the group and culture. But just as there is individual narcissism, there is also social narcissism, and the civil liberties we utilize are not necessarily always helpful for us or for others. Thus, legal rights are often beyond the reach of the disenfranchised. The rights we hold can oppress others, and we justify these rights by force, by legalized violence and by self-serving policies. Within each of us lies a tension between liberty and freedom, and it is only when we fall in love, individually or collectively, that we give up our rights for the well-being of the larger community including all others. Only when we fall in love and learn to care for others, and then for all others, do we experience freedom. In the Garden of Gethsemane, Christ gives up his liberty to live his freedom. Those who struggle against socially unjust structures may find themselves imprisoned, exiled, tortured and even killed, because they seek freedom for the oppressed whose constraints are approved by legislation or social bias.

As we struggle to live in the gift that is the present, we find ourselves in tension, and we are called to be attentive to the ways in which we live the vulnerability such a tension engenders. Because we do not have all the answers or see all the possible outcomes for any proposed plan of action, we are forced to occupy positions of risk. To live in the present is to risk, and we make mistakes because of our limitations. But we can even risk making mistakes when we understand that the God who desires us and who brings all of creation into being—including those elements rejecting their source of life afterwards—can also transform any mistake we make into resurrection. Living consciously connected to God assures us that the love who loved us even when we were sinners loves us now that we are intimates. This love and all the forces of good in creation and the community of those who love the Beloved work together with us to make sure whatever we do builds up the kingdom of God.

Living humbly and open, and assured of God's help, we can risk as we lean into the darkness. The present is not paradise but a place of movement. It is marked by impermanence. This movement is always towards God or away from God. We may have some sense of the direction we are facing as we use the rules for discernment given in Part III. But as a rule of thumb, the movement away from God is distinguished by intensity and self-focus. We experience a lack of openness, humility and joy; we doubt. The movement towards God is shown in the gifts of the Spirit Paul talks about: "love, joy, peace, long suffering, kindness, goodness, faithfulness, gentleness, self-control" (Galatians 5:22). When we are intense, we focus on ourselves; when we are passionate, we focus on the other. Then we move towards self-transcendence. As we move along the path of spiritual intimacy, we love to discover not ourselves but the other, be it God, the community of the human family, or the companion who shares our journey to the fullness of life.

The direction in which we are moving—towards the other or away from the other—shapes how we live the present moment. This moment is never neutral but is filled with conflicting forces, and we are asked in the midst of these to discern which forces we follow and which forces we resist. We can ask, "What is redeeming the present inviting us to do now?" If we know we are rooted in God's love, the gratitude we experience will lead us to the next thing. Often, this is simply to be in the awareness of that gratitude. More often, it is to undertake the next practical thing.

There is a story of an old Buddhist abbot who knew he was to die soon. He called his community to a sitting and told them that the person who best manifested the essence of Zen would become the next abbot. They sat in silence for a long time. Finally, one monk came forward. He took an empty bowl and carefully cleaned it and placed it in front of the abbot. The rest of the community gasped at his insight. Zen is emptiness. The old abbot said nothing. After another long while, a second monk came forward and carefully filled the empty bowl to the brim with clean water. When the water settled and became still, it reflected the surroundings without distortion. Another gasp came from the gathered monks. Zen mirrors reality without bias. Still the abbot did nothing. The silence continued. Finally, in the kitchen, the cook had had enough. The rice was getting cold. He came out and kicked over the bowl of water. In the gasp that followed, the abbot rose and declared that the new abbot was the cook.

Living spiritually in the present does not mean we become lost in piety of one sort or another. It means being practical. We might be riddled with fears and anxieties, angers and regrets. But we do not have to be stopped by them. The gifts permeating our lives liberate us to risk. The grace of the present moment calls us beyond ourselves to a new life.

We cannot hold onto life, but we can live it. In Matthew's gospel, Jesus tells us how.

> I tell you, do not worry about your life, what you will eat or drink; or about your body, what you will wear. Is not life more important than food, and the body more important than clothes? ... For the unbelievers run after all these things, and your heavenly Father knows that you need them. But seek first his kingdom and his righteousness, and all these things will be given to you as well. Therefore do not worry about tomorrow, for tomorrow will worry about itself. Each day has enough trouble of its own. (Matthew 25:32-34)

Living fully in the present does not eliminate troubles. It offers us a rootedness that places those troubles in God's care, allowing us to notice and celebrate the joys that are also part of the present moment. Living in the present links us to the ongoing resurrected presence of the Christ in the world. It is the gift he shares with us here and now. His resurrection is not for our afterlife. It is for our present moment. Resurrection assures us there is no death that will not be transformed.

An Unredeemed Present

But how is destruction to be transformed? We see disorder in the world today and disorder in our own lives. The notion that through spiritual techniques we can reach a perspective where the eschaton is fully now is a fantasy. This fantasy has lots of currency in our contemporary world. Advertisements are built on that fantasy. The perfect car, home, holiday, clothes, partner—even the perfect self, engineered through diet, exercise and dress—are suggested as real possibilities in this world. But those dreams of perfection emerge from the reality of our entrapment in an imperfect world. Our dream of perfection is like the prisoner's dream of freedom. It is a projection of limitations overcome. We might call it heaven, and seek that heaven on earth, or fantasize it as a reward in the afterlife. Both are unreal, because to be a creature is to be limited even in heaven.

We do not live in a perfect world, and we do not even know what a perfect world could be like, given the blindness caused by our own imperfections. We ourselves are not perfect. We are in process and our sense of self is constantly changing and shaped by the circumstances in which we find ourselves. As we change, our notion of perfection changes, but in all these changes we discover ourselves to be unfinished business. How we see and experience ourselves is shaped by the world and by others, including God. These offer us different and conflicting notions of what perfection is. To live in the present requires discernment.

We need to discern the values that seek to define us, and to ask which ones bring us life and which ones take away our joy. The spirit of discernment can be cultivated, as Part III of this book advocates. The daily examens and the experience gained from our earlier histories of being deceived by fantasies promising good, but delivering disappointment and destruction instead, refine our skill in discerning to an instinct. Part of that instinct comes from humility. Realizing our limitations and our bias, we wait to see how things develop, because we know what seems like good can turn out to be evil, and what originally seems bad may really be a blessing in disguise.

The parable of the wheat and the tares (Matthew 13:24-30) illuminates the use of patience in discernment. When wheat and tares spring up, they look alike. They can be distinguished from each other only when they are fully grown. We live in God's world and in God's dispensations, and so to live in the present we learn to hand over our projects and perspectives to God. Living in God's time, rather than in our anxieties, we let God be God. The more we realize our humanity and our limitations, the more we can let God be God. God does things in ways that might surprise us. In the parable of the sower and the seed, we might wonder at a wasteful sower who sows his seed on trodden paths, in shallow soil, among thorns and weeds, as well as in good soil. This is the work of a profligate and exuberant God who gives to all the possibilities of receiving the fullness of life. We cannot deny to others what God wants to give them. God comes to save all, not the already saved—and, importantly, this God comes to those who are most in need of salvation. All we can do is cooperate with God, love others and hope for the best. Our mortality and our own biases limit us, and any awareness of our biases keeps us humble.

Temptations While Trying to Live in the Present

But this does not reduce us to being doormats in an arrogant and aggressive world. Jesus lived in an unredeemed present, focused on the Father. He lived out his life in constant fidelity to the One who loves him. In waiting on the Father, we, like Jesus, do the Father's will. Jesus waited eighteen years after declaring he must be about his Father's business (Luke 2:49) to be publicly acknowledged at his baptism in the Jordan as the Father's "Beloved Son" (Luke 3:21-22). Jesus learned to wait only by waiting. In a time when the life expectancy of a male was between twenty-five and thirty-six years, most of his life was spent waiting on the Father before he began his public ministry. That ministry started immediately after his baptism, when, as Luke's gospel tells us, he is driven out into the desert and tempted. The years of waiting stand him in good stead there. He is hungry after fasting for forty days and trying to discern how to live in the world as God's chosen. The first temptation is to change the stones into bread. What harm would it do? It would deny his humanity. Fasting makes one hungry and vulnerable. Were Jesus to use his divinity to satisfy his hunger, he would be disrespectful to his humanity; he would negate the power of the Incarnation affirming the value of the human. In effect, he would sabotage his mission to live as a human being. His earthly life would be merely a theatrical performance. What Jesus learns in waiting those eighteen years is to be patient and to let the Father minister to him when the Father judges it is the right time. Jesus puts that patience into practice even in his vulnerability.

The second temptation of Christ in Luke's gospel looks not at Jesus' own satisfaction but at his mission of regaining the world for the Father. Satan offered Jesus that world at the price of submission to the evil one. The temptation here is to sacrifice our self for a greater good and to uphold the secular principle that the ends justify the means. Jesus later will sacrifice himself for a greater good, but that sacrifice will be done not to gain the whole world but to maintain his integrity as one totally committed to the Father. Nothing, not even death, stands in the way of his love for the Father. The temptation here attempts to deny Jesus' rootedness in the Father. With love, ends and means are not separate. One loves by loving. We do not love by destroying ourselves or our radical commitment to the source of love. We live in the unredeemed present by loving. Only love transforms the world, and we love by being attentive to our relationship to the Father.

This carries us to the third temptation, in which Jesus is asked how to live that relationship with the Father. Jesus' love for the Father and the Father's love for Jesus let Jesus trust the Father. He does not have to prove the Father's love. He lives his life leaning into that love. He lets the Father show that love in the Father's own time and way. The Father does this by allowing the miracles of Jesus to be worked. They manifest the Father's compassionate mercy. Challenging that mercy by reckless acts of self-interest would be a futile attempt to take away the Father's freedom. This third temptation once again denies Jesus' humanity as a lived relationship of dependence on the Father. The Father is always free. That freedom is finally shown when the Father gives Jesus the gift of resurrection. The Father is not bound by death. At Jesus' death, the Father makes the destroyed body of Christ a resurrected new creation. In death Jesus waits on the Father for resurrection.

Waiting on the Father

Jesus' eighteen years of waiting teach him the patience of waiting on the Father. That waiting occurs throughout Jesus' life. He waits for a human to see he is the Son of God. Until that happens he can only perform miracles and preach. The way he lives the first part of his public life finally allows Peter to acknowledge him as the Messiah. When that crucial moment happens (Matthew 16:13-20), Jesus knows the first part of his mission is over. A human being now sees Jesus the same way the Father sees Jesus. Jesus asks, "Who do you say I am?" Simon Peter answers, "You are the Christ, the Son of the Living God." Jesus replies, "Blessed are you, Simon son of Jonah, for this was not revealed to you by man, but by my Father in Heaven" (Matthew 16:15-17). With this vital connection between the Father and fallen humanity established, Jesus moves on to the second part of his mission: his passion, death and resurrection. But even there he waits on the Father. He waits for the Father to tell him when to go to Lazarus. We know that Jesus can cure from a distance. He does this for the centurion's servant (Matthew 8:5-13). We know Jesus knew Lazarus, his friend, is mortally ill. Yet he does nothing, even though he is sorely grieved. He waits until he is sent to the tomb of Lazarus to liberate him. Jesus waits for the Father in the agony in the garden. He waits for the Father when he dies on the cross, his mission a seeming failure. But the Father resurrects Jesus, and everything changes.

When we live in the unredeemed present, we are often tempted not to wait on the Father. We are tempted to do what we think is appropriate before we receive the grace of knowing what to do and how to do it. Waiting on the Father is the act of love transforming the world, and witnesses to the power of God's love rather than to human ingenuity.

Such waiting does not mean we do nothing. We can live out of the love we have been given and have accepted. This often means we can do many little things to build up the kingdom. We can tell the people we love we love them. We can show this love in the way we live and in the way we treat others. These little acts are covenant moments. They are transformative.

I remember such a moment in my own life. My own father was a sportsman. My two older brothers were sportsmen. I was not. My father and I often disagreed when I was a boy. One night, though he had worked late, he got up early to take me to the airport. I was going off for a short course somewhere. When I got out of the car with my baggage, I thanked him and held out my hand to shake his. Instead, he grabbed me and kissed me on the forehead in front of everyone at the terminal. To this day I remember that simple act as an expression of love. Remembering that act brings back to my memory the other acts of love I so often took for granted: the many sacrifices he made so I could be educated; the time he carried me in his arms to the hospital when I was eleven and had a ruptured appendix and could not walk. I remember how he gave me the freedom to make my way through the world, even though that freedom restricted the family's chances for advancement. Looking back, I realize all the ways he laid down his own life so that his family could have a better life. He never drew attention to what he was doing. He just did those things, loving us and hoping for the best. He lived the graces he was given, and his life allowed others to find their own lives and their own paths through this life.

We can live redeemed in the unredeemed present by living the love we have been given. That love may be the size of a mustard seed, but it still can transform lives. We can offer up to God the broken of the world for whom we are helpless to do anything else. We can breathe love onto them, or imagine an open space through which the Father's love can enter into those destroyed places. And when we encounter people whom we judge to be destructive, we can stand out of the way rather than engaging with them angrily so God may deal with them directly. Mohandas Gandhi said that anger is the enemy of non-violence and pride is a monster that swallows it up.[51] When we are vulnerable, we often use aggression, anger and pride to maintain what we think is right. But being right is different from being righteous. Righteousness is a relationship based on our intimacy with God. Without that intimacy, we are as destructive as those we oppose.

Our work in the unredeemed present is to help transform its disordered aspects presenting themselves to us. Sometimes all we can do is witness to the hope they will be transformed by living our life creatively and serenely in the midst of suffering. Redemption is an ongoing process, and we are still being created. If our unredeemed present is not dealt with, it becomes part of our unredeemed future. The process of healing and redemption extending into the future starts now. We enter this process because no one is fully redeemed until all are. How can you imagine yourself completely happy if someone somewhere is not? Our interconnectedness as the body of Christ makes us responsible for each other. Our present rootedness in the Father, who cares for all, makes us care for all. We are one. We share a common humanity. We are all exposed and complicit in all that is both good and bad in humanity. Even as the dispositions of the people around us directly affect our emotional states—the miserable ones draining us of a sense of joy and life and making us question the presence of God in the world—so, too, our living into a redeemed present by being rooted in God's love can affect the lives of others for the better.

Violence

Miserable people are dissociated from God, and their frustrations turn into forms of aggression and narcissism. Not willing to wait on God, they establish fantasies for well-being imposing violence on others, and ultimately on themselves. Then the kingdom of heaven is overtaken by violence and the violent bear it away (Matthew 11:12). In seeking an order of their own making and by imposing it onto others, disorder is created. This can be seen in the contemporary world where dominant nations use economic sanctions and military power to impose their political systems onto others. Similarly, religious authority is used to reduce community to conformity. Paul rebukes Peter for this bias in the early Christian church. But there is also violence in us: the violence we inherit from living in a discriminatory culture, the violence of family life, and the violence we personally do to ourselves and others. We can acknowledge this violence, but we do not have to live it.

We do not have to be violent in our attempts to help redeem the present. We can live out of our relationship with God and, in the graces of that relationship, we can seek to become peacemakers. The risk we take is that such a stance will destroy us. To live in the present always involves risks. In the beginning of the book of Job, God risks Job to prove to Satan, the accuser, that Job is an inherently good person—he is not good just because of the gifts lavished upon him. Job witnesses to the innate goodness we have been created from. All he has is taken away from him, and he is not even given the comfort of knowing why he suffers. He is left only with his radical dependency upon God. Job maintains this fidelity. Like Job, God also risks us as we live in circumstances that can be personally difficult, for they tempt us to abandon our goodness. We may become so badly burned by the world that we want to have nothing more to do with goodness or with God. We can become so seduced by moral disgust at the corruption and duplicity of those institutions claiming to uphold morals and spiritual values that we distance ourselves from them.

We try to find a path through this world on which we will be unencumbered by simplistic allegiances to distorted interpretations of religion, law and the social contract. We forget the Incarnation invites us not to abandon these narratives, but to explore in them the possibilities of reinterpretation and revitalization for our contemporary world. God is not seduced by a moral disgust for the world. He does not abandon it to its ways, or seek to make apocalyptic moments where all will be wiped out and, maybe, things will start over again. God takes what little good is there and uses it to create something new. The five loaves and two fish feed a multitude. God takes what is destructive and makes it a sign of contradiction. Thus the crucifixion and death of the Christ becomes a witness of supreme love of Christ for the Father and for us. God constantly forgives, redeems and saves. For us, made to love as God loves, there is something similar. When Peter came to Jesus and asked, "Lord, how many times shall I forgive the one who sins against me? Up to seven times?" Jesus answered, "I tell you, not seven times, but seventy-seven times (Matthew 18:21-22). To forgive is to call people to the truth of their lives: that they are lovable, that they can give and receive love. Our witness is to be loving in such a way that others discover a love capable of transforming their violence. Simone Weil observes, "The false God changes suffering into violence. The true God changes violence into suffering."[52] We do not have to repay violence with violence. We do not have to engage in a perpetual dialectic in which one imagined world challenges and tries to absorb another imagined world through power. We must ask a simple question of the imagined worlds our fantasies create in the name of security, or for the sake of belonging, or having a direction in life, or for understanding what is going on: Are these worlds from God? If they are from God, then they are informed by the creativity of God and are distinguished by the presence of the Spirit. They manifest peace, patience, wisdom, joy, compassion, kindness, faithfulness, love and self-control. This does not mean we will never be troubled or harassed, never be at our wits' end or frustrated, and never experience those dark moments when our own violence comes out. To think there could be a life without these feelings is to imagine an unreal life and subscribe to a fantasy. But the awareness of our own brokenness can bring us to places of humility where we want forgiveness from those we have damaged and seek to forgive those who seek to impose their fantasies upon us.

When we do this, we accept, use and share the gift of God's abiding presence with us. We live out of the promise Jesus gave of being with us always, even to the end of time. As we allow the reality of that gift to permeate all the areas of our lives, we discover the things, people and occasions in our present life we can celebrate. When we name and acknowledge them, we find ourselves less trapped by the disorders of the world and we find, through the joy we experience, a path through this damaged world.

The Gifts in the Present

To live in the present is to find what we need to live in the present. The present is a gift; opening that gift means using what the present can offer for our spiritual journey. We may not see what is being given, but this does not mean it is not there.

In 1942, during the Second World War, Picasso used the handlebar and saddle of a junkyard bicycle to create *Head of a Bull*, now on display in the Musée National Picasso in Paris. The two pieces of the discarded bicycle might seem like junk, but in the eyes and hands of a creative person, they come together to form a work of art. What is possible for Picasso is also possible for us in our own ways. Redeeming the present occurs when we use what is given to us in the present to create and celebrate life. To redeem the present, then, is first to be able to see what is in the present with new eyes. This is possible only if we have the vision and the imagination to do so. Such a vision manifests a rootedness in God allowing us to see the world as God sees it. Creation is viewed as unfinished business, capable of transformation, worth saving. This approach allows the creative intimacy of our relationship with the Always Creating Compassionate One to determine our daily lives.

Living in this relationship redeems the present, rather than our fantasy or our penchant for security. Mother Teresa would walk around Calcutta looking for street children to bring back to her ashram so they could be washed, fed, clothed and cared for. One day she found a small dirty boy and brought him to the ashram, but when she went to look for him later, he had gone. She was curious about this. The children she rescued were always content to stay where they could be fed and looked after. But this boy had disappeared. Several days later she saw him back in his original condition and brought him back. Once again he disappeared. Now she became very curious and went out deliberately looking for him. After some time she spotted him. She followed him through the alleyways and open sewers of the slums. He finally ended up with an emaciated woman who was cooking something in a tin can over two cinder blocks. Mother Teresa approached him and asked him why he had run away. He replied, "Because here is home."[53]

The boy's relationship with the one who loved and cared for him was more important than the comfort and security of the or-phanage. That little boy lived in a redeemed present. He knew the difference between security and rootedness. He knew what gave him life. To live in the redeemed present is to know what gives us life, and to choose that life. This is the power of discernment. The previous chapter looked at ways of discernment and ways of refining our skills at discernment so that in the midst of our vulnerability we do not become frozen by fear, unable to distinguish between our needs and our wants, and so confuse imagination and fantasy. Because we are limited beings, we live in conflict between our desires. Jesus himself experienced such a conflict, caught as he was in the Garden of Gethsemane between the fear of death and his desire for the Father. But he knew which path led to life. He did not run from death but chose ongoing intimacy with the Father. His discernment shows a pattern in his life: waiting on the Father and being attentive solely to the Father. For us to discern, even as the little boy in the Mother Teresa story did, we need to know the patterns in our life, for our lives are all a series of patterns, and we need to discover which patterns lead to God and which ones do not.

Because we live out of our desires we are caught in the world of longing, and we must ask ourselves how to live in that world. Which of our longings are manifestations of our life as a desire for God? Which of our longings, separated from our desire for God, lead only to their own satisfaction, and so become destructive? Our separated urges also desire the fullness of life, but they seek it at the cost of our other desires. Our lived experience shows us that only God—not work, or family, or any institution, not even the basic human requirements for food, home, sex or community—satisfies all of our life as desire. Inasmuch as those basic human needs are integrated within our creativity in redeeming the present, they are satisfied without turning us away from our call to the fullness of life. We may derive momentary satisfactions from feeding individual desires, but those transitory pleasures cannot sustain us, and they may become addictive when we expect them to do what only God can do. Since God creates us as desire, God alone fulfills every one of those desires in ways leading us to freedom, to a sense of root-edness and belonging, and to a sense of wonder at the mystery we step into every moment of our lives.

If we accept the radical longing as defining our very sense of being, we can use it to help us discern how to live in the present. This longing purifies us, for we discover nothing and none but God can satisfy us. We acknowledge that longing as the open space inviting the Beloved to enter. We are God's beloved and God so desires us he will not leave us frustrated. But God cannot enter if that empty space is filled up with the preoccupations and idols displacing God. We are not asked to abandon our range of longings.

But we must discover through our lived experience what satisfies those longings and leads us to belong to God, and what does not. This discovery shows us our priorities and our values. It helps us know for ourselves what is more important for our well-being. Not every good thing is good for everyone, and not every good thing is good for the same person all the time. Good spirituality is very practical. It asks a simple question: What is the best thing to be done at this moment?

God desires the best thing for us at every moment, for we are engaged with a God who cares for us at every moment of our lives. So while we yearn for God and for life in all our longings, God also yearns for us. Discernment is not something we do on our own. God is also intimately involved in our discernments, for God desires for each of us the fullness of life. Spiritual intimacy is a two-way street. We might be ready, but we must wait until God is ready to come to us. We might be naked and shameless and say we are ready—as far as we know ourselves—but even so, until God is ready, we must learn to wait until God comes.

Humans do not like to wait. We do not like the sense of emptiness at the root of our life. We do not like the sense of radical dependency on God that is our lot. So we try to fill life up with things. We try one thing and then another to satisfy that emptiness. The social world we live in uses advertisements to suggest what can fill up that emptiness, and we can spend most of our lives accepting those suggestions. T.S. Eliot says that we try everything before we try God.

They constantly try to escape
From the darkness outside and within
By dreaming of systems so perfect that no one will need to
be good.[54]

The postmodern age is distinguished by people who try everything, including the politically correct religious sensibilities available to them today. Some of these are open myths and lead to our immersion in mystery and the drive to community and self-transcendence. Others reinforce our biases and make us self-righteous. Those give us security because they offer us a system in which we abandon our responsibility to be loving and, even more, to accept that we are loved for what we profess, and not simply and absolutely because of who we are, God's beloved. This God gets our attention through covenant moments.

These moments probably occur at every moment of our lives, but those we become aware of emerge when we have tried everything and failed, and have fallen through the cracks of the world. Then we discover our radical dependency on a God we cannot control or coerce. We discover a God who comes to us in our poverty and carries us through our crises into a new and unexpected life. We "find" ourselves when what we have held dear, and have given our lives to, are taken away—be it the loss of loved ones, personal illness, or the termination of a job. We find ourselves held by a God whose care goes deeper than the pattern of habits and the ways we manoeuvre through our daily lives. In the large gap that opens and feels like death, God appears as resurrection. It may take us some time to become aware of a quiet, abiding presence who slowly reweaves our lives into a path offering yet again the fullness of life. Then we discover our present has been redeemed, and, if we reflect, we discover what has redeemed our present is committed to redeeming our present even, and always, now. Redeeming the present always starts with that moment of surrender to, and acceptance of, a love holding all of reality in an abiding and compassionate mercy.

Living in Conflict

In redeeming the present, we realize we are always in conflict between various desires, each longing for satisfaction. We realize to be human is to live in tension, and we seek a peace to resolve that tension. Our desire for peace leads us to ask which desires bring us closer to the peace that passes mere understanding of our human condition and carries us to a place of vulnerability where God can enter our lives and bring us the contentment we seek. It is helpful to list the conflicts in our life and to see which ones are caused by self-interest and are maintained by forms of self-justification, and which ones are caused because we maintain values that rise from our intimacy with God. In his earthly life, Jesus is caught up in this tension, even when he is fully attuned to the Father's love for him and for creation. He himself says of his mission, "Do not think that I have come to bring peace to the earth. I have not come to bring peace, but a sword" (Matthew 10:34). Intimacy with the Father brings us into opposition with those values manifesting other ways of living.

We want to see how we have been conscripted by those values and how they play out in our lives. We can investigate how our self-image contributes to the tensions in our lives because we can dispose ourselves to change those ways that do not make us companions of the Christ. One of the things we can note is our compulsions do not leave us free; some of these compulsions arise because we believe we must maintain the worlds we create. Some of these are established by our raw egoism. Somebody takes away something we feel is ours, or we want, and we become aggressive. We are not free from that aggression precipitating violence. We behave badly. Even as good people we sometimes can be deceived by a lesser good. When we have acted on that lesser good, or on evil presenting itself as a good, and we see the results, we understand how we have been caught. In the play *Hamlet*, the main character says, "I must be cruel, only to be kind."[55] He seeks to revenge his father's murder by his mother's present husband, his uncle Claudius. But in his desire to do good, he causes more deaths than anyone else in the play, and he loses his people's kingdom. We see the same thing happening in our contemporary world. Nations with different value systems from ours are attacked, and in the attempt to bring justice to those we see as oppressed, more chaos and suffering is created. Our domestic lives often reflect the same dynamic. We impose our will on others. This creates resentment, anger and retaliation. Sometimes to maintain our image as tolerant and open, we allow situations to develop that also create destruction. The issue here is not tolerance or intolerance. The self-image we live out of determines how we live in the world.

We can examine ourselves and ask whether our self-image creates violence in ourselves and for others. To redeem the present, we first must allow our self-image to be transformed through our encounter with God, who slowly loves us into changing how we present ourselves to the world. Living in that constant presence of love changes us and allows us to discern what is best in any situation. Discernment frees us from the trap of intensity where we feel compelled to do what we consider to be good and right. It offers us the freedom to do what God would have us do. Our passion for God turns us away from the intensity of justifying ourselves. This passion for God gives us the distance to explore the ambiguities found in every situation and to temper our urges and compulsions to find instant solutions that only exacerbate the situations we find ourselves in. Good spirituality is very political. It realizes we are members of the human family and seeks to make us live as one community rather than as individuals imposing our own particular wishes upon the world. Discernment is never just about ourselves. It always involves those others whose lives will be touched by what we do. It always answers this question: Does what we decide move us all towards the fullness of life, back to the Father?

In his human mission, Jesus places us on this path and on the journey through the beatitudes, carrying us to the stance of peacemakers (Matthew 5:9). These are the ones who accept themselves as the beloved of God and who, like the Christ, bring the compassionate mercy of God into the world by creating community, overcoming the alienation and violence they find in the world.

They lean into the darkness, driven by their longing to be satisfied. They live the beatitude "Blessed are those who hunger and thirst for what is right, they will be satisfied." There is a risk that their sense of emptiness may be prey to addictions, which offer substitutes for God. They need to differentiate between obsessive-compulsive behaviour, which attempts to satisfy their longings, and the invitation to wait on God who does not desire us to be frustrated. Addictive behaviour isolates one aspect of our longing for God, and seeks to satisfy it while ignoring the many other dimensions of that longing. If this behaviour becomes habitual, we end up with divided and conflicted personalities, and experience a struggle for dominance between the different parts of ourselves. As Jesus says in another context, "No one can serve two masters. Either you will hate the one and love the other, or you will be devoted to the one and despise the other. You cannot serve both God and money" (Matthew 6:24). Similarly, our addictive behaviours can drive us away from our ongoing intimacy with God. Addictive behaviours dreadfully take away our freedom and we become trapped.

Their intensity is of quite a different order than the passionate desire we have for God and God has for us. This passionate desire is not loud, quarrelsome, theatrical and self-dramatizing. It is not exclusivist and self-righteous. Its satisfactions do not fill us with shame and regret, or alienate us from others. Instead, God comes to us like the quiet voice who called Samuel to his vocation (1 Samuel 3); often we do not hear it, or we think it is something else. The wisdom of experience allows us to identify this true calling.

In chapter 19 of the first book of Kings, we get a sense of how the passion of God differs from addiction. The prophet Elijah, fleeing from Jezebel, hides out in a cave. There the angel of the Lord comes to him and tells him to stand on the mount of the cave. The Lord passes by, and a great and strong wind tears the mountains and breaks in pieces the rocks before the Lord, but the Lord is not in the wind. And after the wind there is an earthquake, but the Lord is not in the earthquake. And after the earthquake comes a fire, but the Lord is not in the fire. And after the fire there is the sound of a low whisper. When Elijah hears it, he wraps his face in his cloak, goes out and stands at the entrance of the cave. A voice says, "What are you doing here, Elijah?"

The passion between God and us tends to be quiet and found in the ordinary and commonplace. It is, as St. Ignatius says, like water on a sponge, while the work of the enemy of our human nature is like water on a hot rock.

God fills our emptiness quietly and with an intimacy arising from the depths of our being and overflows into our life. That love passes through us into the world as compassionate service redeeming the time. While addiction always results in a self-absorption and taking in life without giving any out, passion, on the other hand, is focused on the other and on the discovery of the other. It differs from narcissism in that it both gives and receives, accepts and offers, in the rhythms of breathing in and breathing out. In fact, one of the ways we can prayerfully get beyond the entrapment of intensity is by attentively following our breath. We can breathe in what we need and we breathe out what arises in us. This breathing in and out as prayer grounds us as creatures held by a loving creator and relates us to the rest of creation as members of one community.

It allows us to relax into who we are, and into a sense of our identity as the beloved of God. We discover we are the pearl of great price God desires. God does not leave us frustrated but rather shares with us his love, values and community. When we accept our radical emptiness, which only God can touch and satisfy, we discover we are that one lost sheep God goes off into the wilderness to find. Poverty of spirit is our human condition. It is the generosity of God to give to such the kingdom of heaven, the fullness of life. We may think it odd of God to leave the ninety-nine sheep and go off into the wilderness to look for the lost one. The wolves might attack those ninety-nine. But they have each other. When attacked, sheep can circle and protect the vulnerable. The lone one is more at risk. Similarly, when we feel isolated and empty, we become more at risk to be tempted, often succumbing to illusions suggesting we can be fulfilled that way. We get trapped and lost, and God must come looking for us, because in our lostness and confusion, we do not know what to do next. We wait to be found, to be comforted, and to have our longings satisfied.

We can pray to the God of excess, who is profligate in love, abounding in mercy, and delights in every aspect of every part of creation, to come and satisfy us. We pray our eyes and hearts be opened to see God already here, attending us, quietly and joyfully. Our sense of longing is to be accepted for ourselves as we are, and if we live out of that sense of longing, we may become more fully who we are: the beloved of God. What that fully means we do not know. We may believe we know ourselves better than God knows us. We may even think if God really knows us as we know ourselves, God will not love us. We forget God loves us even when we sin. In fact, the compassionate mercy of God reveals to us a love that cares for us even when we are separated from God. The Scriptures and our reflections on our lived history reveal to us a God who comes to us to satisfy the longing we are for God.

Often our self-image blocks our acceptance of being loved. Only the encounter with love reveals the distortions of self our self-image maintains. A false self-image, shaped by the values of the world, our perfectionism and bad theology, engenders in us a sense of condemnation and punishment. God does not condemn. God comes to the unloved in love. We are created in love and redeemed by love, and only through love do we return to the fullness of life God offers to all. Rather than hiding those unloved places, we can journey to a more joy-filled life when we bring those unloved places to God and await the transformation he offers. Otherwise we find ourselves trapped in forms of self-destruction, and it feels like hell—that state of being where we do not accept the love always present to us. Accepting the gift of love, living that gift to the extent we can share love, and celebrating the life this sharing gives is the forgiveness redeeming the present and opening it to a creative future.

We find examples of God's unconditional love in some of our own relationships. A friend of mine had a difficult child and was at his wit's end to know what to do. He had tried medication, family therapy and tough love, all with very limited results. The boy kept acting out, which caused major tensions in the family. My friend asked me what should he do, and I wondered aloud if a controlled environment away from the home would be the best solution. We were out driving around a bay as we discussed the problem. In the back seat the son was acting up, kicking and screaming and banging on the windows. As soon as I suggested this solution, it was clear that I had said the wrong thing. My friend fell silent for some time and then spoke. He said, "No, I don't think I will do that. I am going to love him and hope for the best." At this moment I received a revelation years of studying theology had not granted. This is the way God the Father deals with us. He loves us and hopes for the best. This revelation did not end there. The little boy demanded to go swimming even though the tide was out, exposing the mudflats. My friend stopped the car. Father and son stripped down to their underwear, and while I watched from the car, they ran down to the mudflats and rolled around in the red silt, laughing and playing with each other. Watching them, I received a second revelation. This is the way God delights in us.

That was years ago. I have since lost touch with my friend, but I have heard that his son graduated from university after studying child psychology. The love he had received over those long years transformed him and gave him the desire to help others the way he was helped. In such a way we can breathe in and out the love offered to us, and send that awareness to the broken, alienated, frustrated, despised parts of ourselves and the world. We let love do what it desires to do. We allow love to transform the world.

Such a love endures suffering as it holds the forms of destructiveness in the embrace of transformation, as we ourselves suffer while we are loved into being, and love others into the path that leads to life. Love does not escape suffering. Everyone suffers.

We suffer when we are trapped by sin and our identity as loved ones becomes distorted. We are born in a fallen world with a history of violence. No family escapes that violence, though each may experience it in different ways. We ourselves absorb some of that violence and become complicit with it, consciously or not. When we are held by a love that suffers to set us free, we become aware of how we are trapped. We find ourselves in tension between the world to which we have become accustomed and the freedom to which love invites us. There is a life-and-death struggle to abandon the world we know and our familiar ways of knowing. We experience the anxiety of leaving the known for the unknown. We lean into the darkness with fear and trembling because we do not have the hearts to see the love waiting there for us in the darkness. We must wait in that darkness where all our fears and disorders surge up but are not fed, and so wither away. Then we see the love holding us and our families and all of human history from time immemorial so we would not be ravaged by the forces of disorder existentially present in creation.

It is one thing to experience freedom from sin and another thing to learn to live in freedom. Prisoners who are released from confinement may be physically free but may still be emotionally and psychologically trapped by habits of imprisonment. We need to learn how to love as we have been loved. This carries us to the second level of suffering, as we enter the school of charity and first learn to discern between the opposing forces of desire and narcissism lying within us all. We do not have to submit to narcissism if we come to understand its patterns in our lives. It requires an asceticism that facilitates our growth as lovers. We no longer do only what satisfies us. We strive to know and imitate the love journeying with us, through the Incarnation onwards, to the fullness of life. For the Christian, this means developing an intimacy with the Christ, not as a textbook character contained in historical documents, but as the living one whom we have met in our daily lives and in our prayer. There is a cost of discipleship involved in such a relationship. We learn to wait on the Father as a companion of the Christ whose whole mission is to wait on the Father. Intimacy with the Christ manifests itself when we desire to be where the Christ is, and to do what the Christ does. We show our love for the beloved by being where the beloved is. Jesus' invitation to his followers in the Scriptures to come and see where and how he lives is also given to us as his companions in the present day.

We know we respond to the intimacy Jesus offers us when we are willing to be present to him as he goes through his passion, suffering and death on the cross. We all try to avoid suffering, but often it is not possible. It is very difficult to see anyone suffer, and excruciating to be present to the suffering of someone we have come to know and love, especially when we are helpless to do anything about it. When we contemplate the passion and death of the Christ, we see two things happening at the same time. First, we see the love the Son has for the Father is such that nothing, not even a painful, slow and humiliating death, can break that love. We also see the power of the malice of the forces of destruction, which would eradicate love from the world. Jesus' love for the One who calls him "Beloved" is such that he witnesses to his own love for the Father by enduring a painful death. This love allows the Father to transform death into resurrection. Jesus leans into the darkness, where he is exposed to the desolations common to all of humanity: pain, suffering, death. We are daily present to the

Body of Christ suffering, not only in our loved ones or the people we know about, but in all those we encounter. How are we present to them in their helplessness and in ours? We suffer because they suffer, and we cannot turn aside from that suffering even though we are tempted to flee or to anesthetize ourselves to deaden the pain.

Being present to others' suffering carries us to our own depths. We move beyond the boundaries of feeling into what feels like death. We endure that emptiness until life emerges from that place of intimacy where our emptiness and poverty of spirit are touched by God's presence. What comes from that encounter is pure gift. It is resurrection.

Often we live our lives as tragedy, and consider the presence of resurrection in this fallen world as escapist piety or a form of religious sentimentality. We do not dare to expose ourselves to hope, and so hope and the source of hope must come to us. But imagine what is possible if we actually believed in the resurrection. The power of the resurrection is not for an afterlife. It is for this life. What we experienced when we discovered we are freed from the traps that bind us is the presence of the resurrection moving into our lives and changing the stories we live by. Our life as witnesses to resurrection carries us to those places where love is needed, and there we give to others what has been given to us. There is suffering involved in going to the broken places of the world to share life and bring peace. Paul, in his second letter to the Corinthians, lists his sufferings for living the resurrection. He writes,

> Five times I received from the Jews thirty-nine lashes. Three times I was beaten with rods, once I was stoned, three times I was shipwrecked, a night and a day I have spent in the deep. I have been on frequent journeys, in dangers from rivers, dangers from robbers, dangers from my country-men, dangers from the Gentiles, dangers in the city, dangers in the wilderness, dangers on the sea, dangers among false brethren; I have been in labor and hardship, through many sleepless nights, in hunger and thirst, often without food, in cold and exposure. Apart from such external things, there is the daily pressure on me of concern for all the churches. (2 Corinthians 11:24-28)

The lives of the holy ones throughout history reveal similar sufferings they endured in witnessing to the salvation they experienced from God. When we bring love into the world, we also suffer. But there is also another form of suffering worth mentioning. It is the asceticism of joy. We are asked to dispose our lives so as to live joyfully, and this means we cannot live tragically. We are asked to notice, share and celebrate what is good in life, which takes discipline, because we often deny ourselves the joy that is ours. There is a kind of suffering when we have to go against those learned attitudes that being good to ourselves is a selfish thing. It is joy that transforms the world, and living joyfully is a sign of the redeemed present.

That sense of joy struggles against those other forces in our lives ignoring the good always present. We must be watchful and discerning not to be so totally consumed by the bad we ignore the good. We are not to ignore the bad and so live in a world of fantasy, but to acknowledge and celebrate what is daily given. If we are burdened we have to discover ways in which we can live with those burdens—depression or unavoidable painful relationships and situations—so we continue our spiritual journey towards the fullness of life. To do this is to take up our cross and follow Jesus. Jesus says, "If anyone wishes to come after me, let him deny himself, and take up his cross, and follow me" (Mark 8:34). We are not asked to take up Christ's cross—that is Christ's own mission—but to take up our own cross. We also note that Jesus does not say take up your cross and I will follow you, nor does he say take up your cross and don't move. Redeeming the present is admitting the ways in which we suffer, but not becoming frozen by suffering. Someone may be trapped in an abusive relationship and become so traumatized by it, he cannot get free. That person may even come to be so broken by the situation as to believe it is God's will. But God does not desire us to be destroyed, and it is sick to live with that lie.

We live with our humanity as we experience it. We do not deny that humanity, nor do we wallow in our brokenness. We are always invited to live simply and hopefully in that brokenness, waiting for the salvation promised us. As we face the future we can ask ourselves, "What is the love I am invited to? How is it to shape me now? What is the next step?"

We need to let love show us that next step. Years ago, a young medical intern came on retreat. He had just one day to decide what career path to follow. He was concerned with the plight of the poor who lived far away from urban centres, and felt a sense of duty to them. He also wanted to be an anesthesiologist, but he figured he could not justify this since he would be dealing mainly with comatose patients. What was he to do? I asked him if he had asked God. He answered that the only clear direction he had received was to come for this one-day retreat. It was snowing heavily outside, so I suggested he go for a walk in the storm and simply ask God the question. He set out, dubious about the outcome, but willing to give it a try. I must admit to being a little surprised when he came back about an hour later, quite excited. Something had happened during his walk. When he asked God if he was to be a generalist, all he felt was the storm and the cold, but when he asked God if he was to be a specialist, he felt a sense of life and excitement and a quiet joy. He was going to be an anesthesiologist. I do not know why God waited until the snowstorm, but I do know in living a redeemed present, we do not follow our conscripted imaginations but open ourselves in allowing God to re-imagine us. God imagines us beyond our own imagining, and our spiritual journey is always a calling to us to travel beyond ourselves. We do this by accepting the redeemed future offered to us.

Our Redeemed Future

It is our Christian belief that God is more powerful than evil and has chosen to conquer evil in his own mysterious way by allowing Christ to fulfill his identity as a human being. This the Christ does by remaining faithful to his love for the Father even as he is battered by the forces of evil and dies a painful death on the cross. The love the Father has for Jesus transforms the dead Jesus into a new creation offered to us. We are offered salvation by remaining faithful to the Father as Christ in his humanity does. Even when we are not faithful to that relationship, the Father's love comes to us again and again to rescue us from the traps into which our infidelity has led us.

Our Christian belief is God has conquered evil. We are already saved. Our human response is to accept that salvation and to live it in our lives here and now. The gift of redemption does not allow us to escape death, but assures us death is not the end of our life, and it is the work of the Trinity to bring us not only to resurrection but to the fullness of life in communion with all of creation and with the Creator. In this new narrative God offers us, death is not the end but the door to a fuller and newer life. This new life is a journey that leads to the fullness of life. As the book of Revelation tells us, the angel of God is commanded to announce, "These are the words of him who is holy and true, who holds the key of David. What he opens no one can shut, and what he shuts no one can open. I know your deeds. See, I have placed before you an open door that no one can shut" (Revelation 3:7-8). This open door leads to the fullness of life. This door is opened to each one of us, and it is the path, the next step we have to take to the life offered to us. Each step both takes up something new and lets go of something old. Each step is a death leading to a resurrection. One of the gifts of living the redeemed future is the awareness of being always in transition. To be human is to be a pilgrim. Paul's letter to the Hebrews tells us, "Here we have no abiding city, but we look for the city that is to come" (Hebrews 13:14).

We can refuse to accept our pilgrim nature, seeking security instead in what is impermanent. That refusal denies the relationship God establishes with us. Also, there are times when we are forced to accept our pilgrim status, whether we like it or not, and we do so with a sense of fear and anxiety. Then we do not accept or cherish the gift of the new life—that promise of salvation—offered to us. Instead, the unknown terrifies us. But imagine how differently we would live life if we actually believed not only that God can transform every evil into resurrection, but also that this same God desires only our well-being. As Jeremiah points out, God's plans for us are peace and not disaster (Jeremiah 29:11). We can step into the future with the assurance we are saved and loved and looked after. The grace we ask for to live a redeemed future is not only confidence, but also the ability to see truly the open door set before us, and to celebrate that gift given to us by living it joyfully and creatively.

All our paths lead to God. But living in time, we have choices about what paths to take: some paths bring us to God more joyfully than others. There is no mistake God cannot transform in God's own time and freedom into good. God has conquered evil and death. But when or how or where, and by what means given for each of us to share in that victory, is not ours to know. Each of us has a unique path. What we do know is everything will be transformed. "Everyone who belongs to Christ will be given new life. But there is an order to this resurrection: Christ was raised as the first of the harvest; then all who belong to Christ will be raised when he comes back. After that the end will come, when he will turn the kingdom over to God the Father" (1 Corinthians 15:23-4) after conquering everything, including death. We also know why. God loves us. We are his desire and his beloved.

Paul's letter to the Ephesians puts it simply when he prays that

the God of our Lord Jesus Christ, the Father of glory, may give you a spirit of wisdom and of revelation in the knowledge of him, having the eyes of your hearts enlightened, that you may know what is the hope to which he has called you, what are the riches of his glorious inheritance in the saints, and what is the immeasurable greatness of his power in us who believe, according to the working of his great might which he accomplished in Christ when he raised him from the dead and made him sit at his right hand in the heavenly places, far above all rule and authority and power and dominion, and above every name that is named, not only in this age but also in that which is to come; and he has put all things under his feet and has made him the head over all things for the church, which is his body, the fullness of him who fills all in all. (Ephesians 1:17-23)

In this stance of being so loved, we are neither arrogant nor presumptuous. We are not ego-based. We stand in relationship and live out of the relationship of lover to beloved. We live out of the promise Christ has made in Mark's gospel. "I tell you solemnly, whatever you ask for in prayer, believe you have received it, and it will be yours" (Mark 11:24).

It is the nature of love never to leave the beloved abandoned, and never to leave the unloved unlovable. It is the nature of love to bring light and life to the dark places of human existence, and to be loving even in those dark places, so we come to experience transformation into a life we can share and celebrate. We are invited as lovers of the beloved to share in the work of bringing all to the fullness of life. But we first must have significant experiences of being so loved before we effectively cooperate with the grace given to us. Otherwise, we work out of our (often unconscious) biases and, in the name of good, create more chaos. As an old spiritual director once told me in rather simple terms, the goody-goodies often do more damage than the baddy-baddies! Prudent discernment leads us to ask the beloved, "What, if anything, do you want me to do?" We wait for the answer. Sitting with the future as redeemed first means simply allowing ourselves to be present to the gift in a conscious way so it can open and transform us.

The Gift of Resurrection

Dennis and Sheila Linn, along with Dennis's brother, Fr. Matthew Linn S.J., wrote a book on the Ignatian Examen called *Sleeping with Bread*. It opens with this story.

> During the bombing raids of World War II, thousands of children were orphaned and left to starve. The fortunate ones were rescued and placed in refugee camps where they received food and good care. But, many of these children who had lost so much could not sleep at night. They feared waking up to find themselves once again homeless and without food. Nothing seemed to reassure them. Finally, someone hit upon the idea of giving each child a piece of bread to hold at bedtime. Holding their bread, these children could finally sleep in peace. All through the night the bread reminded them, "Today I ate and I will eat again tomorrow."[56]

For us, the lived awareness of our redeemed future is the bread we hold in the darkness of our lives. I have an Irish friend whose grandmother slept with a bottle of gin under her pillow. He said that when she woke up at night, troubled by nightmares and name-less terrors, she would reach under her pillow for the bottle. She was able to sleep knowing it was there. We can ask ourselves what we hold onto that allows us to see the future as not being indifferent to our needs. Evil makes us feel we will not be looked after but will be destroyed. The future makes us vulnerable, because we have little or no control over it. The world we create by our habitual patterns of behaviour may give us the illusion what we have become accustomed to will prevail in the future. But this is simply not true. We are constantly changing and the world around us is changing, too. Habits do not defend us against that reality. All our plotting and scheming, or burying our heads in the sand, or thinking it is "business as usual," all our optimism, pessimism or apathy cannot force the future to conform to our perspectives. The future is a mystery. But when we are trapped by what we want from the future, discernment becomes very difficult, because then the freedom to allow the future to be is compromised and we cannot see what is coming to us.

All we can do is dispose ourselves to receive the future when it comes. Sitting with our redeemed present and with the covenant moments of our redeemed past disposes us to be open to the redeemed future. Then we see that, rather than needing to visit our redeemed future, it comes to us.

Redemption Comes to Us

The Annunciation came to us. Mary was prepared and dis-posed, but she did not go towards the angel. That visitation was pure gift. Similarly, resurrection comes to us. Jesus, in his death, did not resurrect himself. That was the gift of the Father coming to him and to us. This new creation transforms the old into something previously unimagined. Pentecost, that free gift of sharing in the life of the love between the Father and the resurrected humanity of Jesus, also comes to us. Like the disciples in that upper room, trapped in their fear, we also remain caught in our fallen imaginations, until we are liberated into new ways of seeing and living by the coming of the Spirit. Divine love coming into our daily lives exhibits the same dynamics. We wait, love comes, and if we accept it, we are transformed.

In all of this, God searches for us and comes to us bearing gifts of salvation, resurrection and transformation. We cannot go to salvation. It comes to us. All we can do is wait in such a way as to be able to see salvation when it comes to us. In Luke's gospel, we have the story of Simeon and Anna. They are old, and they have lived their lives devoutly in the midst of foreign occupation under a corrupt administration of their religion. Their patient endurance under such trials shows them what does not work. It takes away illusions from their lives but allows them to remain people of the Promise. This purified passion of their desire for the fullness of life allows them to see, in a poor man and woman bringing their little child to the temple, not just another simple family obeying the law of purification, but the Messiah with his mother, Mary, and her spouse, Joseph. And some 33 years later, when that baby has become a man and is executed for breaking religious taboos, two of his disciples encounter someone who opens their eyes and hearts to receive a new story; they encounter the risen Christ on the road to Emmaus.

The earlier disappointment of the two disciples does not close them off from their desire for the fullness of life. In fact, disappointment is the manifestation of that desire and also the manifestation of its purification. There is a world of difference between disappointment and despair. We can hope against even the secular constructions of hope from which no one is exempt. T.S. Eliot reflects on this this idea:

> be still, and wait without hope
> For hope would be hope for the wrong thing; wait without love,
> For love would be love of the wrong thing; there is yet faith
> But the faith and the love and the hope are all in the waiting.[57]

Waiting is not passive or apathetic. Waiting is a form of patience, very much like the dog standing by the window focused and attentive to the return of its owner, while ignoring the cat and the squirrels in the yard or the children playing games in the street. Waiting moves beyond distraction. Indeed, waiting is the way to open the gift of the redeemed future, and just as there are stages in living a gift, so, too, there are stages in waiting. We accept a gift, open it, use it, share it and celebrate it. Waiting is not something we do as a Sunday duty when we attend a religious ceremony, and for that time only are attentive to the values the ceremony addresses.

Waiting shapes every moment of our lives, and even in sleeping, the energies of our life are disposed to that manifestation of human desire. Before we sleep, St. Ignatius suggests we call to mind what we want to be attentive to the next day. That conscious preparation disposes our sleep to the work of a focused awareness even when we are not awake. St. Ignatius further suggests we, when we awaken, turn our awareness to what we desire to contemplate and to do; his introduction to every prayer contains this injunction: "I will beg God our Lord for grace that all my intentions, actions, and habits, may be directed purely to the praise and service of His Divine Majesty" (Sp. Ex. #46). Waiting focuses whatever we do, and in this way we use the gift of the redeemed future. Our focus maintains that intimacy with the Beloved.

As we live this way, we discover it defines who we are and opens us to a community of others who seek or live what we have found. Waiting for our redeemed future creates community with that common value of hope transcending culture or religion. Hope is attentiveness to the redeemed future in our present life. The gift of the redeemed future opens us to each other as members of the human family, each offered a unique path to the fullness of life.

That path does not take us away from the tensions of struggling to be human in a complicated world, but allows us to live more joyfully in the present and frees us from unnecessary anxiety and fear. From our intimacy with God, we know, no matter what can happen to us, nothing will separate us from the love of God (Romans 8:39). But it takes time to accept this love and its gift of the redeemed future. As we stay with this gift and allow it to open us, we become strangers to ourselves, and this leaves us with a sense of wonder. Who am I to be so loved? What does that love desire to show me or lead me to? What is this new world that is appearing to me? While the Socratic ideal is to know ourselves, the ideal in spiritual intimacy is different. It is to lose ourselves. The gift leads us into the unknown. Imagine you have been living in a dark room for most of your life and have become accustomed to the darkness. Then someone turns on the light. At first you are blinded by the light and become panic stricken. You shut your eyes and try to live in a world that now is only a memory. But slowly you become accustomed to the light and start seeing colours and shapes. You can move around the furniture of the room without stumbling into it and hurting yourself. You can even move things around to make an easier living space. Accepting the gift of the redeemed future is like that. It is a stage of falling in love with God. Every new stage on the path of spiritual intimacy is like falling in love for the first time. We are attracted and frightened by what calls us to new forms of delight, but we also regret giving up the comforts of the old, even though we are liberated from its traps.

We experience our ambivalences as consolations and desolations, and so accepting the gift of the redeemed future requires of us the gift of discernment so we do not forsake what the Beloved is offering us. It takes a long time to accept the gifts love offers; often that first embrace of love feels like pain. But it is the pain of withdrawing from addiction to narcissism. At this stage, we must be gentle with ourselves to discover what we can do and what we are invited to do. We do not run ahead of the grace offered to us, and the God who desires us in total intimacy does not abuse us. That sense of discernment is not ideologically driven, nor is it a question of sentimentality or duty. It emerges from a lived sense of life as a spiritual path, and it is felt in the body. The body contains not only our lived histories but also our anticipated future. We experience that future as a sense of expectation.

The power of the Incarnation moving through our lives towards the new creation, which is the fulfillment of resurrection, leads us not just to hope but to expect that redeemed future. We can live our days with that sense of expectation. When I was a child, my parents would put our presents under the Christmas tree a few days before Christmas. We knew they were there, but we did not know what exactly what they were. At night, when everyone was sleeping, one of my sisters would go down to the living room, carefully open the presents, and then seal them up again. As Christmas drew near, she would go around the house telling the others, "I know what you are getting; I know what you are getting." Her knowing and our ignorance increased the level of expectation and excitement to fever pitch. We lived those days like hunting dogs on point, focused on what was ours already but not yet. We felt the anticipation in our bodies, and even when we were somewhat distracted by other things, those wrapped presents with our names on them were always at the edge of our awareness. That awareness engaged and focused our energies, and we lived with the expectation of joy, wonder and delight at what was already given but not yet fully ours. It gave us a concrete sense of being loved and cared for, and we became more attentive to others, filled with a sense of adventure and pleasure in being alive. It shaped what we saw and how we saw it, what we did and how we did it. The presents, unopened, were the redeemed future awaiting us. If I were to extend the analogy a bit further, Jesus is a bit like my sister, knowing what is coming and telling us about it.

Jesus lives the redeemed future in his earthly life. In love he leans towards the Father who in turn leans towards him. What Jesus offers the world is the same spirit he has with the Father. God is not separate from human beings, and we can live our lives with the same expectations Jesus had of the intimacy he shares with his Beloved. He tells us, "Whatever you ask for in prayer, believe that you have received it, and it will be yours" (Mark 24:11). John's gospel gives the basis of that belief. It is a lived intimacy with the Father. In that gospel Jesus says,

> "Believe me that I am in the Father and the Father is in me, or else believe on account of the works themselves. Truly, truly, I say to you, whoever believes in me will also do the works that I do; and greater works than these will he do, because I am going to the Father. Whatever you ask in my name, this I will do, that the Father may be glorified in the Son. If you ask me anything in my name, I will do it." (John 14:11-14)

Living the redeemed future here and now is possible only when we accept an intimacy with the Father offered to all. As John's gospel points out, our work is to believe (John 6:29). And it is work to believe. In a world so marred by tragedy, we are tempted to live tragic lives, and so we need to cultivate the habit of joy. An asceticism is necessary for living joyfully, and it is developed by loving ourselves the way the Father loves all of us. A regular self-reflection focusing on remembering what has been gift in our recent life promotes such a sense of gratitude and trust. But we can also be generous and kind to ourselves.

Often we do not. We deny ourselves what is available and enjoyable to us. I remember once walking past Tiffany's, the jewellery store on Bloor Street in Toronto, with my sister. She saw me looking at their display windows and asked, "Have you ever gone in?" I said no, it was out of my range. We were dressed in jeans and knit shirts and hardly looked like the clientele for a place like that. She grabbed my hand and marched past the armed guard, across the marble floor to the section with the diamond display. We were looking at the rings and brooches in the case when a salesperson came up and asked if we needed help. My sister, who was admiring a diamond necklace of matching stones, said, "That is very beautiful." The salesperson asked if she wanted to see it and she said yes. He took it out of the case, and asked if she wanted to try it on. She said yes. He put it on her. It looked stunning. I remember being filled with a sense of delight. She asked how much it was, and he told her. It was in the upper six figures. She looked at herself in the mirror, touching the stones, and smiling and, after a few seconds, repeated, "It is very beautiful, but we can't afford it." She turned, allowing him to take it off, then we drifted through the store looking at the other precious things, none of which we could afford. Then we left.

My sister may not remember that little incident, but it remains significant in transforming my life story. Often the stories we live out of exclude us from what is free and available to us. We might believe we are not worthy, or that certain gifts are not for us, or we are not aware of what is possible. This is even more so for the gift of the redeemed future, and as a result we live diminished lives.

The gift of the redeemed future assures us that no matter how difficult our lives may be, such a state is not permanent or absolute. In Matthew's gospel, Jesus reminds us we are precious in the

Father's eyes and this same Father cares for us, so much so that he enjoins us not to worry (Matthew 6:25-34). Jesus assures us the Father will give us what we need (Matthew 7:7-11).

Like the characters in the parable of the day labourers (Matthew 20:1-16), we, too, need our daily bread. In fact, we ask for it in the Lord's Prayer. The word "daily" that describes the bread we need for survival is a translation of the Greek word *epiousios*. This word has these four meanings—what we need to survive; our bread for tomorrow; our necessary bread; and our bread for the age to come. The Catholic tradition uses the word *epiousios* literally as "super + substantial." In 1551, the Council of Trent described the Holy Eucharist as supersubstantial bread. What we need to live fully in our present state is spiritual food, the actual presence of the redeemed future transforming how we live our daily lives. The word "eucharist" itself means "thanksgiving." The presence of the redeemed future in our life is both a gift and a living out of that gift gratefully. We celebrate in our very lives what has come to us freely in love.

A celebration of life carries us beyond anxiety and beyond the traps of the unredeemed present; how we live now transforms how we approach the future. The traps of the unredeemed present lie in the false stories we find ourselves in and in the securities they give us about a familiar world. Being rooted in love, we can afford to put down these false myths and with empty arms embrace the Beloved coming to us. In living a redeemed future, we are invited to enter into a reality going beyond the limits of our imagination and find there a love waiting to be found and to embrace us. That reality is present now.

There is an old Hasidic story about Itzak, a very poor man living in a small village in Czechoslovakia. One night Itzak dreamed of a great treasure buried under a bridge in Prague. He believed in dreams, and so he left his family and headed off to Prague to find the treasure. After a long journey, he arrived in Prague and found the very bridge that had appeared in his dream. Itzak began to dig into the earth under that bridge. He dug and dug but found nothing. He fell to the mud and wept.

Soon, along came a policeman, and he nudged Itzak with his nightstick. "What are you doing here, peasant?" asked the policeman. Itzak told the policemen about his dream.

"Oh, what a fool you peasants are," the policeman said. "Who believes in such dreams? Why just the other night I had a dream in which there was an undiscovered treasure that was under the stove in the house of a certain peasant named Itzak in a tiny village of our country. But I would never have wasted such time and energy to have travelled such a distance at such a great cost to myself and my family."

Itzak thanked the policeman and hurried back home. In his house he moved the stove. Under it was the great and unimaginable treasure.[58]

What is present all the time in each of our lives is the unimaginable treasure of the redeemed future, but we live in the poverty of our closed and broken myths as the only reality we accept. The rest seems only a dream. But the openness the redeemed future calls us to allows God to redeem our imagination, and so we start to see what is possible with God. Postmodern epistemology understands we create the reality we see. The redeemed future opens our eyes to see and allows us to live our life in God's time, not our own. In our own time we may ask, "Why does the Father wait so long?" But God's time is strange, and God's ways are not our ways. The prophet Isaiah writes, "'My thoughts are not your thoughts, nor are your ways my ways,' says the Lord. 'For as the heavens are higher than the earth, so are my ways higher than your ways, and my thoughts than your thoughts'" (Isaiah 55:8-9). How else can we understand Paul's letter to the Galatians, where it is written, "When the fullness of time had come, God sent forth his Son, born of woman, born under the law, to redeem those who were under the law, so that we might receive adoption as sons" (Galatians 4:4)? How can the fullness of time occur when, at the time of Jesus' birth, his country was subject to a brutal foreign occupation, corruption of the religious institutions, civil unrest, slavery and abuse of the poor and marginalized? The fullness of time is the moment when a despoiled creation encounters the divine mercy. At that time, creation's desire for the fullness of life, now frustrated by sin, accepts the gift of divine intervention. A young woman risks her present for a redeemed future. She accepts the call of the open myth and gives her life over fully to the Desire who desires all of us. Her name was Mary, and through her radical and total abandonment to Divine Providence, Christ was born into the world.

The fullness of time comes to us, too, when we are willing to risk our present for the redeemed future. We are not asked to throw ourselves into the future as though we were jumping off a cliff's edge. We are asked simply to be open to the future when it comes to us. Mary's readiness did not mean God had to come. God comes when God wants. Living the redeemed future in the present is first and foremost learning how to wait. God is not like the dog outside the door, waiting for the door to open, to leap in and slobber all over us. God has God's freedom. Jesus waits eighteen years after his open declaration that he must be about his Father's business before the Father publicly acknowledges him as his beloved son. The gifts we have, and the crises we see that cry out for salvation, do not compel us into action as we wait on God. Only God's will and time matter. The British poet John Milton (1608–1674) considers this question in his sonnet "On His Blindness."

> *When I consider how my light is spent,*
> *Ere half my days, in this dark world and wide,*
> *And that one talent which is death to hide,*
> *Lodged with me useless, though my soul more bent*
> *To serve therewith my maker, and present*
> *My true account, lest he returning chide,*
> *Doth God exact day-labour, light denied?*
> *I fondly ask; but Patience to prevent*
> *murmur, soon replies, God doth not need*
> *Either man's work or his own gifts, who best*
> *Bear his mild yoke, they serve him best, his state*
> *Is kingly. Thousands at his bidding speed*
> *And post o'er land and ocean without rest:*
> *They also serve who only stand and wait.*[59]

Despite that waiting, Milton's many gifts of rhetoric are not lost, and he is known in English literature as one of its finest poets, author of the magisterial epic poem "Paradise Lost" and its sequel, "Paradise Regained."

Living for the Future

Living for the redeemed future can, at times, seem as if everything we hold dear is lost. Even our experience of our faith, our trust and our relationship in the one we love and who loves us carries us beyond what we expect or wish for. It happened to Martha and Mary when their brother Lazarus fell sick, became gravely ill and died. Jesus did nothing for them at that time. Jesus' raising of Lazarus from the dead restored him to Mary and Martha. But Jesus could have prevented Lazarus's death. Jesus had the ability. Though he grieved the loss of his close friend, he attended the Father's disposition and waited until a rescue seemed impossible to those concerned. Similarly, living the redeemed future asks us to lean into the darkness of the open myth. On one level we might feel lonely and isolated, abandoned, even, but at a deeper level, at times beyond feeling and intuition, we are always connected to the forces of good and to our companions on a similar journey. As Paul reminds us,

> neither death nor life, neither angels nor demons, neither the present nor the future, nor any powers, neither height nor depth, nor anything else in all creation, will be able to separate us from the love of God that is in Christ Jesus our Lord. (Romans 8:38-39)

We are surrounded by love—the forces of good and life, the saints, the angels, God—at every moment of our lives. It is helpful to be aware we are not caught up in some static composition of place. The love surrounding us and holding us is active, involved, concerned and dynamic. This love cares for us and is committed to us. It seeks to share and celebrate with us the life it lives. Often it is quite helpful to sit and allow ourselves to become aware of this ever-present reality. We can breathe it in to every fibre of our being, so we become one with it. We can breathe it out to every aspect of our broken world. In so doing, we share in the work and the life of those who lives are manifestations of love, no matter who or where they are in the spirit. We are both with the community of the good and not fully aware we are with them, being still a pilgrim people journeying to the fullness of life.

We must also be rescued from the traps we find ourselves caught in, and so one aspect of living in the redeemed future is learning how to wait for the beloved to return to rescue us. We wait like a favoured pet at a front window for its owner to return, and all our senses are attuned to that return, for we know nothing and no one else can satisfy so completely. This waiting does not mean we do nothing, but rather that we live in a certain way. If we live out of the expectation love will come to us, we open ourselves to seeing it when it comes, and to see aspects of it in our lives and around us already. Our examen allows it to become part of our daily lived reality, and its presence in our lives allows us to discern properly. It provides a certain resonance between us and those forces of love.

We feel this connection in the body. It feels different than when we are called to do something out of a sense of duty. Usually when that happens, the sensation comes from the head and blocks out alternatives. The rightness of belonging is felt in the guts, or deeper down, where we are rooted. In a film about Jackson Pollock, the American abstract expressionist painter who flung liquid paint onto canvasses, a reporter interviews the painter at work. He asks Pollock how he knew when he was finished. Pollock replies, "How do you know when you're finished making love?"[60] That sense of rightness, completion and union experienced by the painter and the lover is also felt in the body by the one discerning. The body is wise, but the body needs first to be healed and loved into being. Redeeming the past and the present allows this to happen. This does not mean suddenly we are in paradise while the rest of creation suffers. Living a redeemed future is not living in a perfect world. It is about taking up our cross and following Jesus as he faces the future in his return to the Father.

There is a Zen story about a monk who desired enlightenment and visited one famous monastery after another in search of that goal. Nothing happened. Finally, in disgust, he decided to go to a mountaintop and fast until he either received enlightenment or died. On his way up, he passed an old monk carrying his worldly belongings in a sling bag over his shoulder. They stopped to talk and the young monk asked the old one if he had received enlighten-ment. "Yes," said the old man. "And what is it like?" the young one asked. The old man shrugged his shoulders and the bag dropped to the ground. "And what is it like after?" the young monk asked excitedly. At this, the old man picked up his bag, put it back on his shoulder and continued down the mountain.[61]

Developing an intimacy with God does not allow us to escape the trials of this life. It gives us a relationship that allows us not to be destroyed by them but instead to use them to deepen our intimacy with the Beloved. They make us realize even more our absolute dependency on God. We are not God and we should not try to be God. This form of perfectionism is destructive to ourselves and to others. It denies the humility necessary to be human and to live peacefully in relationship with others and with God. When we think we are God, we are always trying to change something, or ourselves, to make it better according to our own value system. In humility we wait on grace to be given before we act, and we discern rather than decide how to act.

In the 1970s, many people were concerned with social justice and threw themselves wholeheartedly into the cause. They picketed, attended demonstrations, lived in poverty and defied with their very bodies oppressive institutions and conglomerates on every social front. Almost all of the ones I knew lost their sense of joy and peace. They became bitter and angry, frustrated and disillusioned. Many in religious life left. They had a vision of a perfect world, and they had the time, energy and, they thought, the means to achieve that perfect world. But they did not. They lost first a sense of prayer, then a sense of a lived relationship with God. They abandoned the friendships of those who did not share their ideological beliefs, and, in losing all this, they lost themselves. The gospel asks, "What does it profit a man to gain the whole world and to lose his soul?" (Matthew 16:26). The failure of those involved in running ahead of grace, without learning to wait on God, carries that stark gospel message even further. What does it profit anyone to try to gain the whole world and in the process to lose her soul? As a recent document on Jesuit religious life points out, a companion of Jesus is not satisfied with just any response to the needs of the times. This response must reveal in all things the initiative of God's love and the Lord's way of proceeding to work in it.[62]

Yet, to lean into the darkness of an open myth does seem like losing our soul. There is a story about St. Ignatius of Loyola when he became the first general of the Jesuits and his conversation with his close companion Jerome Nadal. The two friends were walking and Ignatius asked Nadal, "If you had a choice between dying now, and going to heaven, having the full beatific vision, and living to risk your immortal soul to do something for God, what would you do?" Nadal said he would choose the beatific vision now. Ignatius is reported to have looked at the ground a long time and then replied, "I would do the other thing."[63] Those people who wanted to do something for God and threw themselves, souls and all, into the fight against social injustices risked themselves. We need to ask, then, the question for discernment. What is the difference between them and St. Ignatius?

The answer lies in waiting on the Father. Ignatius learned, in humility, to wait on the Father. He did not run ahead of grace. He never had a vision of a perfect world. What he had was a vision of service, obedient like Christ, always to the Father's will. In fact, if one studies Ignatius's writings—the Exercises, the Constitutions of the Jesuits, his spiritual autobiography and his letters—one discovers not closed systems but actually open and flexible ones allowing a person and a community to discern what is of value in a present situation. A famous incident that took place in the newly formed Society of Jesus involved a Portuguese provincial who was pestering Ignatius about what to do in certain instances. Ignatius sent him back a letter. It was a blank sheet of paper, at the bottom of which Ignatius had signed his name.

That sense of openness and flexibility can emerge only from the lived experiences of being cared for by Divine Providence. It comes only from the mutuality of a spiritual intimacy developed over a lifetime. The fruits of that intimacy are shown in joy—that state of being in which we realize we are looked after, cared for and cherished in all the ups and downs of our life. Joy comes not because we have answers or projects for the future. In fact, God does not give answers. What God gives us are experiences. We learn how to be joyful by being joy-filled, just as we learn to wait by waiting. We cannot program ourselves to be joyful. This comes as a result of being truly intimate with God, and in that intimacy, discovering we are truly loved, cared for and delighted in.

Being joyful is different from being happy. Joy comes when we are aware our consciousness is linked to God so we share the same perspectives and values, delight in the same things, and experience a giving and taking between the lover and the beloved in this relationship. Happiness comes when our energies resonate with what is good in creation—which is different from the Creator. I can be happy by doing good, or when good is done to me, or when a group of us work together for a common good. Then I have a sense of meaning, value, community and belonging. I may know nothing of God, but I know what it is to be in sync with the effects of the energies of God. Contentment comes when we are satisfied with who we are and what we have done. The larger contexts of happiness and joy may be absent, and the object of my contentment, such as a project completed or the acceptance of myself, away from the goad of perfectionism, may be quite limited. Pleasure occurs when my feelings coincide with my sense of self. If I am a thief and I have just stolen something, I may have a sense of pleasure. If I am a parent and my child has done something charming, I experience a sense of pleasure. The context is my own sense of self, so I can take pleasure in the misfortune of others—since misery loves company—as well as in their good fortune. I become the determinant of what gives pleasure or not. Finally, I experience a sense of excitement when my senses are stimulated. I can have adrenaline rushes—by taking risks or using stimulants—and become excited even when the means are destructive to my joy or happiness.

In all of this we do not confuse reality with our feelings. Feelings are signs. They indicate our response or our reading of a particular reality. It is only as such that they allow us a limited access to reality. We are more than our feelings, and our vision of reality is defined by our imagination. Thus, while God can dialogue with us through our imagination, God is more than we can imagine, and while we can enter processes of discernment through our feelings, we are more than our feelings. Reading feelings rightly, instead of fundamentally, is a form of spiritual semiotics. It requires a relationship with Mystery. Ultimately, we are mystery, and made in the image and likeness of the Mystery we name by that other word: "God."

What we do know is God desires us to live joyfully, and so we need to learn how to dispose ourselves to be joyful. We can ask God this simple question: How do you want me to be joyful?

The path to joy comes in accepting a redeemed future, and living joyfully opens the gifts of the future. Joy allows us to anticipate the future so that longing becomes desire incarnate. It allows us to do more than just to vaguely hope; it focuses us so we can discern who and what it is we hope for. It opens our eyes to see the coming of the Messiah, the coming of the Spirit and the coming of the kingdom. It disposes us to work for that coming. It allows us to know the delight of the presence of that kingdom in our very midst here and now. We experience it in the simple love we share with those who love us into being and whom we love into being.

As we accept the gift of the redeemed future, we learn how to open it by living for it. We find ourselves committed to it, and this commitment slowly transforms us as it transformed Peter after his encounter with the risen Christ in John 21. There Jesus asks Peter if he loves (*agape*) him; Peter replies that they are friends (*philia*). Jesus asks again the same question using the same verb and Peter once again replies as he did the first time. The third time Jesus asks Peter the question, he uses the verb *philia*—are we friends? Peter replies, yes they are friends. The rest of Peter's life is a transformation of the relationship from *philia* (friendship) to *agape* (love). This is the same Peter who, on recognizing the Christ, does not ask to walk on water to come to Jesus but leaps into the water and swims to him. This is not the critical response to the beloved manifested earlier in the relationship, when Peter saw the Christ walking on water and said to him, "If it is you, bid me come to you." Jesus bade him come. Peter stepped out of his boat and started to sink. Peter's response after the resurrection is different. It is not critical but passionate. He responds to the love who loves him in an immediate human way. What is transformed from that second moment is a relationship from *philia* to *agape*.

Opened by the Future

As we live the gift of the redeemed future that comes to us in the form of the risen Christ, *philia* becomes *agape* and hope becomes expectation. Then we are like children preparing for Christmas, or like the lover seeking the beloved in the Song of Songs. Our sense of expectancy is not destroyed by the world, and it does not destroy the world. We realize that the world can never be God and we also realize that we can live in the world in a different way, so aware of the vast limitations of the world, we no longer ask the world to be God for us. That focused form of expectant waiting detaches us from all that is not rooted in God. Those things not rooted in God no longer satisfy us, and nothing but God can fill up those newly opened spaces. So we live vulnerably. We wait for the beloved to come and fill us up: to satisfy our longing, to let us experience our rootedness more deeply and delight us with wonder, to let our zeal for our Father's house drive us shamelessly to live freely, and to allow us to see in everyone we meet a similar path to God.

Our waiting is not a passive compliancy where anything and everything goes. Expectant waiting removes a lot of nonsense from our lives. We experiment with how to wait. We may try this and then that, and then discover what works and what does not work. As Teresa of Avila said, mysticism is an experimental science. Expectant waiting makes us mystics. What works brings us into a felt relationship with God. They bring us to those covenant moments that show us what it is to be found by God, intimately and uniquely. These moments sharpen our sense of discernment since we know what true life feels like and how its imitations touch and distress us.

Expectant waiting is the school in which we learn spiritual literacy. We learn to discern, not as the application of a set of techniques, but as the manifestation of a lived relationship with the Desire who desires us. It is like the lover and the beloved discovering their own private codes of communicating with each other leading in turn to greater and greater senses of mutual abandonment to each other and deeper and deeper levels of spiritual intimacy. On one level we have a greater sense of self-awareness, but on another level we become mysteries to ourselves as we are led beyond who or how we presently think of ourselves. A quiet form of adventure manifests itself in our daily life and fills our days with a sense of wonder and gratitude.

This often happens when we have to make key decisions and all the options open to us seem like forms of suicide. It is rather like waiting at the edge of a cliff, when the choice is either to leap off, presuming God will save us, or to return to the situation we are escaping, which seems like abandoning ourselves to martyrdom. Both are false choices. The first recalls the temptation of Christ in the desert, when Satan carries him to the summit of the temple and suggests Jesus jump off to let God save him, since he is God's beloved. Because we are God's beloved, we do not do as we wish. We wait on God. The second choice, to return to places of desolation, is equally destructive, since we give ourselves over to despair and misread it as martyrdom. When we find ourselves caught between these two dreadful alternatives, we are invited to wait at the edge of that cliff for God. A third way opens. We take off and experience once again God's compassionate mercy in rescuing us. Such waiting is not the same as freezing up and becoming a helpless victim. An attentiveness comes from being so vulnerable. We become flexible in that attentiveness and ready to be disposed by God for the new path he opens. There is the element of surprise in all of this, and what we are asked to do is to see and accept the gift of the new way offered to us. We have to wait for that joy to come to us, and be ready to accept it when it comes. Waiting can be painful. We are often inclined to take shortcuts or to distract ourselves. But in the end, we come back to the waiting. In the spiritual life, one stage is built on a previous one. We can spend years avoiding what comes next, but when we discover what we did in the intervening time does not carry us on our spiritual journey, we learn how to wait appropriately and expectantly.

Waiting makes us aware of what it is to be human. To be human is to discover we are not God, and that no one, no institution or community, is God. Christ comes in the Incarnation as a human being not to show us how to become God, but rather to instruct us on how to live as a human being. To live as a human being is to be aware of our radical dependence on the Father, as Christ in his humanity is radically dependent on the Father. Like the Christ, in his human journey back to the Father, as we also journey deeper and deeper into our relationship with God and into love, we discover more and more our creaturehood, and how that creaturehood is loved by God in real, practical and concrete ways. What may seem to be good fortune, luck or coincidence, or what we simply take for granted and overlook in our daily lives, is the abiding providence of God caring for us. Expectant waiting slowly reveals to us just how little control we have over our lives, just how much is gift, and how easy it is to make mistakes or to muck things up. Expectant waiting makes us careful with others and with what we do, because we become sensitive to the fragility of people and their living conditions. It is not as if we become scrupulous, which is a form of narcissism. It is the well-being of the others we encounter that occupies our attention. We extend the care shown to us, willing to take risks with the possibility of making mistakes. We know, despite our stutterings of love, and whatever we may do wrong, we can be transformed by the merciful love of the one who first loved, and continues to love, us into being.

Our growth in sensitivity to the presence of God in the world and to the needs of others we encounter carries us more fully into our own suffering and passion, into our fears, and into the furnaces of affliction encompassing us daily. The more we fall in love with God, the more we find ourselves exposed to the pain of the world and to the forces of destruction seeking to make us all less human. We continue to experience our helplessness, and keep being tempted by the illusions of despair over the heartbreaking cruelty and stupidity of humanity to its own kind. But where else can we be except on the path we walk? As Peter acknowledges when many were turning away from Jesus, "Lord, to whom shall we go? You alone have the words of eternal life" (John 6:68). Like Christ on the cross, we wait to be rescued by the Father in his own time and way. The one who comes to us is a God who heals, redeems, cares for, rejoices in and celebrates us. Even as we suffer this world, we are carried beyond ourselves by this love into places of incredible tenderness and joy where we are overwhelmed and humbled by the simple fact the Lord of all Creation desires to be intimate with us.

As the Psalmist says, "Who are we, mere mortals that you should so care for us?" (Psalm 8:4; 144:3). Truly we do not know ourselves except as the beloved of the Father. All we know about ourselves is that we are drawn by a Desire who desires us, and our way through this world is in response to that desire. As we wait on the Father, such waiting exposes us to the pattern of temptation in our lives. While incidents of temptation might differ because of different circumstances, the pattern and the dynamics of our temptations remain the same, since evil is not creative. Moreover, it is the nature of evil to stop us from going beyond ourselves. It attempts to freeze us so that we remain truncated manifestations of the fullness of life to which we are called. Liberation, on the other hand, is always different. It moves us beyond our expectations. Living our redeemed future transforms our imaginations—and thus our lives—in ways we cannot now imagine. Resurrection is not resuscitation; resurrection transforms us into a new creation. It is not the old creation repaired.

When we wait on God, what happens to us is precisely what happens to Jesus in the temptations in the desert. Our demons emerge and try to make us less than we are. We do not have to feed or indulge them, because that just gives them energy and they become more established in our lives. They become more and more demanding, and they take from us the freedom to walk the path of life we are given or to be present to others.

It is very useful to be aware of how these demonic forces operate in our lives. We need to pray for the grace to become aware of them—for no one is free from them—and also for the grace not to be trapped by them. Anything that encourages our narcissism is destructive, and usually our narcissism is established by the affirmation of, or rejection by, the social world to which we attach ourselves. When we allow that world to define who we are and how we should behave, we give the creation of our identity over to it, rather than to the One who formed us as desire. Then we seek to satisfy our desires in and through the ways established by the world. What the world desires are those things it values, and so the things it values in us are the things it seeks to promote in our lives. Security, social approval, the ability to do what I like, the sense I know what is really going on: all are ways the world behaves and expects us to appropriate for ourselves. These are the things the world deems valuable, and we are seduced by these riches, rather than living in a radical and intimate relationship with God. Based on our creaturehood, this relationship asks us to seek the things of heaven first and to live in the humility of what it means to be human.

It is one thing to be aware of these dynamics in our lives abstractly, but how do we get a sense of their reality? We can first look at incidents of disorder in our lives and then try to see if there is an underlying pattern that traps us within ourselves, even though such patterns may be socially acceptable. We can also examine significant dreams that remain with us. These dreams give symbolic expression to underlying dynamic patterns of our life/death energies. A third way is by imaginative prayer. For example, we can imagine three doors. Behind one door is all we have ever wanted. Behind the second is what stops us from getting what we wanted. Behind the third is the helper who will assist us in getting what we always wanted. In prayer we wait for the doors to open. We do not open them. What is revealed to us in this prayer may surprise us and challenge our self-awareness. I once gave this as a prayer experience to a man at a retreat who did not want to pray and was resistant even to coming for spiritual direction. I was hoping that the novelty might somehow catch his attention. He went off and I did not see him for several days, but on the fourth day of the retreat, he came back quite excited. At first he had thought the experiment was interesting, but intended to do nothing about it. That morning as he was showering, he had an image of the third door opening. Behind it was a heap of broken mirrors. He knew this was significant, but what did it mean? For the first time in his adult life he was presented with a solution to his social remoteness and his inability to get along with others. His self-preoccupation was a form of narcissism. Only by breaking that intense gaze on himself and his needs could he be ready to see what was behind that first door. What was given him in prayer was a breakthrough. He would have to sit with it for some time to allow its power to reveal itself in his daily life, but at least now there was an opening to move forward.

As we move deeper into an attentiveness to the Father, we discover we are not just our individual selves. Our sense of self and concern reaches out to include others. We start to discover our life in the redeemed future is one of growing connectedness with all that exists, and we find ourselves in a set of interrelationships, bondings and intimacies with all different aspects of creation and the human family. We become, as it were, the site for those many interactions to become incarnate, and it is the gift of those interactions to help us in discernments. Life does not become easier, but in the depths of our being we have a sense of rootedness in the mystery we call Father and also in our being woven together with the forces that inform creation. Here we get a glimpse of what Paul proclaims about those who live in Jesus Christ.

> In him we have redemption through His blood, the forgiveness of sins, according to the riches of His grace which he made to abound toward us in all wisdom and prudence, having made known to us the mystery of his will, according to his good pleasure which he purposed in himself, that in the dispensation of the fullness of the times he might gather together in one all things in Christ, both which are in heaven and which are on earth—in Him. (Ephesians 1:7-11)

As we accept the redeemed future and wait in and with Christ on the Father, we find ourselves being gathered into a community returning to the Father. What we are invited to do is to build up that community, and our discernments operate out of this larger vision. We realize no one enters the fullness of life until all are in that fullness of life. We realize our pilgrim journey is to the fullness of life, and even as we journey to this state, we are already surrounded by love, by the Trinity, saints, angels, the people who love us and the forces of good that maintain creation. All of these are companions on our spiritual journey. They intercede for us, support us, counsel and console us, and celebrate with us the joys of our life. The consolations we experience are signs of their presence. We are never alone, no matter how strongly the circumstances of our lives may suggest that we are.

This is not to take away the very real presence of evil in our lives and in our world. Evil seeks to dismember and destroy community, and works actively to break the bonds of love and mutuality that exist among all. Living a redeemed future takes away one illusion evil suggests to us: God's separation from us, and the separation of those who love us from our lives and works. This graced awareness takes away some of the power we might unwittingly give to those false myths diminishing our sense of life. Evil seeks to limit the ways we experience, know and love ourselves. Evil limits our imagination. Covenant moments break the boundaries of those limitations, and we experience transfiguration—not through a glass darkly, but directly. We experience God as God works in this world. In this moment of Christian enlightenment, our awareness of God's connection with us allows us to see as God sees.

We have one such scriptural moment in Peter's confession of faith. When Jesus asks his followers who they think he is, some say Elijah, or John the Baptist back from the dead, or Jeremiah or one of the prophets. Peter alone answers, "You are the Messiah, the Son of the living God." At that moment Peter sees Jesus the way the Father sees Jesus. This perception is a gift from the Father; Jesus acknowledges this gift and also Peter's reception of this gift when he replies, "Blessed are you, Simon son of Jonah, for this was not revealed to you by flesh and blood, but by my Father in heaven." It is from this unity of perspective that the community of believers is established, for Jesus continues, "And I tell you that you are Peter, and on this rock I will build my church, and the gates of Hades will not overcome it" (Matthew 16:13-19).

Of course, Peter's revelation is incomplete, and when Jesus focuses his message on his upcoming passion, Peter falls into the ways of the world, telling the Christ this is not the way God behaves. He thinks he knows better than God how God is to act, and for this, Jesus turns to him and says, "Get behind me, Satan! You are a stumbling block to me; you do not have in mind the concerns of God, but merely human concerns" (Matthew 16:23).

Living a redeemed future is living out of those covenant moments when we are in a manifest union with God, but as even Peter shows here, those ecstatic moments are privileged and foundational. They present us to ourselves in ways that direct and inform the rest of our lives. We build our lives on the reality of those moments and use them as guides for discernment. When we ask ourselves what to do, what is appropriate resonates with those moments; what is inappropriate jars the felt sense of those moments. The latter runs counter to the way Jesus imagines us and asks us to imagine ourselves.

As we make our way through this world and its places of glory and horror, we are given the compass of those covenant moments to guide us. We each of us walk to death and to the gift of resurrection. Every pulse in our body beats steadily against that door, and one day it will open. How we accept the gift reached through death is determined by how we walk our path as we live. We can truly leave this life when we have learned to be grateful for it, and we become grateful for it when we discover it has brought us an intimacy with the Father to be celebrated even more fully, openly and joyfully in resurrection. We can live that intimacy as it is given to us here and now in the midst of our hard times, or in our good times, or even in normal and commonplace times. In all of them, God comes from our past to save us and give us our own personal salvation history. God exists in every present moment, and in this present is our companion and root and life. God also bears in on us from our futures to share with us the abundance of life he offers to all.

The Beloved comes, and we live in expectation of this coming. It helps us discern how to live. Matthew's gospel gives us the parable of the wise and foolish virgins ready to greet the bridegroom when he arrives at the house of his betrothed. The wise virgins and the foolish virgins both have lit lamps. Both expect the bridegroom to come, and both fall asleep. They are all awakened by the approaching sounds of the bridegroom late at night. Why do the wise virgins not share their oil, we wonder? What is the level of preparedness that cannot be shared? The wise are prepared to celebrate the arrival of the groom; the foolish are not. With their oil they can see and celebrate who comes. Without their oil, the foolish ones cannot see or celebrate. It is not a question of charity and of sharing resources. The parable revolves around the question of seeing. The Song of Songs suggests one solution to the question of preparedness. The lover says, "I sleep, but my heart wakes: it is the voice of my beloved that knocks, saying, Open to me, my sister, my love, my dove, my undefiled: for my head is filled with dew, and my locks with the drops of the night" (Song of Songs 5:2). The unawakened heart belongs to those whose attention is not turned to a redeemed future. They cannot celebrate as it is coming to them, and they cannot share in that celebration when it has arrived.

To live expectantly is to have an awakened heart always attentive to what the Beloved desires to give in the various circumstances of this life. It is not ultimately to create those circumstances but to be disposed to finding God in these situations. To be so disposed, we must abandon certain sentimental myths about living in a redeemed future. Redeeming the future is not having a fairytale ending where the "once upon a time" concludes with "and they lived happily ever after." God promises only to be in relationship with us to the end of time. God does not promise us security or a life without care. In fact the covenant relationship God offers us gives us something quite different, as we see when we look at the lives of those who have dedicated themselves to living as God's be- loved. Throughout the ages, we have a cloud of witnesses who have endured suffering, great hardships, abuse, rejection, martyrdom, neglect, insults and injury, loss of family, friends and homeland as they live that relationship.

Falling in love with God does not make life easier. As the two lovers finally discovered at the ending of Chekhov's *The Lady with a Dog*, "it was clear to both of them that they had still a long, long road before them, and that the most complicated and difficult part of it was only just beginning."[64] Before, they were just a dilettante and a married woman manoeuvering through a bourgeois affair, but in the course of their relationship they fall in love and this love imposes its obligations on them. How are they to live their love, given the circumstances of their lives?

When we live any life of love there are always difficulties. We give up our self-direction to live a relationship. When we fall in love with God, developing this relationship brings us to those places where there is a need for healing, reconciliation, transformation and support. It is the nature of Compassionate Mercy to go out to the unloved and unlovable. Where God is, we, as God's companions, are there, too, carrying on the mission of the Christ.

What happened two thousand years ago continued through history and is present even today for those who live out of their intimacy with God. They have fallen in love and they walk towards God with open arms to embrace, and to allow themselves to be embraced by, the One they love. Often when we set out on our spiritual journey, we have lots of gifts to give God; we desire to transform the world for God, and we run towards a God whom we are told is omnipotent, omniscient and all-loving. But when we try to embrace that God, our hands are too full of our gifts, and God's hands are filled with his gifts for us. We cannot hold each other. So God does what God does. He first puts down his gifts, and we discover a vulnerable and broken God, seemingly quite ineffectual in our world. We turn away from such a God and spend our gifts in this world trying to transform it. Our gifts are used up and we are abandoned. Like the prodigal son, we return to the God of empty arms with our own arms empty. Now, with nothing between us, we can embrace. Our mutual vulnerability allows contact and intimacy. Resurrection happens then, and one manifestation of this is the desire to take up God's mission in the world. It is a manifestation of shared intimacy. There is God's vulnerability in entrusting God's mission with us. There is our vulnerability in living beyond our limited sense of self, aware of our radical poverty of spirit. This embrace moves us beyond our understanding of our story as we know it. We enter into God's story for us, becoming living words of the Father. We experience this as a sense of wonder and discovery at what is possible for us, lover and beloved, to do together in this trapped world. Those experiences transform our notion of who God is and how God operates. The love we have for another person and the delight we have in being with the person, even in hard places, reflects some of the delight God has in us. When we fall in love with God and allow ourselves to be loved by God, we find ourselves falling in love with others and even with the world. We start seeing as God sees, and loving as God loves. We no longer act out of a sense of duty or out of a moral law, but from within that sense of shared intimacy. We desire to be where the beloved is, to do as the beloved does, and to live as the desire of the beloved.

In the intimacy shared between the lover and the beloved, we might ask why the Father does not step into the Son's suffering to save him. By extension, we can also ask why the one who loves us does not step into our own suffering to save us. In love we are where our beloved is, and if our beloved is in the pain of the world, showing us how to live in that pain without denying our humanity, then we cannot ask the beloved to deny our humanity and our pain also. Similarly, Jesus' identity, like our identity, is as the beloved of the Father. It is the nature of the world to try to move us from that intimacy so we become its slaves. But the intimacy we share, and the strength it gives us, allows us to say no to the world, and allows us to be true to our calling. Just as God allows the son to walk the path carrying him to his full identity, so, too, in love, the Father allows us, as companions of his Son, to accompany this Son. As in the vision given to St. Ignatius at the little roadside chapel at La Storta, just outside Rome, the Father tells the Christ carrying his cross, "I want you to put this man under your standard." We, like Ignatius, are invited to an intimacy with the Christ—a union in the Father. It allows us to love in such a way that our lives become ones of service in transforming this broken world to a community of love. The love the Father has for us allows us to become who we are.

A Father's Love

When I was growing up, I was the third son. My father played cricket for his country and my two elder brothers were passionate about the game. I hated it. Looking back, I can now see just how much I opposed the life path my father wanted for me. I abandoned a scholarship and entered religious life. I can also see the freedom he gave me to become who I am. I see his concern now, but I also see that open space he allowed me. I also see just how much like him I have become. I once asked him, in one of those rare conversations men have with their fathers, what he thought of me. He paused for a while and then said, "Well, you always seem to know your own mind." I don't know if I know my own mind, but I do know I have a sense of my heart, and have chosen always to live from those intimate spaces.

Jesus also seems to have a sense of his heart, a sense of desire drawing him always towards the fullness of life. His heart gives him the courage to walk into those dark places that try to destroy him. But the Desire who desires him does not allow the Son to be lost in death. The Father's love raises Jesus from the dead, just as the Father's love gives each of us the desire for the fullness of life. This love gives each of us the same grace given to the Christ: the offer and promise of resurrection. When we walk into our dark places, we expect, because of our limited imaginations, to be rescued—resuscitated—in some way. But what happens is that we die. The old narratives by which we lived our lives and which gave meaning to them are taken away. What we are given instead is resurrection. We may bear the scars of dying, as Christ himself bears the signs of the crucifixion in his risen body, but we live a transformed life because of our covenant moments, as the Christ himself did in that covenant moment when he was raised from the dead. He was freed to live a resurrected future.

For us to live the resurrected future, we must let Christ do Christ's work, let the Father do the Father's work, and we also have to do our own work. We cannot bring the dead to life; we cannot bring the dead to resurrection. So what is our work? John's gospel gives us the answer. Our work is to believe in Jesus (John 6:29). He is sent to do the work of the Father so no one will be lost. To believe in Jesus is to live in the same relationship with the Father Jesus has in the Father. He waits on the Father, and we, too, wait on the Father to show us what to do. We have to let God give us the strength to do what we have to do: to wait in the darkness and celebrate the life we find coming to us as we wait. In this we are like the five wise virgins of the parable. We are also invited to bring the dead to God. Sometimes this is as simple as bringing a corpse to a tomb. Other times it is to mourn the dead in our life, or to engage in the work of forgiveness. Then we become the empty space through which the pain of the world meets God and the compassionate mercy of God meets the world. In all of this, we do not run ahead of grace. We wait for it to come and show us what to do and how to do it.

When we do this, we continue the work of Christ in the world. When we live this way, we find ourselves tempted and assaulted, seduced, terrorized and drained by those forces within us and outside of us that seek to diminish us and subvert us from the path leading to the fullness of life. The path exposes us to all that needs conversion. When our vision is crowded by despair, anger, fear or busyness, we do not see the life offered to us even now. These are the forces that need to be brought to the Father's care and creativity. We leave them in God's time, and part of our work is learning to leave ourselves and the damaged parts of creation to God's time. We cannot force God's hand or time in our zeal to bring about our vision of what the kingdom of God will be like. To do that is to be like Judas Iscariot, one of those in Jesus' inner circle, or like contemporary ideologues who agitate for a perfect society of their own making. Even Jesus in his earthly life did not know the time of the full coming of the kingdom. Only the Father knows the time of that coming and the citizens of that kingdom. Our lack of knowledge keeps us attentive and discerning to our relationship with the Father. Being attentive does not give us answers. What we get are experiences that reveal to us how God is with us—or not—as we make our way through this world and this life.

Our growing intimacy with the Father not only brings us to resurrection moments, but carries us further to receiving Pentecost. Then we share the relationship between the humanity of the risen Christ and the Father. This embrace of the resurrected Christ returning to the Father creates Pentecost. That explosion of love, like a spiritual Big Bang, creates new dimensions of intimacy for us. Pentecost is the beginning of the creation of community extending through time until all are caught up again in the mystery we call Father. As we journey towards this fullness of life, we discover in our present lives some of the dimensions of the intimacy God offers us.

We discover our covenant moments, our resurrection stories and our ongoing sharing in the life of the beloved that make us call out to God, "Abba, Father" (Romans 8:14-17). These acts of freedom allow the future to be opened, and they give us a guide about how to live with ourselves and others. There is an asceticism of joy to be established. We need to do the things that give us joy and maintain our joy. Years ago my spiritual director asked me, after I had spent some time complaining about the sorry state of my life, "Why do you give away your joy?" I have carried that question ever since and have used it as a tool in discernment. Often we give away our joy by ignoring the good in our life and the daily moments of gratitude that assure us of God's continuing presence with us. We also give away our joy by not cultivating it in doing good to ourselves and others. The worries of this life can eat away at our peace of mind and heart. The time we can spend with the beloved becomes conditional on other things in our life, and so prayer, the Examen, discernment and even the common delights in living become neglected. We can end up exhausted and alienated from our selves. It is the nature of evil not to let us be joyful, and it is the joy of the resurrection renewing the whole world. We can choose to live joyfully and responsibly. Viktor Frankl, in *Man's Search for Meaning*, writes of his concentration camp experiences.

> We who lived in concentration camps can remember the men who walked through the huts comforting others, giving away their last piece of bread. They may have been few in number, but they offer sufficient proof that everything can be taken from a man but one thing: the last of the human freedoms—to choose one's attitude in any given set of circumstances, to choose one's own way.[65]

We all suffer. It is the First Noble Truth of the Buddha. But we all have a choice in how we respond to our suffering. When Christ came, he showed us how to remain human in our suffering. He depends on the Father, and lives his relationship with the Father. He dies as he lives, in fidelity to that relationship. How we live is how we die. Every moment, the pulse on our wrist beats against the door of death. One day that door opens. This is one way of looking at life, as if life and death were separate. But there is another way. Life and death are the same. Every moment of life carries us to resurrection, and the deaths we encounter on the way to resurrection in this life are many. We are born through death into resurrection. We are changed by this passage. We become transformed by the love greeting us in death and making us new creations. So if every moment is a dying, every moment is also an entry into paradise. There is not one without the other. In fact, both are the same. Living the redeemed future does not allow us to escape suffering and death, but it places those all-too-human conditions in the larger context of the Father's abiding love and care. It places us in a type of purgatory where we endure the purification of our desires by love so that we learn to give up both being terrorized by evil and our complicity in those forms of disorder. We learn to see what stops us from accepting the future as redeemed, and we learn to avoid those traps. Instead, we learn to see and accept the good that is in life and to celebrate this good carrying us to the fullness of life.

Only when we have had the experience of being loved do we realize how different love is from those false gifts trapping us and denying us our voice and vocation. I grew up in the tropics, which had been colonized by the British. Our schooling, language and effective myths were all British. We learned British history and English literature, celebrated Christmas with fake fireplaces and artificial snow, sang Christmas carols about a winter we never experienced, ate British food, watched British films and read British books. We learned that Britain epitomized the values we were enculturated to hold dear, even though those values denied us who we were, our colour, our native land, its heritage and its history, and it taught us to hate ourselves because we could never be British. On one level, it was a gift to be brought up in the British colonial system. It established a horizon of value and belief. But on a deeper level, it taught us to hate ourselves, and that is profoundly unchristian. We are loved by a God who desires us to be who we are, not anyone else, and God desires us to love each other the way we love ourselves. If we do not love ourselves, we cannot love our neighbour as ourselves, and the love we might have for God comes not from our own heart and soul but from a role we have been made to assume. Then, not knowing better, we pretend this is truly ourselves. We mimic living. This is true not just for the colonized. It is true for almost everyone who is socialized into ways of existence denying them their true voice and vocation.

Learning to become ourselves takes a long time. The slow transformation of our lives by love into what is truly loving and lovable means deconstructing those false myths we have lived out of, and accepting for ourselves the story God tells of us. In Jesus' earthly life, he constantly tells his disciples about his future and about theirs. They hear but they do not believe. They are taken up by other stories—stories of privilege and esteem, and of sitting in places of honour in his worldly kingdom. It is through his resurrected state they are converted. The disciples on the way to Emmaus must have the story of their liberation deconstructed and reconfigured so they can see that the person with whom they are travelling is the risen Jesus. Only the presence of love accepted allows us to move beyond our closed and broken myths into an intimacy with the Father. But that acceptance takes time. It takes time to accept that we are loved. It takes time to live out of that love. It takes time to share and celebrate that love in our own life journey.

The gift of Christ's resurrection is not for some other life, but for this life. Experiences of being loved into being affirm our lives and the path of our lives now. Often that gift comes when we have experienced a loss and find ourselves in a very vulnerable space, when what used to make sense no longer does and we have no new narratives to organize the raw experience we now endure. At those times, even our prayer seems detached from us. Into those spaces the Desire we call God comes to us, and this Desire names us so we can find ourselves again in God. This is what happens to Mary Magdalene. She loses a person who healed her of seven devils. He has been crucified and has died. She goes to his tomb to anoint his tortured body. In her anguish, she can do only what she thinks is possible, but after arriving at the tomb, she finds it empty. She cannot even do this one small thing. Into this emptied space of death, the tomb, loss and abandonment, Jesus appears but is not recognized. He must name her first, "Mary," before she can name him, "Rabbouni." In that new level of intimacy between lover and the resurrected Beloved, her life is given a new direction and focus. In early Christian writings, she becomes "the apostle to the apostles."

When we are loved, we are given something we do not expect or figure we deserve. This love is always a free gift, since we cannot make another person love us. It allows us to experience ourselves differently from before. We discover we are lovable, and, furthermore, that we can love. We discover we can live and share what we have been given. We become empowered by the love of the Beloved. We live our lives as expressions of this intimacy. We start to see, know and love ourselves, others and the world as God sees, knows and loves all. We get some sense of God's delight in us and in the creation he makes, sustains, repairs and celebrates. We feel ourselves invited to this celebration and, like the five wise virgins, we prepare to celebrate by accepting the joy and the gifts this life offers now. We discover love does not mean getting what you want, but learning to celebrate the life you have, and to live it in such a way that others are led to the freedom you have been given. What is being described here is how Pentecost manifests itself in our contemporary world.

In Pentecost, as in the Annunciation, the Baptism, Peter's profession of faith, the resurrection and the Second Coming, God comes to a human world to offer us the ever-deepening gift of spiritual intimacy. It manifests itself in ever more inclusive notions of community, moving to that apogee when all of creation concelebrates its existence enfolded back into the Father's love.

To live this resurrected future is to open the gifts of Pentecost. It is to look at ourselves with the eyes of love, and to accept that gaze burning away shame and alienation and bringing us to unsuspected levels of self-acceptance. It is to look at others as invitations rather than as enemies and to celebrate them into our lives with gratitude. It is to look at the world with a sense of wonder and discovery, and finally it is to accept ourselves aligned to the forces of love, and in that community to live creatively and joyfully. We can imagine ourselves surrounded by the heavenly court, in communion with all the blessed, because in fact we are.

All of time, everything and everyone, is held in God's love. Our notion of time is generally sequential. For us, time is a narrative in which one thing follows another. But God's time is not like that. God's time is always now. When we sit in prayer, our notion of time meets God's notion of time. What we read as our past, our present and our future encounters God's sense of our time within his time and care. The incidents from the past, or present concerns, or anxieties about the future that limit our joy in this life become the sites where, in prayer, incarnation occurs. There and then, God enters our narratives so we can enter his. In prayer, our stories are transformed by that encounter, and so we, in prayer, can allow our narratives to be deconstructed and then reconstructed according to the Divine Providence without being retraumatized by what distresses us. At first, the embrace of that love feels like pain, because we have become so identified with our traumas, concerns and anxieties that giving them up feels like a death, or like falling into a depression. Often we hold onto our hurts because we have nothing else to maintain our sense of self. But we discover, in being loved, we can—though it feels like a great risk—give up that false sense of self and identity. Then we find ourselves experiencing a freedom we did not think possible.

What is redeemed is the way we read our experiences. Love changes our vision and outlook on life, and we see the elements of our life differently. Rereading our lives with Christ allows deeper and different dimensions of experience to be brought into consciousness and use, and this gives life.

God's desire for us to be joyful and our desire to share God's joy begins to be realized when we see everything will be transformed into love. This occurs when the unloved become lovable and loving. It is the nature of God's grace to go to the unloved in love. First, it affirms what is good in the unloved. Second, it names the unlovable for what it is so we are not deceived. Third, it allows what is destructive to encounter the compassionate mercy and wisdom of God. We cooperate with that compassion by being patient with ourselves and with the broken ones around us. The patience and mercy of God is time, and living in God's time we are asked to forgive as God forgives, without compromising our integrity or falling into traps of co-dependency where we tolerate others' de-structive behaviour because we ourselves are sinners. We are asked to forgive in such a way that the other is offered hope and direction to a path that gives life, and we ourselves are asked to live among the destructive without destroying ourselves.

All we can do is bring to others the love we have received. We let that love do its work. We remember here the friends who brought the cripple to Jesus and let him down through the roof. It is Jesus who did the work, not the friends. Similarly, it is not the Roman centurion who heals his slave, but Jesus. All the centurion does is bring his concern to Jesus. We let Jesus, the one who loves us, and who is loved by the Father, do his work. All we do is bring that work to God, for we cannot do it for, or by, ourselves. We let Jesus care for us, and we let him care for those we care about. Our radical awareness of our poverty of spirit touches the heart of the One who desires us. He does not leave us abandoned, but instead calls us to a true understanding of ourselves and what we are capable of. Most of us do not have all we need to be as merci-ful as we would like, and so we have to be discerning about what we can do. If we do not have adequate self-knowledge, we can often become overextended and allow our boundaries to break down. Then we stop looking after ourselves and our tendencies to self-destruction emerge. We compensate for our unmet needs in ways that are narcissistic and addictive. We forget our true selves and the path to the fullness of life. Then our desire for the Creator becomes subverted and betrayed to fallen aspects of creation. We find ourselves as lovers trapped and frustrated by sin. Yet we never lose the sense of ourselves as desire. What we lose is the sense of the One who desires us.

Our lives are driven by desire. We are made as desire for God, and made in the image and likeness of God. God is present not only as the answer to our desire, but also as the Desire who desires us. Our whole spiritual life is the coming together of those two desires, and in that coming together, every aspect of our life, from the smallest cell to the totality of our being as a member of the com-munity called creation, is involved and committed. In that coming together, desire becomes hope, hope becomes longing, longing becomes expectation. Faith becomes intimacy; love becomes passion. As we enter our spiritual life more deeply, we become more human, and our love becomes more incarnate. Incarnation moves us through passion and death to resurrection. Resurrection opens us to the lived community created at Pentecost, and this leads to the ongoing shared life in the Spirit, until all is once again caught up in Christ and returned to the Father. We discover our bodies are desire incarnate, and that these bodies, the bodies of our physical selves, the bodies of our social, cultural and communal selves, are all manifestations of the Body of Christ. As we move out of the isolation and fragmentation of our narcissisms into ever fuller senses of being community, we become more human and life becomes more of an adventure. As we set off on this adventure, we try to know ourselves, but as we walk the path of spiritual intimacy, we lose ourselves and we become free. Knowing ourselves—the Socratic ideal—is the human best. In the journey back to the Father, that human best is destroyed for the Divine better. It is the way of Desire becoming passion. Often it seems to the world like the folly of the cross. But in such moments in Jesus' human life, he reached out to the Love that named him and called him even in and through death. It might seem stupid, crazy or eccentric to walk such a path. But it is the path of the saints. It is a path that leads to the fullness of life, and it is the path offered to all of us.

Conclusion

There are many paths through the darkness. Our lives are a mystery: that mystery encounters the mystery of the world we live in and the Mystery we call God. There are no techniques to translate our pilgrim ways into a comprehensive program covering all the eventualities of life. The unexpected happens. Even what we expect and plan have dimensions we cannot prepare for, because we are unaware of them. What we know is very limited. What we *know* we do not know is larger; what *we do not know* that we do not know is beyond our imagining. This is part of the human condition. But it is also the human condition to be in relationship with God. How this relationship is understood and lived varies, of course, from person to person. Some deny the relationship. Others read it in purely natural terms. Still others understand it in terms of law and duty.

Our task in this book has been to read our lives in terms of desire and to see desire as the source of spiritual intimacy. The desire God has for us and the desire we are for God come together in an unfolding relationship. It takes us on a path leading to the fullness of life. On that path we find ourselves being constantly called to discern how we are, who we are, where we are and what we need to do next. These are all interrelated questions. They influence each other's answers and we cannot simply separate one from the other and give it a priority status. Who we are depends on where we are and how we understand ourselves in that context. But the context is shaped by our perception of ourselves and what we are doing. And what we do and how we do it reveal who we are to ourselves. These forms of mutuality make discernment difficult, since our lives are sites where many different forces are dynamically present. Some compete for our attention; still others we take for granted, and there are some who prefer to work their way unnoticed.

Our Present Times

We are living in a time of great transition. The dynamic forces that make up our lives as individuals and as members of a culture and a world offer us differing views of ourselves and of our path. Even families no longer share a common sensibility, and this is even more so among different elements of our nations or cultures. These conflicting voices, each claiming to be of significant value, force us into ourselves to discover what we truly value and aspire to. We discern to discover how to be in the world. The four approaches examined in this book are aids to discernment. These are not comprehensive guides. If we were to look at our history of making good decisions, we could discover that there is an underlying pattern to it. That pattern could be different for different people, and that pattern could be different for different decisions. The same thing could be noted about the bad decisions we make. Discernments involve our cooperation with the creativity of God in particular situations. This creativity cannot be reduced to techniques. What techniques do is to dispose us to this creativity and attune us to accepting this creativity when it manifests itself. As a Buddhist master once famously said, enlightenment is an accident; when queried about the long, hard discipline of zen-sitting, he replied that techniques just make us accident-prone.

The Path of Contemplation

The first approach this book examined is a phenomenological reading of the sequence of traps that stop us from achieving the freedom to make and maintain good discernments. To gain freedom, we need to be aware of how fear traps us in forms of security and limits our options for life. When we admit our fears and examine where they come from and how they shape our lives, we take away their power. We confront our fears, not to kill them off but to discover how to admit them without giving in to them. Courage is not the absence of fear. Courage involves not indulging fear. When we leave the comfort zone our fear protects, we begin to see more clearly things we took for granted, and we see how the world operates. We gain a clarity into how things and people and situations work.

While this is a growth into liberation, it can quickly become a trap, because then we think we understand things. We do not realize the underlying mystery of things. We do not realize just how limited and limiting our knowing really is. Giving up clarity does not justify stupidity. It is a form of humility that accepts that we are not God and, like Job, we do not understand the workings of the universe or the human heart or the mind of God. What clarity gives us is a system based on our experiences of the world. In a real sense, we are still trapped by the world when we exercise clarity. We see the implicit order of the world with clarity, while with fear we experience the explicit order. But as we journey into liberation, realize the boundaries of clarity and tap into the dynamics of mystery underlying our spiritual journey, we find ourselves becoming powerful and creative. The energies we have liberated in moving beyond the structures of the world turn their attention to reshaping that world. We have discovered how the world traps us and how our way of understanding that world traps us, and now we discover how easily we can be seduced in using our knowledge and our sense of freedom to order that world as we think it should be ordered. Power is a trap because it enflames our ego and gives us status in this world. To share power or to use it as a gift to benefit others is the lesson to be learned in overcoming this third trap. When we do this, we become further liberated. But we discover the forces of the world and the cumulative effects of human disorder can take what has been created good and beneficial for all, and distort it for selfish ends. We can become disillusioned and burned out in trying to be good and to bring good to our world. We can become cynical and despairing. Here we face the final trap and must learn how to live with a sense of integrity and joy in the midst of the violence and malice we discover in our own contexts.

In looking at the traps stopping us from discerning, we notice each trap focuses us on ourselves in relationship to the world. What is left out is our relationship to God. Despite those traps, our lives also experience the power of God to liberate us and move us towards the fullness of life we desire. God moves us out of fear by giving us a sense of being deeply rooted in him. We are liberated from clarity by the sense of mystery in our lives. It opens us to the gift of awe and wonder. These gifts unleash creativity, which we use to spiritually free others instead of focusing on forms of self-indulgence and self-serving social liberties. Our freedom moves us beyond political pragmatism. We dispose our power to building up the kingdom as God desires it. Living in the world, we notice often good ideas and projects becoming corrupted by the unscrupulous, and so being woven back into self-serving social structures. We may become disillusioned by this and be tempted to give up the struggle for the fullness of life for all. We can become content with our despair and seek the comfort of like-minded companions, ignoring the broader call to a community including all, even those with whom we disagree. As those called to be the living words of the Father, we are always invited to go beyond our despair and to live deeply trust in God's mercy, which transforms every death into resurrection.

Fear, clarity, power and despair prevent us from discerning. To be aware of their dynamics in our lives is one thing, but we also need the grace to overcome them. Both our awareness and that particular grace deal with our negativity. We must also be aware of what promotes discernment and ask for the grace to develop these. What promotes discernment is a rootedness in God's love supplanting our need for security; a sense of wonder opening us to Mystery and carrying us beyond the systems of meaning the world offers; a freedom expressing our relationship with the Father and allowing us to give up our civil liberties for that greater good; and, finally, a working relationship emerging from a trust in the mercy of Divine Providence refusing to be overwhelmed by the destructiveness of the world. Instead of the closed and broken myths the world offers as a way of living, we can choose instead to live out of an open myth that lets God enter into human history and into our personal lives.

A Map of the Journey

The second section of the book looks at what happens when we live out of that open myth. Driven by our desire for God, we walk into, through and past those stages of spiritual growth leading to an ever-growing awareness of our changing relationship with the divine. This is manifest in the different ways in which we live our attentiveness to the One who loves us into the fullness of being. We start off by following our discontent at our present state of life. Using our discontent as a discerning tool, we seek to satisfy our desire for a more meaningful life. We experiment to discover what leads us to that satisfaction. We discover moments of consolation and they show us we are on the right path. We seek to consolidate those moments by choosing a life path that facilitates this choice. In living out that choice, we discover we must discipline ourselves, like an athlete in training, to bring the disordered and undeveloped aspects of ourselves into conformity with our life choice. We stop worrying about what to do with our lives and instead focus on our concern with how to live what we have chosen in the best possible manner. When the habits of perfection have become established in our daily living, we even forget ourselves.

From that state of well-being, the Desire who calls us moves us to a deeper level of abandonment to love by removing from us, at the depths of our being, our dependence on those structures that have constructed our life. We experience a radical poverty of spirit that manifests itself in a felt sense of nothingness. The love we have been living opens itself to this spiritual intimacy. Nothing lies between us and God, and we are rooted in God at that level of nothingness that goes beyond perception, feeling and insight. In Zen Buddhism, this may be taken as a moment of enlightenment. Incarnating this enlightenment state radically adjusts the way we are in the world, and often that adjustment is experienced as anxiety. Kierkegaard calls this anxiety the dizzying experience of freedom. Spiritual freedom is not the luxury of doing what we like, which presupposes an established ego. Nor is it the complacency of being able to access civil liberties, and still less is it the religious indifference of the earlier stages of spiritual development, where we are disposed only to God and what God desires. Even then we have an ego in conformity with the divine. In this present stage of attentiveness, we lose the sense of our ego as a concrete entity, and so lose the compass of our relationships with everything else, even though we still exist in the world and go about our daily business. As we slowly accept this state of being we start seeing things, people and relationships as they are in their impermanence. We see them arising from that nothingness we experience and returning to that nothingness from which they have come. We learn how to celebrate what is passing without asking it to be more or less than what it is. Living this freedom, we engage in the world as a spiritual pilgrim. Through our emptiness, the mercy of God can enter the world. Through our emptiness the pain and suffering of the world can encounter God. Through that same emptiness, God's delight in his creation can be celebrated in the world; through that emptiness, what is good in creation can be acknowledged and affirmed by God.

Techniques of Discernment

As we journey through this world, we are still being formed. We do not come to the end of love or of loving. We remain imperfect. We still need to discern. The third section of this book looks at discernment as a way of walking through the mystery calling us always beyond ourselves. There are four different types of discernment. We may want to make a decision or to understand what is going on. We may want to know the spirit behind what is going on. We may even want to have a way of improving our daily relationship with God in the context of that spirit.

All discernments presuppose a living relationship with God. In fact, discernment is the way we live our relationship with God. The dialogue with God, as well as the mutual accommodation of lover and beloved, not only reveals what is happening and why, but also provides ways of overcoming disorder and of discovering what are the best possible strategies to help build up the kingdom. Discernment starts by becoming attentive. Then we notice the things bringing us closer to God and how we experience them, and we notice things separating us from God and how we experience them. When we are turned away from God, the seductions to self-satisfaction are laden with false promises. But they cannot give us true life. Indulging in them increases our alienation. When we are turned away from God, we experience the call to conversion in forms of guilt, remorse, fear. Similarly, when we are coming closer to God, we can feel the call in terms of delight, peace, patience, creativity and compassion. The evil spirit tries to disturb that consolation through various deceptions, not the least of which is pretending to offer an apparent good which, if accepted, leads to destruction and a weakening of our faith, hope and love. These are all general rules of thumb and operate from the principle that when we are rooted in God's love and engaged in God's work, this sense of connection and intimacy can withstand the assaults of evil. Such good is supported by God and is maintained by God. What is seemingly good is not rooted in God's love, and so leads to forms of destructive behaviour.

One of the ways we can learn discernment is by looking at our past, our present and our future. When we look at our past, we can see the good decisions we have made and thus can see our pattern of making good decisions. Then we can look at the bad decisions we have made and look for our pattern of making bad decisions, and the underlying forces that habitually structure our bad decisions. What is crucial in this second reflection is the pattern of making seemingly good decisions, which turn out to be unhelpful. For instance, we might be predisposed to a spontaneity that wants to be helpful, and so we commit ourselves to projects without having examined the longer-term consequences. Or we may be so cautious that we rarely commit ourselves to anything and so lead diminished lives. In all of these cases, looking critically at our past helps to give us some insight into how we habitually behave.

Discernment is also available in the present, when we do our particular and our general examens. Our particular examen is what we do daily to correct a fault. When we become attentive to a particular fault—such as being prone to negative thoughts and comments—we can correct it by becoming aware of when, why and how often we fall into this trap. This self-awareness is remedial and helps us see our present in more positive terms. Also very helpful is the general examen we use to advance on our spiritual path. Once a day we can sit in the presence of God and allow our gratitude for that intimacy to show us the things in our day that have brought us closer to God, as well as those things that have taken us away from God. We celebrate the good and we ask for help to overcome the bad. In doing this, we rededicate ourselves to our spiritual path, conscious always of being held in God's compassionate love that desires only the fullness of life for us all.

There are times when to walk to a fuller spiritual life we need to make significant decisions about our future. To do this in ways that do not trap us in an apparent good, we must be suitably disposed not to make a decision from a narcissistic perspective. We must be aware of our patterns of entrapment and of liberation. None of us is without this tension in our lives. We must desire truly to follow the path of liberation, and in this desire we make a choice. Still, we are aware, at times, our desires are conflicted. We may use different approaches to resolve this situation. When we are conflicted, we find ourselves in turmoil. Ignatius suggests we examine all the reasons both for and against following a particular option or not following it. This process is rather like a court case where both defender and prosecutor look at all sides of an issue. In so doing, we discover hidden agendas and perspectives capable of stimulating our prayer either to consolation or to desolation.

We might also use role-play. In the first scenario, we give advice to someone in a similar situation to ours, and then follow that advice ourselves. Or we might imagine ourselves on our deathbed, ask ourselves what method we would use to arrive at a decision, and then follow that method to make the present decision. Finally, we might imagine ourselves dead, surrounded by God, the saints and angels, and all of created good. In this context of all-encompassing love, we ask ourselves what we would have done if we were still living. This is the decision we adopt now.

Discernment allows us to walk through mystery. In all of this we have a guide. God gives us the helps we need not to become lost or confused. God does not give answers. God gives experiences. We learn to read those experiences through the understandings given to us by our past, by the way we live in the present, and how we create for the future.

Redeeming the Time

In living our relationship with God, our call is to redeem the time. Time is redeemed when the compassionate mercy of God is discovered, accepted, lived and celebrated in time. For most of us, our past is a mixture of positive and negative experiences. The positive ones have given us a healthy self-image and an inner strength allowing us to be with others without eroding our boundaries or giving ourselves away in destructive relationships. We are able to live with ambiguity and have confidence in God as a companion on our life journey. We know these positive experiences from the sense of gratitude we experience when we recall them. These gifts have opened us up to life, to others and to God. It is helpful to recall those experiences and to celebrate them the way we celebrate birthdays, weddings or other significant events in our life. They give us a sense of ourselves as loved and called to life.

We have also had experiences that were not life-giving at the time. The life we knew was taken away, and we found ourselves vulnerable and raw, seemingly caught in the chaos of the world. Only years later, when we look back, do we discover that these experiences liberated us from false and limiting notions of ourselves or what we were capable of. They were "passover" experiences. Like the Israelites, we found ourselves in forms of slavery, but the compassionate mercy of God entered those situations and led us out of the traps snaring us then. At first we had to struggle against ways of behaving and believing we brought with us. We had to learn new ways, develop new values, see things differently. All this took time. It changed us. Now we can look back and see the blessings of those difficult moments. These have become covenant moments where we were lost but found, liberated when we were trapped, held in love when all we could experience was pain and suffering. Recalling these moments is crucial for us, because they allow us to see ourselves as still being formed by God.

God does not desire we live limited lives. If we are honest with ourselves, we must admit that some things in our past have not yet been resolved to the extent that we can see and celebrate them as redeemed. We may have learned ways of coping with these experiences, but their effects remain with us and shape how we behave in the present. We are still traumatized by what has happened to us. When we are hurt, we tend to close in on ourselves and shut down. We freeze, and if we are badly hurt, we remain frozen. A hard shell grows around that vulnerable and damaged place festering under our armour. Only when that armour encounters love can healing begin. Becoming unthawed takes time and patience. Just as we learn to wait on God in our spiritual journey, we also need to learn to wait on ourselves with equal patience. Part of the process of healing includes forgiving those who have hurt us, but before this stage can be reached, we must learn how to forgive ourselves. We must admit first of all we have been hurt, and sit in the presence of love to see the damage the hurt has done to us. We can ask in prayer if part of that damage has been due to our egos. We see if there are patterns in our lives that lead us to be victimized. Using the particular and general examens, we can work, with God's help, to transform those habits.

But we are hurt not only by ourselves. Others hurt us, too. As we sit in God's love, we might discover this love allows us to release our tensions from being hurt, and so we do not hold grudges or seek revenge or do further damage to ourselves and others. But sometimes as we sit in this love holding us to life, we discover we are unable to forgive aspects of ourselves or others. We find ourselves trapped and helpless. Like the woman suffering from hemorrhage for twelve years without finding a cure, we, too, can turn to Jesus and ask for help. Jesus' mission is to bring forgiveness, and in turning to Jesus, we admit our vulnerability, our need and our helplessness. This form of openness allows God to enter our lives and those damaged areas. Here we abandon ourselves to the divine providence and mercy, and wait on God to be liberated. We note we are part of the suffering body of Christ who waits on the Father to bring him, and us, to resurrection. We also note that on the cross, Jesus does not forgive his enemies. He asks the Father to forgive them. His role in this act of forgiveness is offering his enemies up to the Father for the Father to offer those violent ones a path leading to life and a sense of their common humanity. Like

Christ on the cross, we, too, in seeking to be liberated, can ask the Father to do for us what he has done for his Son.

Like Christ after his resurrection, we will carry on our bodies and into the rest of our lives the scars of the hurts done to us. Maybe one day they will become signs of our humanity and of our covenant moments with God. We will look at them and remember how we have been rescued. But for the moment, all we know is we are a work in progress, held in the hands of God. Our redemption has not yet been fully realized, but we lean into the love that leads us, and all, to the fullness of life.

The path to the fullness of life starts here and now, in the present moment. We are always invited to live in the present moment, but we realize only God lives fully in the present. We bring the past with us and anticipate the future as we live in the present. When the past is unredeemed, our hurts shape the way we see and react to the present, and this causes us to look at the future with anxiety and despair. Redeeming and celebrating the past liberates the present and opens us up to embrace the future with hope and anticipation. We are not fully attentive to the present when we are preoccupied with past concerns and future projects. Both are aspects of the present, but they are not the whole of the present. Similarly, the present moment is not the fullness of the present. To live in the present as present is to have that present linked to the past and future, and it is to experience the integration of these three dimensions of time. If we isolate the present from past and future, we fall into the trap of irresponsibility. Like children, we feel only what is immediate matters, and so we ignore consequences or causes. Then we are unable to distinguish between what seems to be good and what really is valuable. This is spiritual immaturity masquerading as enlightenment.

If time is experienced as a continuum, to live spiritually in the present is to extend the space of that continuum we designate as the present to what is normally considered past and future. A spiritually present moment broadens to encompass dimensions of past and future in an integrated unity. As we journey closer and closer to God, we discover the present to be more and more encompassing of reality. We become more aware of connections between things and of a sense of our interrelatedness to them all. It is our rootedness in God that allows us this gift. We do not become the centre of the universe, with all things gravitating towards us in our egocentric present. No, we find ourselves, as it were, swimming through a large ocean, with a limited perspective but with the awareness there is no separation between ourselves and that ocean of time. With this perspective, we discover every moment of time offers us an encounter with the divine celebrating our life or reconciling it with the love we are invited to live. Each moment opens to eternity and to the fullness of time.

Living the redeemed present means living with that awareness. Even under the most dreadful circumstances, one can be aware that creation is a work in progress. Despite the painful reality of evil in the world and in our own lives, there is the broader reality of God holding all of creation, in spite of its self-destructiveness, in his Love. We may be tempted to wonder why, if that is so, there is evil, why people suffer and why they hurt each other. As humans, with limited perspectives, we do not know the answers to these questions. Not knowing is part of the human condition. We are not God. But we can ask another question: How can I find, share and celebrate life in the situations I find myself in?

This is a question for discernment. It asks us how we imagine reality to be. Imagination shapes our vision. As the poet William Blake insists, we see not *with* our eyes but *through* our eyes. We see with our imagination, which needs conversion so we can have the eyes to see how it is possible to live humanely in our present situations. We remember Christ came not to make us divine—to believe that would be to succumb to the temptation of Eve in the garden of Eden—but to show us how to live full human lives. To live as Christ does in his humanity, we, like him, learn to wait on the Father. Christ's human discernments are done through being attentive to the Father. He responds to the delight the Father has in creation and to the concern the Father has for creation. Living the present as fully as we can, we can also celebrate what is good in our situation and cooperate with grace given in transforming what is destructive in our world. In doing this, we do no more and no less than what Christ does in living his earthly present two thousand years ago, today and throughout human history. The Christ given to us in the gospels does not do everything. In fact, he disappointed those who wanted him to overthrow Roman occupation, to re-establish religious orthopraxis and to conform to the expectations of those who desired a utopia on earth. For them, his mission on earth was a failure. They read him through worldly eyes, looking for specific results. He lived his life differently. He was attentive to the Father. He was always present to the Father. In living our present, we also are invited to be present to the Father, whatever that might mean. As Mother Teresa of Calcutta once observed, "We are not called to be successful; we are called to be faithful."[66] Living in the present is a witness of fidelity. We wait on the Father to come to us, name us and mission us. Our discernments dispose us to that mission.

In the history of salvation, we notice the Annunciation, the nativity, Jesus' baptism, Peter's confession of faith, Jesus' resurrection, Pentecost and the Second Coming all come to us. We do not go to God. God comes to us. All we can do is dispose ourselves to be able to recognize and accept that present when it comes to us. We can live in anticipation of that coming in our present lives.

To live a redeemed future is to expect the coming of God ever more into our lives, and to live out of that expectation. The fullness of life is always offered to us by God, and our spiritual journey is entering into that fullness of life at ever deeper and more com-prehensive levels. We are always surrounded and interpenetrated by the love of God and the community of God's beloved—saints, angels, good and holy people, the ordered aspects of creation—interceding for us, protecting and defending us, celebrating us, advising and guiding us, supporting and weaving us ever deeper into the divine life. This community is actively present in each of our lives. We may not always be aware of it or attentive to it, but it remains true nevertheless. To journey into our redeemed future is to become aware of what is always and everywhere present. When we say that Christian eschatology—the end times—is already now and, at the same time, not yet, we may understand this state as already present, though we need to be converted to see this. Our spiritual journey is one of a deepening conversion as we step into mystery.

This journey, with all of its ebbs and flows, advances and reversals, is a journey into mystery. While dimensions of illusion are removed from our lives in this journey, we also encounter more and more layers of what stops us from seeing, knowing and loving ourselves, others and creation as God sees all. These blocks are existentially manifest in our lives and in the worlds we inhabit. There are wars, disease, violence, poverty, starvation and corruption, and they exist outside of our imaginations. They are real in their unreality, and they impact upon us and on all we hold dear. A change of perspective does not make them go away or become acceptable. The journey to the fullness of life engages itself with these forms of destruction. Indeed, inasmuch as we are living into a redeemed future and are companions of the risen Christ and his community, we are committed to transforming our world into a community of mutual sharing and respect. How this engagement takes place is the matter for discernment. As we enter that process of discernment, we discover how closely we are woven into the divine life and into the community of those who, through the ages, have witnessed by their love the same mission to which we are committed. We discover we are not alone. We discover we are loved, and that we can, and do, love. That love is manifest in the celebration of all the good crossing our path. It is also manifest in the ways in which we live our lives as peacemakers. The path of the beatitudes in Matthew's gospel carries us to this way of being. In fact, the journey to a redeemed future is the life of the blessed. For such people, Jesus says,

> Blessed are the poor in spirit, for theirs is the kingdom of heaven.
> Blessed are those who mourn, for they shall be comforted.
> Blessed are the meek, for they shall inherit the earth.
> Blessed are those who hunger and thirst for righteousness, for they shall be satisfied.
> Blessed are the merciful, for they shall obtain mercy.
> Blessed are the pure in heart, for they shall see God.

Blessed are the peacemakers, for they shall be called sons of God.
Blessed are those who are persecuted for righteousness' sake, for theirs is the kingdom of heaven.
Blessed are you when people revile you and persecute you and utter all kinds of evil against you falsely on my account. Rejoice and be glad, for your reward is great in heaven. They persecuted the prophets before you the same way. (Matthew 5:3-12)

As we walk into the redeemed future awaiting us, we discover more and more our poverty of spirit and our radical dependence on God. We mourn what has been lost or destroyed, and we commit ourselves to a humility that counteracts the aggression of a fallen creation. In a world seemingly given over to license of self-righteousness, we experience in our very bodies the passionate desire for us all to be converted to communities of love. We do what we can to share the love we have personally experienced and that has liberated us from our traps to care for others. In our concern for others, we discover more and more we must abandon our narcissisms and see others as God sees all.

Even more than seeing them with the eyes of love, we are invited to live that love in real and practical ways. Here we wait upon God and attend to those God sends us in following the example and the ministry of the Christ. No matter how the world treats us, we walk this path to the redeemed future. This path leads us and all to the fullness of life. When we do this, the Jesus of Matthew's gospel tells us we become salt of the earth and light for the world (Matthew 5:13-14). When we do this, we live the redeemed future here and now. We celebrate in our very bodies the kingdom of God among us. We realize we have become that kingdom of God.

Notes

1   Part I builds on an article I wrote for *Review for Religious* (published over two issues), which was later reprinted in *Best of Review for Religious 4*. Monty Williams SJ, "The Path of Contemplation, 1," *Review for Religious*, Vol. 47, No. 6. Nov./Dec. 1988, 918–33; and "The Path of Contemplation, 2," *Review for Religious*, Vol. 48, No. 1, Jan./Feb. 1989, 95–111. I am grateful to the journal for allowing me to use the article here.

2   T.S. Eliot, "East Coker," II. 179–80, section 5, from *Four Quartets*, http://www.tristan.icom43.net/quartets/coker.html. Accessed January 2, 2012.

3   http://www.marxists.org/reference/archive/wilde-oscar/soul-man/index.htm. Accessed January 2, 2012.

4   http://www.history.ucsb.edu/faculty/marcuse/classes/201/articles/1914FreudRemembering.pdf. Accessed January 2, 2012.

5   *Journal of Behavioral Medicine*, Vol. 10, 139–44; also *Psychology Today*, August 1987, 54.

6   Saint Teresa (of Avila), *The Life of Teresa of Jesus: The Autobiography of Teresa of Avila*, translated by Edgar Allison Peers (New York: Doubleday: Image Books, 2004), 12.

7   St. Ignatius of Loyola. *The Spiritual Exercises of St. Ignatius: Based on Studies in the Language of the Autograph*, translated by Louis J. Puhl, SJ (Chicago: Loyola University Press, 1975). All other references to the Spiritual Exercises will appear in parentheses in the text.

8   http://www.sufi.ws/rahbaran-tarighat/55-en.php. Accessed January 2, 2012.

9   http://graham.main.nc.us/~bhammel/wilde.html. Accessed January 2, 2012.

10 T.S. Eliot, "East Coker," l. 180, section 5.

11 Thomas Aquinas, Prologue to the Commentary on Boethius' De Hebdomadibus in *The Classics of Western Spirituality: Albert & Thomas, Selected Writings*, edited and translated by Simon Tugwell (New Jersey: Paulist Press, 1988), 527–28.

12 William Blake, "The Everlasting Gospel" ll. 97–100, in *The Complete Poetry & Prose of William Blake*, edited by David Erdman (New York: Anchor Books, Doubleday, 1988), 520.

13 Martin Buber, *Tales of the Hasidim* (New York: Schocken Books, 1975), 112.

14 Martin Heidegger, *Being and Time*, translated by John Macquarrie and Edward Robinson (New York: Harper, 1962).

15 "The eye by which I see God is the same as the eye by which God sees me. My eye and God's eye are one and the same—one in seeing, one in knowing, and one in loving." Quoted in *The Man from Whom God Hid Nothing: An Essay on Johannes Eckhart*, by Arthur Brown, at http://www.philosophos.com/philosophy_article_105.html. Accessed January 2, 2012.

16 The Ten Oxherding Pictures illustrations are by Tomikichiro Tokuriki, in *Zen Flesh, Zen Bones: A Collection of Zen and Pre-Zen Writings* (North Clarendon, VT: Charles E. Tuttle Co. 1957, 1985). Used by permission of the publisher. The poems are my own translation.

17 T.S. Eliot, "Little Gidding," section 5, from *Four Quartets*, http://www.tristan.icom43.net/quartets/gidding.html. Accessed January 2, 2012.

18 http://timjohnsonphotoandink.blogspot.com/2009/08/what-to-write-maybe-question-would-be.html. Accessed January 2, 2012.

19 Michel Serres, *Genesis*, translated by Genevieve James and James Nielson (Ann Arbor, MI: University of Michigan Press, 1995). See also Wallace Stevens, "Connoisseur of Chaos," in *The Collected Poems of Wallace Stevens* (New York: Vintage Books, 1990), 215: "A: A violent order is disorder and B: A great disorder is an order. These/ Two things are one."

20 Geshe Tenzin Wangyal teaches this five-stage Dzogchen meditation. It is the heart instruction of Dawa Gyaltsen, a Bön meditation master who lived in the eighth century. The meditation is found at http://www.purifymind.com/DiscoverNatureMind. htm. Accessed January 2, 2012.

21 William Faulkner, *As I Lay Dying* (New York: Random House, 1957), 92.

22 Faulkner, *As I Lay Dying*, 29.

23 http://rpo.library.utoronto.ca/poem/2618.html. Accessed January 2, 2012.

24 T.S. Eliot, "Little Gidding" section 5, from *Four Quartets*.

25 http://en.wikipedia.org/wiki/Serenity_Prayer. Accessed January 2, 2012.

26 William Blake, "Milton," Book 2: ll. 42–45, in *The Complete Poetry & Prose of William Blake*, 136.

27 George A. Aschenbrenner, SJ, "Consciousness Examen," reprinted in David L. Fleming, SJ, ed. *Notes on the Spiritual Exercises of St Ignatius of Loyola* (St. Louis, MO: Review for Religious, 1981), 175.

28 Aschenbrenner, "Consciousness Examen," http://ignatianspirituality.com/ignatian-prayer/the-examen/consciousness-examen. Accessed January 2, 2012.

29 Those four stages as a growth to spiritual intimacy with the Father are described in Monty Williams, SJ, *The Gift of Spiritual Intimacy* (Toronto: Novalis, 2009). Anyone seeking to understand these stages further in that light can find them there.

30 www.shakespeares-sonnets.com/sonnet/129. Accessed January 2, 2012.

31 http://www.goodreads.com/author/quotes/10994.Blaise_Pascal. Accessed January 2, 2012.

32 http://ignatianspirituality.com/ignatian-prayer/prayers-by-st-ignatius-and-others/fall-in-love. Accessed January 2, 2012.

33 See Williams, *The Gift of Spiritual Intimacy*.

34 Keats's letter of Sunday, 21st. December, 1817 to George and Tom Keats, in *The Letters of John Keats*, edited by Hyder E. Rollins (Cambridge, UK: Cambridge University Press, 1958), I, 193–94.

35 William Wordsworth, "Expostulation and Reply," ll. 17–24 in www.bartleby.com/145/ww133.html. Accessed January 2, 2012.

36 Julian of Norwich, *The Showings of Divine Love*, ch. 5, in http://www.umilta.net/love1.html. Accessed January 2, 2012.

37 Julian of Norwich, *The Showings of Divine Love*, ch. 5.

38 Faulkner, *As I Lay Dying*, 29.

39 William Shakespeare, *King Lear*, Act III, Scene 4:100–02.

40 http://www.dwildepress.net/critica/mystic7.html. Accessed January 2, 2012.

41 Soren Kierkegaard, *The Sickness Unto Death: A Christian Psychological Exposition for Upbuilding and Awakening* (Kierkegaard's Writings, Vol. 19, translated and edited by Howard V. Hong (Princeton, NJ: Princeton University Press, 1983).

42 http://www.ocf.org/OrthodoxPage/liturgy/liturgy.html. Accessed January 2, 2012.

43 Buber, *Tales of the Hasidim*, 112.

44 http://www.poemhunter.com/poem/requiem. Accessed January 2, 2012.

45 http://www.poemhunter.com/poem/requiem.

46 http://www.poemhunter.com/poem/requiem.

47 William Blake, "Proverbs of Hell," in "The Marriage of Heaven and Hell," l. 10, in *The Complete Poetry & Prose of William Blake*, 36.

48 http://www.nasrudin-stories.com/mullah-nasrudin-and-the-key. Accessed January 2, 2012.

49 William Blake, "The Marriage of Heaven and Hell", plate 14 in *The Complete Poetry & Prose of William Blake*, 39.

50 Teilhard de Chardin, *The Divine Milieu* (New York: Harper Colophon Books, 1960), 76.

51 http://sourcesofinsight.com/gandhi-quotes. Accessed January 2, 2012.

52 Simone Weil, *Gravity and Grace* (New York: Routledge, 2004), 72.

53 Told to me by someone who had spent time with Mother Teresa in Calcutta.

54 T.S. Eliot, "The Rock," in *Collected Poems 1909–1935* (New York: Harcourt, Brace & World, 1936).

55 William Shakespeare, *Hamlet*, Act III, Scene 4:194.

56 Dennis Linn, *Sleeping with Bread: Holding What Gives You Life* (New York: Paulist Press, 2002), 1.

57 T.S. Eliot, "East Coker," Section 3, ll. 23–26, from *Four Quartets*.

58 http://www.vedanta-atlanta.org/stories/YourDream.html. Accessed January 2, 2012.

59 http://www.wussu.com/poems/jmblind.htm. Accessed January 2, 2012.

60 *Pollock*, directed by Ed Harris (USA: Sony Picture Classics, 2000) http://www.imdb.com/title/tt0183659/quotes. Accessed January 2, 2012.

61 This story was told to me years ago by a Zen student of long standing.

62 *Jesuit Life & Mission Today: The Decrees of the 31st–35th General Congregations of the Society of Jesus*, edited by John W. Padberg, SJ (St. Louis: Institute of Jesuit Sources, 2009). GC34, #542, 660.

63 This story was told to me in my novitiate by John English, SJ. I have not found the written source for it, but include it here because it fits into the spiritual profile of St. Ignatius.

64 http://www.online-literature.com/wilde/1297. Accessed January 2, 2012.

65 http://www.pbs.org/wgbh/questionofgod/voices/frankl.html from Viktor Frankl, *Man's Search for Meaning: An Introduction to Logotherapy* (Boston: Beacon Press, 1992).

66 http://www.osv.com/OSV4MeNav/BlessedMotherTeresa/WeAreCalledToBeFaithful/tabid/3143/Default.aspx. Accessed January 2, 2012.